The Languages of the World

Kenneth Katzner

The Languages of the World

FUNK & WAGNALLS
New York

 Published simultaneously in Canada by Fitzhenry & Whiteside Limited, Toronto.

Designed by Dennis J. Grastorf

Manufactured in the United States of America

Library of Congress Cataloging in Publication Data

Katzner, Kenneth.
The languages of the world.

1. Language and languages. I. Title.

P201.K35 400 74-13158
ISBN 0-308-10120-0

2 3 4 5 6 7 8 9 10

CONTENTS

FOREWORD

IT HAS BEEN said that living in the world and speaking only one language is somewhat equivalent to living in an enormous mansion and staying in only one room. Those who acquire more than one language find fascinating new and different vistas opening before them, not only of practical opportunity but for the fulfillment of intellectual curiosity and the fascination of looking at the world from a background and viewpoint of another culture.

There are three or four thousand languages still spoken in the world today—several thousand fewer perhaps than were spoken before the leveling surge of the great world languages of the present time, but nevertheless an awesome figure to the nonlinguist. Of this number over two hundred are widely enough used to be classed as languages of international importance, in consideration either of the number of native speakers or of the extent of the area over which the language is spoken.

The Languages of the World offers an excellent aid not only to linguists, to whom its importance is obvious, but for anyone interested in international affairs or even curious about the other inhabitants of our planet. The classification chart of the world's languages at the beginning of the book and the informative and comprehensive explanations of language families and their interrelation comprise an easy-to-understand and entertaining course in linguistics.

The choice of a typical excerpt from each of the more important two hundred languages in its own language script should make this book a *livre de chevet* for all linguists as well as a collector's item for those in allied fields.

To return to the metaphor of the mansion with many rooms, here, in seeing the scripts, one can admire the furnishings of the "other rooms," the beautiful curving and sweeping scripts of the Middle East, the decorative ideographic writing of the Far East, as well as the curling and circular scripts of Southeast Asia. Having examples of these scripts at hand would enable even an amateur linguist to identify foreign scripts with ease and satisfaction.

The extensive country-by-country survey should be of special use to those involved in travel, industry, education, and diplomacy. Information given in the description of each language is fascinating to any reader. Among the many items of information in this section are some potential conversation stoppers, such as: There are still several hundred languages spoken by only 50,000 surviving Australian aborigines; There is a language called "Police Motu" spoken originally by the New Guinea constabulary; One of the few English words accepted by the French Academy is *le bulldozer* (pronounced bool-do-ZAIR); There are more than a thousand separate languages among the Indians of North and South America; Henry IV was the first English king since 1066 who spoke English as a native language.

The author is to be commended for his choice of excerpts that not only show the intricacy and beauty of foreign scripts but, when translated on the same page, give a brief glimpse of the national culture as well as the language whose description follows below. The concise and informative descriptions of these several hundred languages furnish the reader with a view of world history, anthropology, relationship of peoples, and even something of their traditions, customs, and way of life which is, of course, the essence of individual languages.

Charles Berlitz

PREFACE

For as far back as we can trace his history, Man has always spoken many different languages. If at one time he spoke a single language, from which all other languages subsequently descended, linguistic science is unlikely to uncover any hard evidence to confirm such a fact.

In the 19th century scholars made a concerted effort to reconstruct what was then assumed to be Man's original language. Major contemporary languages were exhaustively analyzed in the hope of discovering some common elements that might point to a single primeval source. Languages of isolated primitive peoples were examined in the hope of finding a revealing "fossil" tongue. But the search was in vain. Today linguists realize that a clear picture simply cannot be obtained of events that occurred perhaps a million years ago. We are faced with a complete lack of data about the beginnings of language, and any study of its subsequent evolution must be confined to the more recent historical period. Yet even in this limited aspect of the inquiry, we find ourselves confronted with a myriad of languages.

At present the languages of the world number in the thousands. To establish an exact or even an approximate number is out of the question, for many are scarcely known and it is impossible to draw a clear-cut distinction between language and dialect. In many cases, as one travels across a region the language gradually merges into a neighboring one and it becomes impossible to state for certain just what language is being spoken. But although exact numbers are unavailable, we do know that the American Indian languages number more than a thousand, the languages of Africa close to a thousand, and the single island of New Guinea contributes some 700 more. India has over 150, the Soviet Union 130, while China has several dozen, as do a number of other countries. Even in the United States more than fifty different Indian languages are spoken.

It is important, however, to view these figures in their proper perspective. A single statistic tells a great deal: of the several thousand languages of the world, fewer than 100 are spoken by over 95 percent of the earth's population. One language, Chinese, accounts for 20 percent all by itself, and if we add English, Spanish, Russian, and Hindi, the figure rises to about 45 percent. German, Japanese, Arabic, Bengali, Portuguese, French, and Italian bring the figure to 60 percent, while the next dozen most important languages raise it to 75 percent. When we realize that the last 5 percent speak thousands of different languages, it is clear that the great majority of these languages are spoken by tiny numbers of people—a few thousand in some cases, a few hundred in others, many in only a single village, some by only a few families, some even by only one or two people. As the number of speakers diminishes in each case, a fateful decision must inevitably be made: the members of the rising generation must abandon their mother tongue and adopt instead a more widely-spoken neighboring language that will be of greater use to them. By such a decision the lesser language is literally condemned to death, its ultimate passing awaiting only the death of the last surviving speaker. This process is going on at present more rapidly than is generally realized, having been greatly accelerated by the advent of mass communications which propagate major languages in areas where hitherto only minor languages were spoken. The days of most of the Indian languages of the United States are probably numbered, and in Black Africa, with the emphasis on English, French, Swahili, and other major languages, many hundreds of lesser languages will probably also gradually disappear.

The chart on the following pages lists some 500 different languages. The number is arbitrary and could easily have been larger or smaller, but it attempts to cover the entire world without burdening the reader with a multitude of unfamiliar and unimportant names. For names that are unfamiliar, the index at the back will direct the reader to information about where each language is spoken. Sample texts and translations have been provided for nearly 200 of the languages.

The chart has been arranged to show the major language families of the world. While it is impossible to establish a single protolanguage as the ancestor of all others, it is clear that many modern languages do descend from a common ancestor, as evidenced by basic similarities in their vocabulary and grammatical structure. Those exhibiting such similarities are combined into familiar groupings such as the Romance, Germanic, and Slavic languages. These in turn are grouped into families whose various branches, though having diverged farther back in time and thus evincing less obvious similarities, are nonetheless also of common ancestry. The largest family of languages by far is the Indo-European, whose speakers now embrace approximately half the world's population. It was the discovery of the existence of the Indo-

European family that led linguists to seek more tenuous links to other families and thus to prove the existence of an original common language for all of mankind. But here the effort broke down, and at this stage we must content ourselves with the existence of some twenty important language families and perhaps fifty or more lesser ones. Again the figure is imprecise, for the question of whether certain families are related to each other is still open to debate. And to complicate the picture further, a few languages such as Basque seem to defy all linguistic classification and show no similarity whatever to any other existing language.

The chart is followed by a brief description of each language family. This in turn is followed by individual descriptions of the more important languages, beginning with a sample text and translation. The final section of the book contains a country-by-country breakdown.

Part I

LANGUAGE FAMILIES OF THE WORLD

THE LANGUAGE FAMILIES OF THE WORLD

Family	Subgroup	Branch	Major Languages	Minor Languages
Indo-European	Germanic	Western	English, German, Yiddish, Dutch, Flemish, Afrikaans	Frisian, Luxembourgian
		Northern (Scandinavian)	Swedish, Danish, Norwegian, Icelandic	Faroese
	Italic		Latin	
	Romance		Italian, French, Spanish, Portuguese, Rumanian	Catalan, Provençal, Rhaeto-Romanic, Sardinian, Moldavian
	Celtic	Brythonic	Welsh, Breton	
		Goidelic	Irish (Gaelic), Scottish (Gaelic)	
	Hellenic		Greek	
			Albanian	
	Slavic	Eastern	Russian, Ukrainian, Belorussian	
		Western	Polish, Czech, Slovak	Sorbian (Lusatian)
		Southern	Bulgarian, Serbo-Croatian, Slovenian, Macedonian	
	Baltic		Lithuanian, Latvian (Lettish)	
			Armenian	
	Indo-Iranian	Iranian	Persian, Pashto, Kurdish, Baluchi, Tadzhik, Ossetian	
		Indic	Sanskrit, Hindi, Urdu, Bengali, Punjabi, Marathi, Gujarati, Bihari, Rajasthani, Oriya, Assamese, Kashmiri, Nepali, Sindhi, Sinhalese	Bhili, Romany, Maldivian

Family	Subgroup	Branch	Major Languages	Minor Languages
Uralic	Finno-Ugric	Finnic	Finnish, Estonian, Mordvin, Udmurt (Votyak), Mari (Cheremis), Komi	Lappish
		Ugric	Hungarian	Ostyak (Khanty), Vogul (Mansi)
	Samoyed			Nenets (Yurak), Selkup (Ostyak-Samoyed), Nganasan (Tavgi), Enets (Yenisei-Samoyed)
Altaic	Turkic	Southwestern (Oghuz)	Turkish, Azerbaijani, Turkmen	
		Northwestern (Kipchak)	Kazakh, Kirgiz, Tatar, Bashkir	Kara-Kalpak, Karachai, Balkar, Kumyk, Nogai
		Southeastern (Chagatai)	Uzbek, Uigur	Salar
		Northeastern		Altai, Khakass, Tuvinian
			Chuvash	
				Yakut
	Mongolian		Mongolian	Buryat, Kalmyk
	Tungusic	Northern		Evenki (Tungus), Even (Lamut)
		Southern (Manchu)		Manchu, Nanai (Gold), Sibo

Family	Subgroup	Major Languages	Minor Languages
Caucasian	Southern	Georgian	
	Western		Kabardian, Circassian, Adygei, Abkhazian, Abazinian
	Eastern		Chechen, Ingush
	Dagestan		Avar, Lezgin, Dargin, Lak, Tabasaran
Independent			Basque
Dravidian		Telugu, Tamil, Kanarese (Kannada), Malayalam	Gondi, Kurukh (Oraon), Kui, Tulu, Brahui
Munda			Santali, Mundari, Ho, Savara (Sora), Korku
Independent			Burushaski
Sino-Tibetan	Sinitic	Chinese	
	Tibeto-Burman	Burmese, Tibetan	Yi (Lolo), Lisu, Nakhi (Moso), Lahu, Karen, Kachin (Chingpaw), Chin, Bodo, Garo, Meithei, Lushei, Newari, Murmi, Jonkha, Lepcha
	Tai	Thai, Lao	Chuang, Puyi (Chungchia), Tung, Nung, Shan
	Miao-Yao		Miao, Yao
Independent		Japanese	
Independent		Korean	
Independent			Ainu
Mon-Khmer		Khmer (Cambodian)	Mon, Palaung, Wa (Kawa), Bahnar, Sedang, Khasi, Nicobarese
Independent		Vietnamese	Muong

Family	Subgroup	Major Languages	Minor Languages
Malayo-Polynesian (Austronesian)	Indonesian	Indonesian, Malay, Javanese, Sundanese, Madurese, Tagalog, Visayan, Malagasy	Minangkabau, Achinese, Batak, Buginese, Balinese, Ilocano, Bikol, Pampangan, Pangasinan, Igorot, Maranao, Jarai, Rhade, Cham
	Micronesian		Marshallese, Gilbertese, Chamorro, Ponapean, Yapese, Palau, Trukese, Nauruan
	Melanesian		Fijian, Motu, Yabim
	Polynesian		Maori, Uvea, Samoan, Tongan, Niuean, Rarotongan, Tahitian, Tuamotu, Marquesan, Hawaiian
Papuan			Enga, Kâte, Kiwai, Orokolo, Marind, Nimboran, Baining
Australian			Aranda (Arunta), Murngin
Paleo-Asiatic			Chukchi, Koryak, Itelmen (Kamchadal), Nivkh (Gilyak), Ket (Yenisei-Ostyak), Yukagir (Odul)
Eskimo-Aleut		Eskimo	Aleut

Family	Subgroup	Branch	Major Languages
Niger-Congo	Western Sudanic	Mande	Mende, Malinke, Bambara, Dyula, Soninke, Susu, Kpelle, Vai, Loma
		West Atlantic	Fulani, Wolof, Serer, Dyola, Temne, Kissi, Gola, Balante
		Gur (Voltaic)	Mossi (Moré), Gurma, Dagomba (Dagbane), Kabre, Senufo, Bariba
		Kwa	Yoruba, Ibo, Ewe, Twi, Fanti, Ga, Adangme, Fon, Edo, Urhobo, Idoma, Nupe, Agni (Anyi), Baule, Kru, Grebo, Bassa
	Benue-Congo	Bantu	Swahili, Luba, Kongo, Lingala, Mongo, Ruanda, Rundi, Kikuyu, Kamba, Sukuma, Nyamwezi, Hehe, Chagga, Makonde, Yao, Ganda (Luganda), Nkole (Nyankole), Chiga (Kiga), Gisu, Toro, Nyoro, Nyanja (Chewa), Tumbuka, Bemba, Tonga, Lozi, Lwena (Luvale), Lunda, Shona, Fang, Bulu, Yaundé, Duala, Bubi, Mbundu, Chokwe, Ambo, Herero, Makua, Thonga (Tsonga), Sotho, Tswana, Pedi, Swazi, Zulu, Xhosa, Venda
			Efik, Ibibio, Tiv
	Adamawa-Eastern	Adamawa	Mbum
		Eastern	Zande, Sango, Gbaya, Banda
			Ijo (Ijaw)

Family	Subgroup	Branch	Subbranch	Major Languages
Afro-Asiatic (Hamito-Semitic)	Semitic	North Arabic		Arabic, Maltese
		Canaanitic		Hebrew
		Aramaic		Syriac, Aramaic, Assyrian
		Ethiopic		Amharic, Tigrinya, Tigre, Gurage, Harari, Geez
	Berber			Shluh, Tamazight, Riffian, Kabyle, Shawia, Tuareg (Tamashek)
	Cushitic			Somali, Galla, Sidamo, Beja, Afar, Saho
	Egyptian			Coptic
	Chadic			Hausa

Chari-Nile (Macro-Sudanic)	Eastern Sudanic	Nubian		Nubian
		Nilotic	Western (Nilotic)	Luo, Dinka, Nuer, Shilluk, Lango, Acholi, Alur
			Eastern (Nilo-Hamitic)	Teso, Karamojong, Masai, Turkana, Bari, Lotuko
			Southern	Nandi, Suk (Pokot)
	Central Sudanic			Sara, Mangbetu, Lugbara, Madi
Saharan				Kanuri, Teda (Tibbu)
				Songhai, Djerma
Maban				Maba
				Fur

Khoisan				Bushman, Hottentot, Sandawe, Hatsa (Hadzapi)

NORTH AMERICAN INDIAN

Family	Major Languages
Algonkian	Ojibwa (Chippewa), Cree, Naskapi, Blackfoot, Micmac, Cheyenne, Arapaho, Fox, Delaware, Passamaquoddy
Wakashan	Nootka, Kwakiutl
Salishan	Flathead, Lillooet, Shuswap, Thompson, Okanagan
Athapascan	Navajo, Apache, Chipewyan, Carrier, Chilcotin
	Tlingit
	Haida
Penutian	Yakima, Nez Perce, Klamath, Tsimshian
Yuman	Yuma, Mohave
Iroquoian	Cherokee, Seneca, Mohawk, Oneida
Siouan	Sioux (Dakota), Assiniboin, Winnebago, Crow, Omaha, Osage
Caddoan	Caddo, Pawnee
Muskogean	Choctaw, Chickasaw, Creek, Seminole
Keresan	Keresan
Uto-Aztecan	Papago, Pima, Hopi, Ute, Shoshone, Paiute, Comanche, Kiowa, Nahuatl, Tarahumara, Mayo
Tanoan	Tewa, Tiwa, Towa
Zuñian	Zuñi
Oto-Manguean	Otomi, Mazahua, Mixtec, Zapotec, Mazatec, Chinantec
	Tarasco
Zoquean	Mixe, Zoque
	Totonac
Mayan	Maya (Yucatec), Tzotzil, Tzeltal, Chol, Chontal, Huastec, Quiché, Mam, Cakchiquel, Kekchi

CENTRAL AND SOUTH AMERICAN INDIAN

Family	Major Languages
Macro-Chibchan	Miskito (Mosquito), Lenca, Guaymi, Cuna, Bribri, Cabecar
Ge-Pano-Carib	Carib, Ge, Panoan, Chiquito, Tacana
Andean Equatorial	Quechua, Aymara, Jivaro, Araucanian, Guarani, Tupi, Arawak

ARTIFICIAL

	Esperanto, Occidental, Interlingua

PIDGIN AND CREOLE

	Pidgin English, French Creole, Papiamento, Taki-Taki, Saramacca, Krio, Kituba, Fanakalo, Police Motu

Indo-European Languages

THE INDO-EUROPEAN FAMILY of languages is the world's largest, embracing most of the languages of Europe, America, and much of Asia. It includes the two great classical languages of antiquity, Latin and Greek; the Germanic languages such as English, German, Dutch, and Swedish; the Romance languages such as Italian, French, Spanish, and Portuguese; the Celtic languages such as Welsh and Gaelic; the Slavic languages such as Russian, Polish, Czech, and Serbo-Croatian; the Baltic languages, Lithuanian and Latvian; the Iranian languages such as Persian and Pashto; the Indic languages such as Sanskrit and Hindi; and other miscellaneous languages such as Albanian and Armenian. In Europe only Basque, Finnish, Estonian, Hungarian, Turkish, and a few languages of Russia are not of this family; the others have apparently all descended from an original parent tongue.

Who were the original Indo-Europeans and when and where did they live? Since they left no written documents, which are, after all, the basis of history, the answers to these questions can be best obtained by attempting to reconstruct their language. If we may assume that a word that is similar in most of the Indo-European languages designates a concept that existed in the original Indo-European society and that, on the other hand, a word that varies in most Indo-European languages designates a concept not discovered until later, we may then draw certain tentative conclusions. It would appear that the Indo-Europeans lived in a cold northern region, that it was not near the water, but among forests, that they raised such domestic animals as the sheep, the dog, the cow, and the horse, that among wild animals they knew the bear and the wolf, and that among metals they probably knew only copper. Many believe that it was the use of the horse and chariot that enabled them to overrun such an enormous expanse of territory.

The general consensus is that the original Indo-European civilization developed somewhere in eastern Europe about 3000 B.C. About 2500 B.C. it broke up; the people left their homeland and migrated in many different directions. Some moved into Greece, others made their way into Italy, others moved through Central Europe until they ultimately reached the British Isles. Another division headed northward into Russia, while still another branch crossed Iran and Afghanistan and eventually reached India. Wherever they settled, the Indo-Europeans appear to have overcome the existing population and imposed their language upon them. One must conclude that they were a most remarkable people.

The possibility of so many languages having descended from a common ancestor was first suggested in 1786, though the similarity of Sanskrit and Italian was noted as early as the 16th century. By 1818 more than fifty separate languages were established as Indo-European; Albanian was added to the list in 1854 and Armenian in 1875. The total number of Indo-European speakers is about 1,875,000,000 people, approximately half the earth's total population.

The table below, giving the equivalents of six English words in numerous languages, will serve to illustrate the basic interrelation of the Indo-European languages, as contrasted with the languages of other families.

INDO-EUROPEAN LANGUAGES

English	month	mother	new	night	nose	three
Welsh	mis	mam	newydd	nos	trwyn	tri
Gaelic	mí	máthair	nua	oíche	srón	trí
French	mois	mère	nouveau	nuit	nez	trois
Spanish	mes	madre	nuevo	noche	nariz	tres
Portuguese	mês	mãe	novo	noite	nariz	três
Italian	mese	madre	nuovo	notte	naso	tre
Latin	mensis	mater	novus	nox	nasus	tres
German	Monat	Mutter	neu	Nacht	Nase	drei
Dutch	maand	moeder	nieuw	nacht	neus	drie
Icelandic	mánuður	móðir	nýr	nótt	nef	þrír
Swedish	månad	moder	ny	natt	näsa	tre
Polish	miesiąc	matka	nowy	noc	nos	trzy
Czech	měsíc	matka	nový	noc	nos	tři
Rumanian	lună	mamă	nou	noapte	nas	trei
Albanian	muaj	nënë	i ri	natë	hundë	tre, tri
Greek	men	meter	neos	nux	rhīs	treis
Russian	mesyats	mat'	novy	noch'	nos	tri
Lithuanian	mėnuo	motina	naujas	naktis	nosis	trys
Armenian	amis	mayr	nor	kisher	kit	yerek
Persian	māh	mādar	nau	shab	bini	se
Sanskrit	mās	matar	nava	nakt	nās	trayas

NON-INDO-EUROPEAN LANGUAGES

	(*month*)	(*mother*)	(*new*)	(*night*)	(*nose*)	(*three*)
Basque	hilabethe	ama	berri	gai	südür	hirur
Finnish	kuukausi	äiti	uusi	yö	nenä	kolme
Hungarian	hónap	anya	új	éjszaka	orr	három
Turkish	ay	anne	yeni	gece	burun	üç

The various branches of the Indo-European family are of sufficient importance to merit a brief discussion in their own right. We shall therefore touch upon the Germanic, Romance, Celtic, Slavic, Baltic, Iranian, and Indic languages.

GERMANIC LANGUAGES. The Germanic languages include English, German, Dutch (or Flemish), and the Scandinavian languages—Swedish, Danish, Norwegian, and Icelandic. Yiddish and Luxembourgian are offshoots of German, and Afrikaans is based on Dutch. Frisian, spoken in northern Holland, developed independently, as did Faroese, a Scandinavian language spoken in the Faroe Islands.

It is generally assumed that by the first century B.C. Germanic peoples speaking a fairly uniform language were living on both sides of the North and Baltic seas. In time there developed the so-called West, East, and North Germanic dialects. The West Germanic tribes settled in the lands between the Elbe and Oder rivers, and it is here that the German language gradually evolved. The East Germanic tribes settled east of the Oder River, but their languages have long since become extinct. In Scandinavia the North Germanic tribes spoke a language we now call Old Norse, the ancestor of the modern Scandinavian languages. In the 5th century A.D. three West Germanic tribes, the Angles, Saxons, and Jutes, crossed the North Sea into Britain, bringing with them a language that would later be known as English. And in the 9th century Old Norse was carried far westward to Iceland.

In the development of any language or language family, certain mutations inevitably occur that set it off from other languages or language families with which it shares a common origin. One such example is the sound shift that gradually occurred in the Germanic languages in the first millennium B.C. A number of Indo-European consonants acquired different values in the Germanic languages, as may be shown by a comparison between Latin, which retained the Indo-European consonants, and English, a Germanic language which did not. The Indo-European consonant *d* became *t* in the Germanic languages (*e.g.*, Latin *duo*, English *two*), *k* or *c* became *h* (*collis*/hill), *t* became *th* (*tonitus*/thunder), *p* became *f* (*piscis*/fish), and *g* became *k* or *c* (*ager*/acre). This phenomenon was first described in detail in the 19th century by the German philologist Jacob Grimm (perhaps better known as the author, together with his brother Wilhelm, of *Grimm's Fairy Tales*). Known as Grimm's Law, it was a landmark in the development of modern philology.

ROMANCE LANGUAGES. The Romance languages are the modern descendants of Latin, the language of the Roman Empire. Of the modern Romance languages, Italian, French, Spanish, Portuguese, and Rumanian are each the language of an entire nation, while Catalan, Provençal, Rhaeto-Romanic, Sardinian, and Moldavian are confined to smaller areas within individual countries.

As the armies of Rome extended the boundaries of the Empire into much of the continent of Europe, Latin was introduced everywhere as the new language of administration. Spoken Latin remained fairly uniform in the beginning, though it already differed markedly from the Latin of classical literature. But as the Empire began to crumble, and Roman administrators began to disappear, the Latin of each region began to develop in its own individual way. Separated from each other by great distances, and naturally influenced by the speech of surrounding peoples, each developed its own distinctive characteristics to the point where it became a separate language.

Since we are dealing here with a slow and imperceptible process, it is impossible to say when spoken Latin ends and Romance begins. But the divergence was certainly under way by the 5th century, and by the 8th century we can detect unmistakable differences in the basic vocabulary and grammar of the various Romance dialects. The oldest text in a Romance language is the Oaths of Strasbourg, a document in Old French dating from A.D. 842.

The evolution of the Romance languages continued into modern times, each continually influenced by new geographic and ethnic factors. Each language has borrowed heavily from various non-Romance languages—French from Germanic and Celtic, Spanish and Portuguese from Arabic, and Rumanian from Slavic, Hungarian, Albanian, and Turkish. Many words exhibit remarkable uniformity throughout—*e.g.*, bread: *pane* (Italian), *pain* (French), *pan* (Spanish), *pão* (Portuguese), *pîine* (Rumanian)—while others clearly show the effects of isolation and borrowing—*e.g.*, child: *bambino* (Italian), *enfant* (French), *niño* (Spanish), *criança* (Portuguese), *copil* (Rumanian).

CELTIC LANGUAGES. The Celtic languages (the initial *c* may be pronounced as either *s* or *k*) are the indigenous languages of Ireland, Scotland, and Wales. They include Gaelic (known as Irish in Ireland), Welsh, and Breton, the latter spoken in northwestern France.

The Celts were once a powerful people who dominated the area of southern Germany and the northern Alps in the first millennium B.C. About the beginning of the 5th century B.C. they began to migrate in all directions, reaching the remotest parts of Europe in a number of successive waves. The date of their arrival in the British Isles is unknown, but we are certain that when the Anglo-Saxons arrived in the 5th century A.D. they were met by a people speaking a Celtic language. In time the Celts were pushed back by the English into the west and north, leaving only Wales and the Scottish Highlands Celtic-speaking. In the 6th century one large group of Celts emigrated from Cornwall and southern Wales to Brittany, in northwestern France, where today they still speak the Celtic language known as Breton.

The Celtic languages are, sad to say, the one branch of the Indo-European family whose very survival is seriously endangered. Cornish, another Celtic language, became extinct in the 18th century, while Manx, spoken for centuries on the Isle of Man, died out only recently. While Welsh and Irish still show signs of vitality, both are continually losing ground to the all-pervasive influence of English. Attempts to encourage the teaching and speaking of the Celtic languages have met with some success, but with each passing generation the number of speakers diminishes.

SLAVIC LANGUAGES. The Slavic languages, spoken in the Soviet Union, Poland, Czechoslovakia, Yugoslavia, Bulgaria, and a small part of East Germany, form another major division of Indo-European. The modern Slavic languages number eleven: Russian, Ukrainian, Belorussian, Polish, Czech, Slovak, Bulgarian, Serbo-Croatian, Slovenian, Macedonian, and Sorbian (Lusatian).

The origin of the Slavic people is clouded in obscurity. Their homeland appears to have been the area between the Vistula and Dnieper rivers, in present-day Poland and Russia. Perhaps by the 7th century B.C. they could be identified as a distinct ethnic group. In later centuries they began a slow and steady migration in different directions, eventually dividing into the three distinct groups evident in the Slavic languages of today. The western Slavs (ancestors of the Poles, Czechs, and Slovaks) migrated toward the Elbe and Oder rivers in Germany and Poland, where they eventually adopted the Roman Catholic faith. The southern Slavs (ancestors of the Yugoslavs and Bulgarians) moved into the Balkans, where some (the Serbs and the Bulgarians) adopted the Greek Orthodox faith, while others (the Croats and the Slovenes) adopted Roman Catholicism. The eastern Slavs made their way into Russia, where they too, in the 10th century, adopted Greek Orthodoxy.

The first Slavic language used for literary purposes was Old Church Slavonic, written in the Cyrillic alphabet devised by the Greek missionaries Cyril and Methodius in the 9th century. As individual alphabets were later developed for the various Slavic languages, the choice was made entirely by religion. The Cyrillic alphabet was adopted by the Orthodox Russians, Ukrainians, Belorussians, Bulgarians, Serbs, and Macedonians, while the Latin script was adopted by the Roman Catholic Poles, Czechs, Slovaks, Croats, Slovenes, and Sorbs. Only the use of two alphabets distinguishes Serbian from Croatian, which are otherwise, for all practical purposes, one and the same language: Serbo-Croatian.

BALTIC LANGUAGES. The Baltic languages presently number only two—Lithuanian and Latvian—several others having died out centuries ago. They are the most conservative of the Indo-European languages, retaining a number of archaic features of Indo-European that vanished from the others long before they were committed to writing. The Baltic languages share a number of common features with the Slavic languages, leading some scholars to suggest a Balto-Slavic subgroup within the Indo-European family.

The original Baltic peoples are believed to have moved into western Russia about 2000 B.C. during the great migrations of the Indo-European tribes. For centuries they occupied a large area extending from the Oka River, near present-day Moscow, westward as far as the Baltic Sea. About the 6th century A.D. the eastern Balts were forced to move westward by the more numerous Slavs, and soon afterward settled in their present homeland. By the 10th century Lithuanian and Latvian were clearly distinct languages. Today the two are not mutually intelligible, but even a cursory comparison of their vocabulary is sufficient to show their common origin.

IRANIAN LANGUAGES. The Iranian languages are dominated by Persian, a major language of antiquity and spoken today by over 25 million people. Others include Pashto, spoken in Afghanistan and Pakistan; Kurdish, the language of the Kurds; Tadzhik and Ossetian, spoken in the Soviet Union; and Baluchi, spoken in Pakistan and Iran.

The Iranian languages and the Indic languages, described below, together form what is known as the Indo-Iranian subgroup of the Indo-European family. While the other Indo-European migrations appear to have been toward the west, the Indo-Iranians headed southeast, toward the Caspian Sea and on to Iran and Afghanistan. After traversing arid deserts and great mountains, they finally reached India at a date estimated at about 1500 B.C. By perhaps 1000 B.C. the dialects of India and Iran were sufficiently different to be considered separate languages.

The 7th century B.C. witnessed the rise of the great religion of Zoroastrianism, whose sacred texts, the *Zend Avesta*, were written in an ancient Iranian language called Avestan. By the following century the might of the Persian Empire had made Persian the dominant language of the ancient world.

Since the conquests of Islam in the 7th century A.D. the Iranian languages have been written in the Arabic script. Prior to World War II the Soviet government created Cyrillic-based alphabets for Tadzhik and Ossetian, as well as for Kurdish as spoken in the Soviet Union.

INDIC LANGUAGES. The Indic languages, also known as Indo-Aryan languages, are spoken over a vast area embracing the northern two-thirds of India, as well as most of Pakistan, Bangladesh, Sri Lanka (Ceylon), and Nepal. In India the most important Indic languages are Hindi, Urdu (which closely resembles Hindi), Bengali, Punjabi, Marathi, Gujarati, Oriya, and Assamese. Urdu and Punjabi, as well as Sindhi, are also spoken in Pakistan, while Bengali is also the dominant language of Bangladesh. Another Indic language, Sinhalese, is the principal language of Sri Lanka, while Nepali is spoken in Nepal, and Kashmiri in Kashmir. Romany, the language of the Gypsies, is also of this family.

The Indic languages are the modern descendants of Sanskrit, brought to India by Indo-European settlers about 1500 B.C. The language of the sacred Hindu scriptures, it gradually gave way to the Prakrit, or Middle Indic, languages. It is out of these that the modern Indian languages eventually evolved. The date of their appearance cannot be fixed precisely but the first literary documents began to be available about 1200 A.D.

The majority of the Indic languages are written in variations of a script known as Devanagari, which appeared in India about the 7th century A.D. The Indic languages of Pakistan—Urdu and Sindhi—are written in the Arabic script.

Uralic Languages

OF THE FEW non-Indo-European languages of Europe, the majority belong to the Uralic family. Of the approximately 20 million speakers of Uralic languages all but the 30,000 Samoyeds speak one of the Finno-Ugric languages.

The ancestors of the Uralic peoples are believed to have occupied a broad belt of central European Russia about six thousand years ago. In the third millennium B.C. they began to migrate in different directions, eventually settling in lands far removed from their original home. Some moved to the northwest as far as Estonia and Finland, others moved due north, while still others migrated north and east into the lands of western Siberia. Their subsequent history is best discussed under the terms Finno-Ugric and Samoyed.

The Finno-Ugric languages are further subdivided into the Finnic branch, of which the most important language is Finnish, and the Ugric, of which the most important is Hungarian. The Finnish tribes probably came to Finland about the beginning of the Christian era. Those that settled south of the Gulf of Finland eventually produced a dialect of Finnish that we now call Estonian. Probably the only people living in Finland at this time were the Lapps, who were driven farther north into the Arctic regions. Since the Lapps are of different racial stock than the other Finno-Ugric peoples, it must be assumed that they once spoke a non-Finno-Ugric language of their own. If so, it was completely lost in the wake of the Finnish invasions, and efforts to spot a single word of the ancient language in modern Lappish have been unsuccessful.

About 2½ million speakers of Finno-Ugric languages are still to be found in central European Russia. Mordvin, Udmurt (Votyak), and Mari (Cheremis) are spoken over an area approximately coinciding with the original homeland of the Uralic peoples. Apparently these peoples did not participate in the great Uralic migrations, or at least they did not migrate very far. The fourth Finno-Ugric language of the Soviet Union, Komi, is spoken farther to the north, probably the result of a migration that paralleled that of the Finnish tribes to the northwest.

The term Ugric is derived from Ugra, an old Russian name for western Siberia. It was to this area that the Ugric peoples migrated in the first centuries of the Christian era. Not long afterward, however, they began a long and slow migration westward, eventually reaching present-day Hungary in the 9th century. Thus we have the rare phenomenon of Hungarian, completely unrelated to the languages of neighboring countries.

In every migration there are always some that remain behind, and this explains the remote Ostyak (Khanty) and Vogul (Mansi) languages of western Siberia. The former is spoken by about 15,000 people along the Ob River and its tributaries, the latter by about 4,000 along the Sosva and Konda rivers, tributaries of the Ob and Irtysh rivers respectively. Only these languages bear a close resemblance to Hungarian. To encourage their use, Cyrillic-based alphabets were developed by the Soviet government in the late 1930s. The area in which the people live has been designated the Khanty-Mansi National District and its capital called Khanty-Mansiisk.

The second branch of the Uralic family consists of the remote Samoyed languages. They are only four in number and of these, two have fewer than 1,000 speakers each. The most important is Nenets, formerly called Yurak, with about 25,000 speakers spread over a vast area of the northern tundra region, between the city of Archangel on the west and the Yenisei River on the east. Next in importance is Selkup, formerly Ostyak-Samoyed, spoken by about 2,000 people somewhat to the south, on both sides of the Taz River in western Siberia. The other Samoyed languages are Nganasan (Tavgi), with about 750 speakers on the Taimyr Peninsula (the northernmost area of mainland Russia), and Enets (Yenisei-Samoyed), with about 300 speakers near the mouth of the Yenisei River.

The separation of the Samoyed and Finno-Ugric peoples is believed to have taken place more than five thousand years ago. The Samoyeds probably headed east and remained for a long time on the taiga of western Siberia. Some time at the beginning of the Christian era they began to migrate northward and westward, eventually to settle over scattered areas of the far north. During the late 16th century, with the first major Russian penetration into Siberia, the Samoyeds came under Russian rule.

The Samoyed languages were never committed to writing in tsarist Russia but in 1931 the Soviet government introduced a Roman-based alphabet for the Nenets and Selkup languages. Between 1937 and 1940 this was replaced with the Cyrillic. Today, textbooks, newspapers, and some native literature are published in Nenets and, to a lesser extent, in Selkup. Both languages are also taught in the schools.

Altaic Languages

THE ALTAIC LANGUAGES are spoken over a vast expanse of territory extending from Turkey on the west, across Soviet Central Asia, into Mongolia and China, and on to the Pacific Ocean. The name Altaic is derived from the Altai Mountains of western Mongolia where the languages are believed to have originated. Speakers of the Altaic languages number about 80 million. The family consists of three divisions: Turkic, Mongolian, and Tungusic.

The Turkic languages are a homogeneous group of about twenty languages, which are for the most part mutually intelligible. The most important, of course, is Turkish, which accounts for about half of all the speakers. To the east of Turkey, in Iran and the Azerbaidzhan S.S.R. of the Soviet Union, Azerbaijani is spoken. To the north, in the area known as the Caucasus, there are Karachai, of the Karachai-Cherkess Autonomous Region (capital: Cherkessk); Balkar, of the Kabardin-Balkar A.S.S.R. (capital: Nalchik); Kumyk, of the Dagestan A.S.S.R. (capital: Makhachkala); and Nogai, spoken in a number of different republics. Across the Caspian Sea, in Soviet Central Asia, there are Turkmen, Uzbek, Kazakh, and Kirgiz, each spoken in a union republic of the same name, as well as Kara-Kalpak, of the Kara-Kalpak A.S.S.R. (capital: Nukus). In European Russia, Tatar and Chuvash are spoken in the region of the Volga, while Bashkir is spoken in the foothills of the Ural Mountains. In southern Siberia, in the vicinity of the Altai Mountains, there are Altai, of the Gorno-Altai Autonomous Region (capital: Gorno-Altaisk); Khakass, of the Khakass Autonomous Region (capital: Abakan); and Tuvinian, of the Tuvinian A.S.S.R. (capital: Kyzyl). Far to the northeast, in the Yakut A.S.S.R., Yakut is spoken. In western China the most important language is Uigur, which also has some speakers in the Soviet Union.

The Mongolian branch of Altaic consists basically of Mongolian proper, the other languages being little more than dialects of it. Mongolian was the language of the great Mongol Empire established by Genghis Khan in the 13th century. In the 14th and 15th centuries a number of offshoots developed, but even today these are largely intelligible to Mongolian speakers. The two most important Mongolian languages other than Mongolian itself are spoken in the Soviet Union. One is Buryat, spoken in the area around Lake Baikal; the other, Kalmyk, is spoken to the west of the Volga River delta. Other dialects of Mongolian are spoken in northwestern China.

The Tungusic languages account for less than one-tenth of one percent of all Altaic speakers. They are spread over a vast area of Siberia and part of China. A northern branch includes Evenki, or Tungus, and Even, or Lamut, both spoken in central and eastern Siberia, the former as far east as Sakhalin Island. The southern branch includes Sibo, spoken in northwestern China, and Nanai, or Gold, spoken both in China and the Soviet Union, near the city of Khabarovsk. Another Tungusic language is Manchu; spoken by the once great Manchu Dynasty, it has all but died out in the 20th century.

To point to a single people living in a certain place at a certain time as the progenitor of the modern Altaic speakers is simply not possible at the present stage of linguistic scholarship. The oldest known Turkic people are the Kirgiz, of whom documents exist dating as far back as 200 B.C. The Turks seem originally to have been a woodland, hunting people in the Altai Mountain region. In the 6th century A.D. they ruled an empire that extended from the borders of China to the Black Sea. Probably by this time their language had already become distinguishable from Mongolian. In later centuries most of the Turkic peoples fell under the domination of the Mongol Empire. As for the Tungus, virtually nothing is known of their development prior to the 17th century.

The Altaic and the Uralic languages show sufficient similarity in grammar and phonology to lead some linguists to think of them as two branches of a single family, the so-called Ural-Altaic family. A good case can be made for this point of view, for both lack any forms expressing gender, both indicate various grammatical relationships by the addition of numerous suffixes, and both observe a principle known as vowel harmony, in which only front vowels or only back vowels appear in an individual word. But in the crucial matter of vocabulary, almost no correspondences (other than recent borrowings) can be found, and for this reason it is probably best to regard them as separate families. The term Ural-Altaic, therefore, will not be used in this book.

Caucasian Languages

THE CAUCASIAN LANGUAGES are spoken in the region known as the Caucasus, lying both north and south of the Caucasus Mountains, between the Black and the Caspian seas. This relatively small area, now in the Soviet Union, is one of extraordinary linguistic diversity, with languages often varying from town to town and even from village to village. All together about fifty languages are spoken here, of which about forty are of the Caucasian family. Speakers of the Caucasian languages number about 5 million.

Of the forty or so Caucasian languages, only twelve have been committed to writing, and all but one of these only in the 20th century. The remainder are spoken by tiny pockets of people, ranging in number from a few hundred to a few thousand, and some confined to a single village. It is safe to assume that these unwritten languages will eventually die out and we shall therefore confine our discussion here to those that have been reduced to writing.

The Caucasian languages are dominated by Georgian, spoken by more people than all the rest put together, and the only one with an ancient literary heritage. Georgian, together with a few minor dialects, constitutes the so-called Southern branch of this family, but it is far from certain whether it is actually related to the others. It has been placed in the Caucasian family primarily on a geographic basis, with further research necessary to determine whether it belongs linguistically as well.

The other branches of the Caucasian family are the Western, the Eastern, and the Dagestan. In the Western branch there is Abkhazian, spoken by about 80,000 people in the Abkhazian A.S.S.R. (capital: Sukhumi), in the northwestern corner of the Georgian S.S.R. facing the Black Sea. Directly to the north, in the Adygei Autonomous Region (capital: Maikop), Adygei is spoken by about 100,000 people. To the east, in the Karachai-Cherkess Autonomous Region (capital: Cherkessk) and the Kabardin-Balkar A.S.S.R. (capital: Nalchik), there are about 320,000 speakers of Kabardian. (Karachai and Balkar each refer to a Turkic language also spoken in these regions.) Adygei and Kabardian are closely related and are sometimes referred to collectively as Circassian, a language also spoken in Turkey and Syria. A minor language of the Western branch is Abazinian (25,000 speakers), also of the Karachai-Cherkess Autonomous Region.

The Eastern Caucasian branch consists of Chechen (600,000 speakers) and Ingush (150,000), both spoken in the Chechen-Ingush A.S.S.R. (capital: Grozny). Farther east, in the Dagestan A.S.S.R. (capital: Makhachkala, on the Caspian Sea), no fewer than thirty Caucasian languages are spoken. Five have been reduced to writing, of which the most important is Avar (400,000 speakers) of western Dagestan. In the southeast, in an area that includes the city of Derbent, there is Lezgin (300,000), which is also spoken in the neighboring Azerbaidzhan S.S.R. Between the two lie three lesser languages—Dargin (225,000 speakers), Lak (80,000), and Tabasaran (50,000).

The Caucasus has had a turbulent history since ancient times and has often served as a refuge for persecuted peoples who fled into the mountain villages to seek protection against invaders. Over the centuries it has been overrun by the Persians, Macedonians, Romans, Arabs, Mongols, and Turks, and it was finally incorporated into the Russian empire about 1865. The great linguistic diversity of the region is not a recent phenomenon, for it was noted by Greek and Roman travelers before the Christian era. Arab geographers later referred to the Caucasus as a "mountain of languages."

Dravidian Languages

THE DRAVIDIAN LANGUAGES are found principally in southern India and, to a lesser extent, in Sri Lanka (Ceylon) and Pakistan. Though there are about twenty of these languages in all, four major ones account for all but a few million of the approximately 135 million Dravidian speakers.

In southern India the Dravidian languages are dominant. Since the recarving of the country's provincial boundaries along linguistic lines in 1956, each of the four major languages is spoken in a single state. On the eastern coast Telugu is spoken in Andhra Pradesh (capital: Hyderabad), while Tamil is spoken in Tamil Nadu (capital: Madras). On the western coast Kanarese, or Kannada, is spoken in Karnataka (capital: Bangalore), while Malayalam is spoken in Kerala (capital: Trivandrum). Tamil is also spoken in northeastern Ceylon. Tamil and Malayalam are closely related and together with Kanarese form one branch of the family. Telugu, which differs more noticeably from the others, forms a separate branch.

Of the other Dravidian languages, only five need be mentioned here, the rest spoken by small numbers of people in extremely isolated areas. Three of the five are spoken in central India, where the Indo-European languages generally prevail. The most important is Gondi, spoken in Madhya Pradesh and northeastern Maharashtra. Kui is spoken in southern Orissa, and Kurukh, or Oraon, in Bihar, Orissa, and Madhya Pradesh. One other Dravidian language, Tulu, is spoken in the south, on the western coast around the city of Mangalore. Finally there is

Brahui, spoken in the province of Baluchistan, southwestern Pakistan.

The Dravidian languages are known to have been spoken in India before the arrival of the Indo-Europeans about 1000 B.C. It is considered likely that at one time they were spoken over much of central, and perhaps even northern, India. If this is true then we must assume that the bulk of the Dravidians were driven south by the Indo-Europeans, with only those living in isolated mountain regions remaining behind. The few pockets of Dravidian speakers in central India would appear to lend weight to this theory.

Munda Languages

THE MUNDA LANGUAGES are spoken in scattered sections of northern and central India, mostly in the east, though there is one in the west. Speakers of the Munda languages number only 5 million, less than one percent of India's population.

The family comprises about a dozen languages, only five of which need be mentioned here. The most important is Santali, spoken in the states of Bihar, West Bengal, and Orissa. Santali has about 3 million speakers and is the only one of the Munda languages that has been reduced to writing. To the west of Santali are Mundari and Ho, each with about 750,000 speakers. Both are spoken in southern Bihar, Mundari to the north of Ho, but a second group of Mundari speakers is located to the south in Orissa. Santali, Mundari, and Ho are closely related and are sometimes grouped under the single name of Kherwari. Another Munda language, Savara, or Sora, is spoken by about 250,000 people in southernmost Orissa. Finally there is Korku, spoken far to the west, in western Madhya Pradesh and northeastern Maharashtra, by about 200,000 people.

Like the Dravidian languages, the Munda languages are known to predate the Indo-European conquest of India and were at one time undoubtedly spoken over a much larger area than at present. Over the centuries they have receded into the more remote areas under the impact of peoples with more advanced cultures. One theory links the Munda languages with the Mon-Khmer languages of Southeast Asia, the two sometimes combined into a broader grouping known as the Austro-Asiatic family.

Sino-Tibetan Languages

THE SINO-TIBETAN FAMILY consists first and foremost of Chinese, plus four other national languages—Thai, Burmese, Lao, and Tibetan—and an undetermined number of lesser languages spoken in China, Burma, India, Nepal, and other countries. Chinese speakers today number perhaps 800 million; speakers of the other Sino-Tibetan languages number about 100 million.

It is customary to divide the Sino-Tibetan family into four branches. Chinese forms a separate branch of its own. A second branch consists of the so-called Tibeto-Burman languages, which include Burmese, Tibetan, and more than a hundred lesser languages. Among the most important are Yi (Lolo), Lisu, Nakhi (Moso), and Lahu, all spoken mainly in China; Karen, Kachin (Chingpaw), and Chin, spoken mainly in Burma; Bodo, Garo, Meithei, and Lushei, spoken in Assam, India; Newari and Murmi, spoken in Nepal; Jonkha, spoken in Bhutan; and Lepcha, spoken in Sikkim. A third branch consists of the Tai languages, including Thai and Lao, as well as Chuang, Puyi (Chungchia), and Tung, spoken in China; Nung, spoken in China and Vietnam; and Shan, spoken in Burma. Finally there are two other languages of China and Southeast Asia, Miao and Yao, which form a separate branch.

That the languages of each of the four branches are genetically related to those of the other three is still far from certain. No comprehensive study has been made of these languages as in the case of the Indo-European family, where the relationships of its members have been clearly defined. It remains for future scholarship to work out a more definitive classification, and to establish their connection with other Asian languages such as Vietnamese.

Mon-Khmer Languages

THE MON-KHMER LANGUAGES are spoken in Southeast Asia. Their name is derived from the two most important members of the family—Khmer, the national language of Cambodia, and Mon, a relatively minor language today, but at one time one of the most influential in the region.

Other members of the Mon-Khmer family include Palaung, spoken in Burma; Wa, or Kawa, spoken on both sides of the border between Burma and China; Bahnar and Sedang, spoken in Vietnam; and Khasi, spoken in Assam, India. Another Mon-Khmer language, Nicobarese, is spoken on the remote Nicobar Islands in the Bay of Bengal by only 12,000 people.

The Mons are known to have lived in Burma long before the beginning of the country's political history. After the Mongol conquest of Burma in the 13th century they formed their own kingdom, which for the next 250 years was a great center of Buddhist culture and had wide contacts with the outside world. The Mon alphabet, which was borrowed from southern India, was later adopted for writing Burmese. Today the Mons live mainly in Burma, with a minority across the border in Thailand.

The Khmer empire was dominant in Southeast Asia from the 9th through the 12th century. The famed ruins of the capital city of Angkor date from this period. Later the Khmers were overcome by the Thais and toward the end of the 14th century their empire was destroyed.

Today speakers of the Mon-Khmer languages number about $7\frac{1}{2}$ million. Khmer speakers account for about five-sixths of the total. The Mon-Khmer languages are sometimes combined with the Munda languages of India to form a broader family known as the Austro-Asiatic languages.

Malayo-Polynesian Languages

THE MALAYO-POLYNESIAN, or Austronesian, family of languages extends more than halfway around the globe—from Madagascar, off the southeastern coast of Africa, through the Indonesian archipelago, the Philippines, and across the Pacific Ocean. Its speakers number perhaps 175 million, all but one million of whom speak a language of the so-called Indonesian branch. There are three other branches: Micronesian, Melanesian, and Polynesian.

Four members of the Indonesian branch are the official language of an independent country: Indonesian in Indonesia, Malay in Malaysia, Tagalog in the Philippines, and Malagasy in the Malagasy Republic. In Indonesia there are also Javanese, Sundanese, Madurese, Minangkabau, Achinese, Batak, Buginese, and Balinese. In the Philippines there are also Visayan, Ilocano, Bikol, Pampangan, Pangasinan, Igorot, and Maranao. In Vietnam there are Jarai, Rhade, and Cham, the last mentioned also spoken in Cambodia. And on Taiwan the 200,000 aborigines speak a number of languages which are also of this family.

Hundreds of Malayo-Polynesian languages are spoken on the countless islands that dot the Pacific Ocean. In Micronesia, generally north of the equator and west of the International Date Line, there are Chamorro, of Guam (40,000 speakers); Gilbertese, of the Gilbert Islands (40,000); Trukese, of Truk Island (25,000); Marshallese, of the Marshall Islands (20,000); Ponapean, of Ponape Island (15,000); Palau, of the Palau Islands (10,000); Yapese, of Yap Island (5,000); and Nauruan, of Nauru Island (5,000). In Melanesia, south of the equator, the most important language is Fijian (200,000 speakers), but more than a hundred other Melanesian languages are spoken in New Guinea, New Britain, New Ireland, the Solomon Islands, New Hebrides, and New Caledonia. Generally east of the International Date Line are the far-flung Polynesian languages. Traveling from west to east we come upon Maori of New Zealand (100,000 speakers); Uvea of the Wallis Islands (5,000); Samoan (150,000); Tongan of Tonga (75,000); Niuean of Niue Island (5,000); Rarotongan of the Cook Islands (5,000); Tahitian (50,000); Tuamotu of the archipelago of the same name (5,000); Marquesan of the Marquesas Islands (5,000); and finally the language of Easter Island. Far to the north is Hawaiian, with about 7,500 speakers at present. Despite the enormous distances between them, the Polynesian languages show a remarkable degree of uniformity, and in some cases there is even a certain degree of mutual intelligibility.

The background and the details of the great Malayo-Polynesian migrations are still largely unknown. It is safe to assume that the original homeland of the people was somewhere in Asia, perhaps in India or in present-day Malaysia or Indonesia. There are signs that the settlement of the islands of the Pacific began as early as 1500 B.C., about the same time that some of the Indo-European tribes were settling in their new homelands. One westward migration of the Malayo-Polynesians stands out in sharp contrast to the others—the remarkable journey of the ancestors of the present inhabitants of Madagascar from Indonesia some 1,500 to 2,000 years ago.

Papuan Languages

THE PAPUAN LANGUAGES are spoken principally on New Guinea, though some extend eastward into New Britain and the Solomon Islands. The term Papuan is more geographic than linguistic, for the languages exhibit such wide variations among themselves that it seems hardly likely that they belong to a single family. There are more than 500 of these languages, but only about 2 million speakers. Few of the languages have more than 10,000 speakers, and many have only a few hundred.

In the western half of New Guinea, now the Indonesian province of West Irian, two of the better known languages are Marind and Nimboran. In the eastern half, now known as Papua New Guinea, there are Enga, Kâte, Kiwai, and Orokolo. On New Britain there is Baining.

The interior of New Guinea is one of the most inaccessible regions on earth, with many of the inhabitants still living in the Stone Age. Adjacent villages separated by a valley or two often speak mutually unintelligible languages. Some of the Papuan languages are virtually unknown, and serious study of them began only after World War II.

Australian Languages

THE TERM "AUSTRALIAN LANGUAGES" refers to those spoken by the Australian aborigines. About 50,000 in number, they speak several hundred different languages. The rest of the population of Australia, of course, speaks English.

The aborigines are found in all parts of the continent. That their languages actually form a single linguistic family is doubtful, though certain words are the same in virtually every language. Since Australia has been an island as long as man has inhabited the earth, the aborigines must have come by water, but from where and approximately when are matters of pure conjecture.

Among the more important Australian languages are Aranda, or Arunta, spoken in the center of the continent, and Murngin, spoken in Arnhem Land, the northernmost part of central Australia. A few aborigine words have entered the English language: *boomerang*, *kangaroo*, *wallaby*, and *koala*.

Paleo-Asiatic Languages

THE TERM "PALEO-ASIATIC" is a somewhat imprecise designation for a number of minor languages spoken in northern and eastern Siberia. It includes a small group of related languages plus three additional languages having no genetic link either with each other or with any linguistic family.

The most important of the Paleo-Asiatic languages is Chukchi, with about 12,000 speakers in that part of Siberia nearest Alaska. Related to Chukchi is Koryak, with 6,000 speakers in the Koryak National District, covering the upper two-thirds of the Kamchatka Peninsula. Within the Koryak National District a third related language, Itelmen, formerly Kamchadal, is spoken by about 500 people.

Three other languages included in the Paleo-Asiatic family actually defy linguistic classification. Nivkh, or Gilyak, is spoken by 2,000 people along the lower course of the Amur River and also on Sakhalin Island. Ket, or Yenisei-Ostyak, has about 1,000 speakers along the banks of the Yenisei River in central Siberia. Lastly there is Yukagir, or Odul, with only 300 speakers in the Yakut A.S.S.R. and Magadan Oblast.

Some authorities also include the Eskimo and Aleut languages in this family, while others add Ainu, spoken in Japan. Since no genetic relationship is involved here, the question of classification becomes purely a matter of personal preference. It seems best, however, to confine the Paleo-Asiatic family to the Soviet Union, placing the languages of other countries elsewhere.

Despite the small numbers of speakers of the Paleo-Asiatic languages, Cyrillic-based alphabets have been devised by the Soviet government for Chukchi, Koryak, and Nivkh.

Eskimo-Aleut Languages

THE ESKIMO-ALEUT LANGUAGES number exactly two—Eskimo and Aleut. The former is spoken by about 85,000 people in Greenland, Canada, Alaska, and Siberia. The latter is spoken by about 1,000 people in the Aleutian Islands and one hundred more on the Commander Islands of the Soviet Union. Though undoubtedly related to each other, the two languages are vastly different, having obviously begun to diverge several thousand years ago. Attempts have been made to link Eskimo and Aleut with certain Indian languages of Alaska, with the Chukchi language of Siberia, with Ainu of Japan, and even the Uralic and Indo-European languages. Though some interesting similarities have been noted, it seems best at this stage to regard the Eskimo-Aleut languages as a separate family.

Niger-Congo Languages

THE NIGER-CONGO FAMILY of languages is the largest in Africa. It extends from Senegal, in westernmost Africa, across the "hump" to Nigeria, and then down the southern half of the continent as far as South Africa. South of the equator almost all the languages of Africa are of the Bantu group, the largest subdivision of Niger-Congo. There are many hundreds of Niger-Congo languages, with perhaps as many as 200 million speakers.

Leaving Bantu for last, we may distinguish six other branches of Niger-Congo. The Mande branch includes Mende, of Sierra Leone; Malinke, of Senegal, Gambia, Guinea, Mali, and Ivory Coast; Bambara, of Mali; and Kpelle, of Liberia. The West Atlantic branch includes Fulani, spoken over much of West Africa; Wolof and Serer, of Senegal; and Temne, of Sierra Leone. The Gur, or Voltaic, branch includes Mossi, of Upper Volta; Gurma, of Ghana, Togo, and Upper Volta; Dagomba, of Ghana; and Senufo, of Mali and Ivory Coast. The Kwa branch includes Yoruba and Ibo, of Nigeria; Twi and Fanti, of Ghana; Ewe, of Ghana and Togo; Fon, of Dahomey; and Kru, Grebo, and Bassa, of Liberia. The Benue-Congo branch, which includes Bantu, also contains a small group of languages in Nigeria, including Efik and Tiv. An eastern branch, called Adamawa-Eastern, includes Zande, of Zaïre and the Sudan, and Sango, of the Central African Republic.

Though only a subdivision of Niger-Congo, the Bantu languages in themselves constitute one of the major families of the world. They are spoken south of what is sometimes called the "Bantu line," extending from Cameroon on the west to Kenya on the east. The most important

Bantu language by far is Swahili, now the most widely spoken African language of East Africa. Other major Bantu languages are Luba, Kongo, and Lingala, of Zaïre; Kikuyu, of Kenya; Ruanda, of Rwanda; Rundi, of Burundi; Ganda, of Uganda; Nyanja, of Malawi and Zambia; Bemba, of Zambia; Shona, of Rhodesia; Tswana, of Botswana and South Africa; Sotho, of Lesotho and South Africa; and Zulu and Xhosa, of South Africa. There are more than 300 Bantu languages in all, with as many as 100 million speakers.

Linguistic evidence seems to point to the area of Cameroon—the northwestern corner of Bantu-speaking country—as the original homeland of the Bantu people. They are believed to have migrated into the rain-forest area to the south and east about 2,000 years ago, perhaps because it was better suited to the raising of certain crops they had acquired from Southeast Asia. In any event, they displaced the indigenous inhabitants of the area almost entirely, with the result that only a few isolated pockets of non-Bantu speakers now remain in southern Africa.

Afro-Asiatic Languages

THE TERM "AFRO-ASIATIC" is a recent coinage, having replaced the older term Hamito-Semitic. The family embraces five groups of languages spoken by people of vastly different racial, religious, and cultural origin, but today there is little doubt among linguists that their languages are interrelated. Speakers of the Afro-Asiatic languages number about 175 million.

The five branches of Afro-Asiatic are Semitic, Berber, Cushitic, Egyptian, and Chadic. The Semitic languages include Arabic, Hebrew, and a number of languages of Ethiopia. The Berber languages are a homogeneous group spoken in Morocco, Algeria, and a number of other countries. The Cushitic languages are spoken principally in Ethiopia and Somalia. The Egyptian branch consisted originally of ancient Egyptian, but is now represented by Coptic. The Chadic branch is dominated by Hausa. In former systems of classification the Berber, Cushitic, and Egyptian languages were grouped together under the single term Hamitic.

The terms Hamitic and Semitic are derived from the names of two of the sons of Noah in the Bible, Ham and Shem. It is now generally agreed that the original home of the Hamitic peoples was North Africa, and that of the Semitic peoples South Arabia. The undoubted kinship of their languages suggests that at one time they were one people, but if so it would have to have been in prehistoric times. Perhaps one of these peoples once migrated from the homeland of the other, but no one really knows.

Further details on the Semitic, Berber, and Cushitic languages are presented under separate headings below.

SEMITIC LANGUAGES. In addition to Arabic and Hebrew, the Semitic languages include Amharic, the national language of Ethiopia, plus a number of other languages of Ethiopia—Tigrinya, Tigre, Gurage, and Harari. Maltese, spoken on Malta, is also Semitic, as is Syriac, now mainly a liturgical language. The family is, of course, dominated by Arabic, the official language of more than fifteen countries, and spoken by over 100 million people. Hebrew, the language of the Old Testament, was revived as a spoken language in the 19th century.

The Semitic languages may be traced back some 5,000 years. The oldest of which we have any knowledge is Akkadian, spoken in ancient Mesopotamia about 3000 B.C. Two dialects of Akkadian, Assyrian and Babylonian, were widely spoken in the Near East for the next 2,000 years. By the 8th century B.C. they had given way to Aramaic, which served as the common language of the Near East until well into the Christian era. With the rise of Islam in the 7th century, Arabic, originally a minor language of the Arabian Peninsula, was spread all the way across North Africa to the Atlantic Ocean.

Perhaps as early as 1000 B.C. Semitic peoples from South Arabia crossed the straits of Africa into Ethiopia. Under the influence of native dialects their language developed into Geez, spoken until the 11th century, and still the classical literary language of Ethiopia. Out of Geez emerged the modern Ethiopic languages that are spoken today.

It was the Semitic peoples who introduced the alphabet to the world. Credit for this landmark in human history goes to the Phoenicians, the date being no later than the 15th century B.C. Later Phoenician writing was adopted by the Hebrews and the Arameans. The Greeks borrowed this alphabet about 1000 B.C. and it later spread all over the world.

BERBER LANGUAGES. The Berber languages are spoken in North Africa, principally in Morocco and Algeria, and to a lesser extent in Niger, Mali, and other countries. The Berbers have been known since ancient times and their language at one time was probably spoken over most of North Africa.

Speakers of the Berber languages number some 8 million—5 million in Morocco, $2\frac{1}{2}$ million in Algeria, and 500,000 in other countries. In Morocco the most important languages are Shluh, spoken by a people of the same name in southern Morocco, and Tamazight, spoken by a people called the Beraber in the central part of the country. Each numbers over 2 million. Another Berber language, Riffian, is spoken in the north by about 500,000 people.

In Algeria the principal language is Kabyle, with over 2 million speakers in the mountains east of Algiers. Just to the south and east of this area, Shawia is spoken by about 150,000 people. Far to the south, in scattered oases of the Sahara Desert, live the Tuaregs, who number about 300,000 in Niger and 200,000 in Mali. The Tuaregs, whose language is known as Tamashek, are also to be found in small numbers in Algeria, Libya, and Upper Volta.

The Berber languages are quite similar to each other, so much so that some authorities often speak of a single Berber language. No Berber alphabet exists today, though some transcriptions have been made into Arabic. The Tuaregs have a script of their own called Tifinagh, which dates back to ancient times. It is used mainly for inscriptions, however, and no books or periodicals in it as yet exist.

CUSHITIC LANGUAGES. The Cushitic languages are spoken mainly in Ethiopia and Somalia, though they also extend into Kenya and the Sudan. In Ethiopia they are spoken by more than half the population, while in Somalia the Somali language is spoken everywhere. The Cushitic languages of Ethiopia are Galla, Sidamo, Beja, Afar, and Saho, as well as Somali. Galla and Somali are also spoken in Kenya, while Beja is also spoken in the Sudan.

In the Bible Cush was the son of Ham, the son of Noah, and the name became the biblical word for Ethiopia. The Cushitic peoples are believed to have arrived in Ethiopia from North Africa some time before the Semitic peoples arrived from Arabia. At present Somali is the only Cushitic language with a formal system of writing.

Chari-Nile Languages

THE CHARI-NILE LANGUAGES, formerly known as Macro-Sudanic, are spoken mainly in the Sudan, Uganda, Kenya, and Chad, and to a lesser extent in Tanzania, Zaïre, and the Central African Republic. Though figures are imprecise, a rough guess as to the number of speakers would be in the vicinity of 10 million.

Of the two branches of Chari-Nile, Eastern and Central Sudanic, the former is by far the larger. It consists of Nubian, spoken in the Nile Valley of the Sudan, plus the large family of Nilotic languages. A western branch of Nilotic includes Luo, of Kenya; Dinka, Nuer, and Shilluk, of the Sudan; and Lango, Acholi, and Alur, of Uganda. An eastern branch, also known as Nilo-Hamitic, includes Teso and Karamojong, of Uganda; Masai, of Kenya and Tanzania; Turkana, of Kenya; and Bari and Lotuko, of the Sudan. A southern branch includes Nandi and Suk (Pokot), of Kenya. The other branch of Chari-Nile, Central Sudanic, includes Sara, of Chad; Mangbetu, of Zaïre; and Lugbara and Madi, of Uganda.

The Chari-Nile languages are sometimes grouped with the Saharan languages, which include Kanuri, of Nigeria, as well as with Songhai of Mali, Djerma of Niger, Maba of Chad, Fur of the Sudan, and other languages, to form the larger Nilo-Saharan family.

Khoisan Languages

THE FEW NON-BANTU LANGUAGES of southern Africa are of the Khoisan family. The two most important are Bushman and Hottentot, each with about 50,000 speakers. The former is spoken in Botswana, South West Africa, and South Africa; the latter entirely in South West Africa. Two other Khoisan languages are Sandawe and Hatsa (Hadzapi), of Tanzania, the former with about 25,000 speakers, the latter with fewer than 1,000.

The name Khoisan is composed of the word "Khoi," the Hottentot word for Hottentot, and "San," the Hottentot word for Bushman. The most distinctive feature of the Khoisan languages is the presence of the so-called click consonants, made by drawing air into the mouth and clicking the tongue. While a few such sounds are found in other languages such as Xhosa and Sotho, they are known to have been borrowed from the Khoisan peoples who presumably created them. The relationship between the two branches of Khoisan is remote yet fairly certain. But the questions of how and when they drifted so far apart are as yet unanswered.

American Indian Languages

THE AMERICAN INDIAN LANGUAGES present a bewildering picture of more than a thousand languages, the vast majority spoken by small tribes numbering a few thousand people or less. Over one hundred Indian languages are spoken in the United States and Canada, over three hundred in Mexico and Central America, and perhaps a thousand in South America. There are about 20 million Indians in the Western Hemisphere.

The staggering task of sorting out these languages began more than a hundred years ago and is still going on. In North America alone there are believed to be some fifty different families. These in turn have been grouped into a few great superfamilies, but the designations are still tentative and subject to further revision. One of the largest North American families is the Algonkian, which includes Ojibwa (Chippewa), Cree, Blackfoot, Cheyenne, Fox, and Delaware, spoken mainly in the northern Midwest, Montana, and south-central Canada. The Athapascan languages, originally spoken in Canada, include Navajo, of the American Southwest, now the most widely spoken Indian language in the United States. The Iroquoian languages include Cherokee, of Oklahoma and North Carolina, and Seneca and Mohawk, of New York. The Siouan languages, also spoken mainly in the northern Midwest, include Sioux, or Dakota, as well as Crow, of Montana, and Osage, of Oklahoma. In the Muskogean family are Choctaw, Chickasaw, and Creek, all spoken mainly in Oklahoma. The Uto-Aztecan family includes Papago, Pima, Hopi, Ute, Shoshone, Paiute, and Comanche, spoken throughout much of the American Southwest.

Mexico, the home of the once great Aztec and Maya civilizations, still has a large Indian population. The Aztec language, known as Nahuatl, is still widely spoken in the states adjacent to Mexico City. It is also of the Uto-Aztecan family. Mayan languages are spoken in both Mexico and Guatemala, while Mixtec, Zapotec, and Otomi, all of the Oto-Manguean family, are spoken in southern Mexico. South of Mexico the most important Indian language by far is Quechua, spoken in Peru, Bolivia, and Ecuador. Once the language of the great Inca Empire, it now has at least four times as many speakers as any other Indian language. Next in line in South America are Guarani, of Paraguay, and Aymara, of Bolivia and Peru, while others include Tupi, of Brazil; Jivaro, of Peru and Ecuador; and Araucanian, of Chile.

Arawak and Carib are spoken by small groups of people in Colombia, Venezuela, Guyana, and Brazil; Carib is also spoken in Honduras, British Honduras, and Surinam. The countless Latin American Indian languages have been grouped into three great families: Macro-Chibchan, Ge-Pano-Carib, and Andean Equatorial.

It is now generally agreed among scholars that the Indians came to America from Asia, the migration beginning perhaps as long ago as 25,000 years. Small bands of hunters wandered across the land bridge that spanned the Bering Strait and over the centuries their descendants gradually drifted southward. So slowly did these movements take place that probably no single generation was conscious of a migration. These people were not all alike, but differed markedly from each other in physical appearance, customs, and language. Eventually they would inhabit the entire hemisphere—from the Arctic to the southernmost tip of South America.

By the time of the arrival of the white man, the Western Hemisphere was already well populated with diverse cultures ranging from rudimentary hunting and gathering economies to the highly developed Aztec, Maya, and Inca civilizations. The Mayas went farthest in the art of writing, their remarkable hieroglyphs having eluded decipherment to the present day. Because of the Indians' Asian origin their languages have been carefully compared with the various languages of Asia, but thus far no significant similarities have been discovered.

Dozens of modern English words have their origin in one or another Indian language. The Algonkian languages seem to have contributed the most: *moose*, *skunk*, *chipmunk*, *raccoon*, *opossum*, *persimmon*, *squash*, *hominy*, *squaw*, *papoose*, *wigwam*, *powwow*, *moccasin*, *wampum*, and *tomahawk*. *Woodchuck* comes from Cree, *toboggan* from Micmac, *tepee* from Sioux, and *totem* from Ojibwa. From Nahuatl come *tomato*, *chocolate*, *avocado*, *coyote*, and *ocelot*, while *maize*, *potato*, *hammock*, *barbecue*, *canoe*, *cannibal*, and *hurricane* come from various Indian languages of the West Indies. Among South American Indian languages Quechua has contributed *llama*, *puma*, *vicuña*, *quinine*, and *coco*, while from Tupi come *jaguar*, *tapir*, *tapioca*, *petunia*, and *jacaranda*. The word *poncho* comes from Araucanian.

But it is in the geographic place names of the North American continent that the Indian influence is most clearly seen. About half of the fifty United States, including virtually all the Midwestern states, derive their names from an Indian language. Mississippi means "great river" in Ojibwa; Minnesota means "sky-blue waters" in Sioux;

Oklahoma means "red people" in Choctaw. Saskatchewan means "swift-flowing" in Cree. Among the many American cities with Indian names there are Milwaukee, from *Mahn-a-wakee-Seepe* ("gathering place by the river"), Winnipeg ("muddy water"), Tallahassee ("old town"), Tuscaloosa ("black warrior"), Chattanooga ("rock rising to a point"), Kalamazoo ("boiling pot"), Nantucket ("the faraway place"), Pawtucket ("the place by the waterfall"), Woonsocket ("at the very steep hill"), and Walla Walla ("place of many waters").

Independent Languages

BY THE TERM "INDEPENDENT LANGUAGES" we mean those that do not belong to any specific family and in general are unrelated to any other language. In the classification used in this book, seven languages—three major and four minor ones—fall into this category.

The major languages are Japanese, Korean, and Vietnamese. Japanese and Korean may be related to each other, while Vietnamese is related to Muong, a minor language of Vietnam. The other minor languages are Basque, of northeastern Spain and southwestern France; Burushaski, spoken in northwestern Kashmir; and Ainu, spoken on Hokkaido, Japan. Attempts have been made to link these languages with virtually every other language family of the world but thus far without success.

Artificial Languages

THE TERM "ARTIFICIAL LANGUAGES" refers to those that have been artificially constructed, each in the hope that it might eventually become a universal tongue. Although a number of such languages have been created, only one, Esperanto, has achieved a significant measure of international recognition.

The first attempt at an artificial language was Volapük, which appeared about 1880. Though difficult to learn and as a result short-lived, it did inspire others to attempt a better system. In 1887 L. L. Zamenhof, of Warsaw, Poland, introduced Esperanto, with its greatly simplified grammar and logically constructed vocabulary. Esperanto ("one who hopes") soon developed a large following of dedicated speakers, and later a significant body of literature. Many of the world's literary masterpieces have been translated into Esperanto. Numerous attempts to improve or reform it were in the end abandoned, and today it remains basically the same as designed by Zamenhof.

In the 20th century Occidental and Interlingua appeared, but these are designed primarily for scientific and technical use and stress recognizability rather than active speech. The great advantage of artificial languages lies in their simplicity and the absence of irregular grammatical forms. However, they suffer from the lack of native speakers and national prestige, and in recent years interest in them has generally declined. The tremendous increase in the use and study of English since World War II has led many to believe that English, rather than an artificial language, has the best chance of eventually becoming a universal tongue.

Pidgin and Creole Languages

PIDGINS AND CREOLES are languages that arise to bridge the gap between people who could not otherwise communicate with each other. A pidgin language is one with sharply reduced vocabulary (usually between 700 and 1,500 words) of English, French, Spanish, or Portuguese origin, to which a sprinkling of native words have been added. In some cases, however, it is merely a simplified form of a local language, often with borrowings from another. A pidgin language has no native speakers; *i.e.*, it is always spoken *in addition to* one's mother tongue.

When a pidgin eventually becomes the mother tongue of a group of people it is thereafter referred to as a creole language, and is said to have become "creolized." As such its vocabulary must greatly expand, or re-expand, to accommodate its users' everyday needs. Creoles are rarely written down, but otherwise function in a manner not unlike that of any natural language.

Pidgin English and French Creole are two notable examples of these languages. Pidgin forms of English have existed in a number of countries, but the most important one in use today is the Melanesian

Pidgin of eastern New Guinea and nearby islands. As the indispensable lingua franca of the region, it has been accorded official status in the new country of Papua New Guinea. French creoles, in many different varieties, are spoken in Louisiana, Haiti, Guadeloupe, Martinique, St. Lucia, Trinidad, and French Guiana, as well as Mauritius and Réunion in the Indian Ocean.

A number of other pidgins and creoles have gained considerable currency in individual countries. Papiamento, based principally on Spanish, is widely spoken on Curaçao and other islands of the Netherlands Antilles. In Surinam (Dutch Guiana), in South America, a language called Taki-Taki ("talkee-talkee"), based on English with numerous Dutch words, has become the lingua franca, while Saramacca, a creole based on English but containing several features of African speech, is spoken by the Bush Negroes, the descendants of former African slaves. Africa too has its share of such languages, including a Pidgin English spoken in Cameroon, another known as Krio spoken in Sierra Leone, and a Portuguese creole spoken in Guinea-Bissau and the Cape Verde Islands. Kituba, a simplified form of the Kongo language, is widely spoken in the Congo, while Fanakalo, based largely on Zulu with many English and some Afrikaans words added, is spoken in South Africa among those employed in the mines.

In Papua, in southeastern New Guinea, another pidgin language, Police Motu, has become the lingua franca of much of the region. It is a simplified form of a language known as Motu, which became the trading language between the Motuans and their customers along the shores of the Gulf of Papua. Police Motu derives its curious name from the fact that it was used by the prewar Papuan native police force, which drew its recruits from all parts of the territory.

Part II

INDIVIDUAL LANGUAGES

LANGUAGES OF EUROPE

English

OLD ENGLISH

Beowulf maþelode, bearn Ecgþeowes:
"Ne sorga, snotor guma; selre bið æghwæm
þæt he his freond wrece, þonne he fela murne.
Ure æghwylc sceal ende gebidan
worolde lifes; wyrce se þe mote
domes ær deaþe; þæt bið drihtguman
unlifgendum æfter selest.
Aris, rices weard, uton raþe feran
Grendles magan gang sceawigan.
Ic hit þe gehate, no he on helm losaþ,
ne on foldan fæþm, ne on fyrgenholt,
ne on gyfenes grund, ga þær he wille.
Ðys dogor þu geþyld hafa
weana gehwylces, swa ic þe wene to."

Beowulf spoke, the son of Ecgtheow: "Sorrow not, wise warrior. It is better for a man to avenge his friend than much mourn. Each of us must await his end of the world's life. Let him who may get glory before death: that is best for the warrior after he has gone from life. Arise, guardian of the kingdom, let us go at once to look on the track of Grendel's kin. I promise you this: she will not be lost under cover, not in the earth's bosom nor in the mountain woods nor at the bottom of the sea, go where she will. This day have patience in every woe—as I expect you to."

—*Beowulf*

The spectacular advance of English across the face of the globe is a phenomenon without parallel in the history of language. Observe a German tourist talking to a Japanese shopkeeper in Tokyo, or an African diplomat to his counterpart from Asia, and the medium of communication will almost certainly be English. Though the French and the Russians may sharply disagree, English is already well on its way to becoming the unofficial international language of the world community.

English is the principal language of the United States, Canada, Great Britain, Ireland, Australia, New Zealand, and of such newly independent countries as the Bahamas, Jamaica, Barbados, Grenada, Trinidad and Tobago, and Guyana. It is the official language of more than a dozen African countries, as well as of various British dependencies such as British Honduras, Gibraltar, Hong Kong, and numerous islands in the Caribbean, and the Atlantic, Indian, and Pacific oceans. In India it has the title of "associate official language" and is generally used in conversation between people from different parts of the country. In dozens of other countries throughout the world it is the unofficial second language. All told, English is the mother tongue of about 300 million people, making it second only to Chinese in this regard. But the number of people who speak English with at least some degree of proficiency totals many millions more and, unlike Chinese, extends to every corner of the globe.

In tracing the historical development of the English language, it is customary to divide it into three periods: Old English, which dates from earliest times to 1150; Middle English, 1150–1500; and Modern English, 1500 to the present. Since this book deals basically with foreign languages—languages largely unfamiliar to us—we shall confine our discussion here to the early periods.

The history of the English language may be said to have begun with the arrival in Britain of three Germanic tribes about the middle of the 5th century. Angles, Saxons, and Jutes crossed the North Sea from what is present-day Denmark and the coast of northwest Germany. The inhabitants of Britain prior to this invasion spoke a Celtic language which seems to have quickly given way to the new Germanic tongue. The Jutes, who came from Jutland, settled in Kent, the Isle of Wight, and along part of the Hampshire coast. The Saxons, who came from Holstein, settled in the rest of England south of the Thames. The Angles, who came from Schleswig, settled in the area extending northward from the Thames as far as Scotland, and it is from them that the word "English" evolved. They came from the "angle" or corner of land in present-day Schleswig-Holstein. In Old English their name was Engle and their language known as *englisc*.

In the next several centuries four distinct dialects of English emerged. The Humber River divided the northern kingdom of Northumbria, where Northumbrian was spoken, from the kingdom of Mercia, in central England, where Mercian was spoken. South of the Thames the West Saxon dialect developed in the kingdom of Wessex, while Kentish was spoken in Kent. In the 7th and 8th centuries Northumbria enjoyed political and cultural ascendancy in England, but in the 9th century both Northumbria and Mercia were utterly devastated by the invasions of the Vikings. Only Wessex preserved its independence and by the 10th century the West Saxon dialect came to be the official language of the country. Since most surviving Old English works are those written in West Saxon, our knowledge of Old English is derived mainly from this dialect.

The Germanic peoples in early times used a form of writing known as runes. Its letters were made up mainly of straight lines, so as to be suitable for inscriptions carved on wood or stone. With the arrival of Christian missionaries from Ireland and Rome, however, the runes gradually gave way to the Roman alphabet. A few letters were retained —the þ and ð, both of which represented the *th* sound (*e.g.*, *wiþ*—with, *bæð*—bath), either voiced or unvoiced. Another was the *æ*, which represented the *a* sound of the word "hat" (*bæc*—back). The sound of *sh* was represented by *sc* (*sceap*—sheep), and the sound of *k* was spelled *c* (*cynn*—kin). The letters *j*, *q*, and *v* were not used, and *f* served for both *f* and *v*.

The Old English vocabulary consisted of a sprinkling of Latin and Scandinavian (Old Norse) words over an Anglo-Saxon base. Latin words included *street*, *kitchen*, *kettle*, *cup*, *cheese*, *wine*, and, after the adoption of Christianity, *angel*, *bishop*, *abbot*, *martyr*, and *candle*. The Vikings brought many Old Norse words (*sky*, *egg*, *cake*, *skin*, *leg*, *window*, *husband*, *fellow*, *skill*, *anger*, *flat*, *odd*, *ugly*, *get*, *give*, *take*, *raise*, *call*, *die*), as well as the personal pronouns *they*, *their*, and *them*. Celtic has left its mark mostly in place names (*Devon*, *Dover*, *Kent*, *Carlisle*), and in the names of most English rivers (*Thames*, *Avon*, *Trent*, *Severn*).

Many Old English words and their Old Norse counterparts competed vigorously with each other for supremacy in the language. Sometimes the Old Norse word won out, sometimes the English, in some cases both words remained in use. For "window" the Norse *vindauga* ("wind-eye") won out over English *eagthyrl* ("eye-hole"), but the English *nosthyrl* ("nose-hole") became the modern "nostril." Norse *anger* now takes precedence over English *wrath*, while English *no* and *from* enjoy supremacy over Norse *nay* and *fro*. But standing side by side in modern English are Norse *raise* and English *rear*, Norse *ill* and English *sick*, as well as other such pairs as *bask/bathe*, *skill/craft*, *skin/hide*, and *dike/ditch*. As can be seen, the *sk* sound was most typically Old Norse, and often competed with the English *sh* in the same word. Thus in modern English we have such doublets as *skirt/shirt*, *scatter/shatter*, and *skip/shift*, which began to diverge in meaning only with the passage of centuries.

The Norman Conquest of 1066 brought the French language to England. For about two centuries after the conquest French was the language of the English nobility. Its impact upon English was tremendous. Thousands of new words were introduced into the language, touching upon the fields of government, religion, law, food, art, literature, medicine, and many others. As with the case of Old Norse,

MIDDLE ENGLISH

Bifel that, in that seson on a day,
In Southwerk, at the Tabard as I lay
Redy to wenden on my pilgrimage
To Caunterbury with ful devout corage,
At night was come in-to that hostelrye
Wel nyne and twenty in a companye,
Of sondry folk, by aventure y-falle
In felawshipe, and pilgrims were they alle,
That toward Caunterbury wolden ryde;
The chambres and the stables weren wyde,
And wel we weren esed atte beste.
And shortly, whan the sonne was to reste,
So hadde I spoken with hem everichon,
That I was of hir felawshipe anon,
And made forward erly for to ryse,
To take our wey, ther as I yow devyse.

It happened that, in that season on a day,
In Southwark, at the Tabard as I lay
Ready to wend on my pilgrimage
To Canterbury with a fully devout heart,
At night there came into that inn
Full nine and twenty in a company,
Of sundry folk, by chance fallen
Into fellowship, and pilgrims were they all,
That toward Canterbury would ride;
The chambers and the stables were large,
And well we were treated with the best.
And briefly, when the sun had gone to rest,
So had I spoken with them every one,
That I was of their fellowship forthwith,
And made an agreement to rise early,
To take our way, as I shall tell you.

—CHAUCER, *The Canterbury Tales*

the infusion of French words produced numerous synonyms (English *shut*, French *close*; English *answer*, French *reply*; English *smell*, French *odor*; English *yearly*, French *annual*), as well as many other pairs of words offering subtle distinctions of meaning (*ask/demand*, *room/chamber*, *wish/desire*, *might/power*). It is interesting to note that while the names of meat-producing animals such as *ox*, *cow*, *calf*, *sheep*, *swine*, and *deer* are English, the words for the meats derived from them (*beef*, *veal*, *mutton*, *pork*, *bacon*, *venison*) are all French. And to the already existing synonyms, English *wrath* and Old Norse *anger*, the French added a third word—*ire*.

But despite the great flood of words into English from Latin, Old Norse, French, and later other languages, the heart of the language remained the Old English of Anglo-Saxon times. While fewer than 5,000 Old English words remain unchanged and in common use today, these constitute the basic building blocks of our language. They include the everyday household words, most parts of the body, as well as the numerous pronouns, prepositions, conjunctions, and auxiliary verbs that hold the language together. It was this basic stock, onto which was grafted a wealth of contributions from numerous other sources, that in the end produced what many people today believe to be the richest of the world's languages.

In the 14th century English finally came into its own in England. Between 1350 and 1380 it became the medium of instruction in the schools and the language of the courts of law. King Henry IV, who ascended the throne in 1399, was the first English king since the Norman Conquest whose mother tongue was English. By the close of the 14th century the dialect of London had emerged as the literary standard and Geoffrey Chaucer had written his immortal *Canterbury Tales*.

All great languages have humble beginnings. In the case of English it was the arrival in Britain of a small Germanic tribe from an "angle" of land on the Continent.

Welsh

Pam y caiff bwystfilod rheibus
  Dorri'r egin mân i lawr?
Pam caiff blodau peraidd ifainc
  Fethu gan y sychdwr mawr?
Dere â'r cafodydd hyfryd
  Sy'n cynyddu'r egin grawn,
Cafod hyfryd yn y bore
  Ac un arall y prynhawn.

Gosod babell yng ngwlad Gosen,
  Dere, Arglwydd, yno dy Hun;
Gostwng o'r uchelder golau,
  Gwna dy drigfan gyda dyn;
Trig yn Seion, aros yno,
  Lle mae'r llwythau yn dod ynghyd,
Byth na 'mad oddi wrth dy bobl
  Nes yn ulw yr elo'r byd.

Why are ravenous beasts allowed
  To trample the tender grapes?
Why must sweet flowers
  Fail in the great drought?
Send the healing showers
  To increase the vine shoots,
A healing shower of the first rain
  And another of the latter rain.

Pitch thy tent in the land of Goshen,
  Come thyself, Lord, to abide there;
Descend from the bright heights,
  Make thy dwelling among men.
Abide in Zion, remain there,
  Whither the tribes go up,
Do not ever abandon thy people
  Even to the annihilation of the world.

—WILLIAM WILLIAMS PANTYCELYN

Welsh, the language of Wales, is spoken by about 600,000 people, or less than 25 percent of the Welsh population. Like Gaelic, spoken in Ireland and parts of Scotland, it is one of the Celtic languages, which constitute one of the many branches of the Indo-European family. Celtic tribes entered Britain sometime after the 5th century B.C. The Anglo-Saxon invasions many centuries later drove the Welsh into the west, where they retained their Celtic speech and remained a distinctive people.

The Welsh call their country *Cymru* and their language *Cymraeg*. The alphabet lacks the letters *j*, *k*, *q*, *x*, and *z*, while a number of other consonants are pronounced quite differently from the English. The letter *w* is a vowel, pronounced *u* as in "put," thus giving rise to such words as *gwr* (man) and *bwyd* (food). *Ch* is pronounced as in German (*e.g.*, *chwaer*—sister). The letter *f* is pronounced *v* (*nef*—heaven), the *f* sound rendered by *ff* (*ceffyl*—horse). Two special Welsh letters are the *dd*, pronounced as a voiced *th* (*dydd*—day), and *ll*, pronounced approximately *thl*. The latter appears at the beginning of many Welsh city names such as Llandudno, Llangollen, and Llanfyllin. Welsh towns bear some of the most picturesque names of any in the world. A few examples are Betws-y-Coed, Penrhyndeudraeth, and Pent-bont-rhyd-y-beddau.

Gaelic

Ba ṁinic do ṡíl Nóra go mba ḃreá an saol ḃeiṫ ag imeaċt roimpi ina seaḃac siúil gan beann aici ar ḋuine ar biṫ—bóiṫre na hÉireann roimpi agus a haġaiḋ orṫu; cúl a cinn leis an mbaile agus le cruatan agus le crostaċt a muintire; í ag siúl ó ḃaile go baile agus ó ġleann go gleann. An bóṫar breá réiḋ roimpi, glasra ar gaċ taoiḃ de, tiṫe beaga cluṫara ar ṡleasaiḃ na gcnocán.

Ba mhinic do shíl Nóra go mba bhreá an saol bheith ag imeacht roimpi ina seabhac siúil gan beann aici ar dhuine ar bith—bóithre na hÉireann roimpi agus a haghaidh orthu; cúl a cinn leis an mbaile agus le cruatan agus le crostacht a muintire; í ag siúl ó bhaile go baile agus ó ghleann go gleann. An bóthar breá réidh roimpi, glasra ar gach taobh de, tithe beaga cluthara ar shleasa na gcnocán.

Several times before Nora had thought of what a fine life she would have as a tramp, independent of everybody! Her face on the roads of Ireland before her, and her back on home and the hardship and anger of her family! To walk from village to village and from glen to glen, the fine level road before her, with green fields on both sides of her and small well-sheltered houses on the mountain slopes around her!

—PADRAIC PEARSE, *The Roads*

Gaelic is spoken both in Ireland and in Scotland, in two distinct varieties that are generally referred to as Irish Gaelic and Scottish Gaelic. Like Welsh, it is one of the Celtic languages and thus part of the Indo-European family. Gaelic is also sometimes referred to as Erse.

Irish Gaelic, often known simply as Irish, is an official language of the Republic of Ireland. Although spoken by only 500,000 people, or about one-sixth of the population, its use has been strongly encouraged by the government and it is taught in all Irish schools. The traditional Gaelic alphabet, the first of the two samples above, was evolved from the Latin about the 5th century. It contains only five vowels and thirteen consonants—the letters *j*, *k*, *q*, *v*, *w*, *x*, *y*, and *z* are missing. An acute accent over a vowel indicates that it should be pronounced long, while a single dot over a consonant indicates that it should be aspirated. Nowadays Gaelic is generally written in modern English characters. In the new orthography the dot was dropped and the letter *h* placed after the consonant instead (*e.g.*, *ċ* became *ch*).

About the 5th century Gaelic was carried from Ireland to Scotland. With the passage of time the Scottish variety diverged to the point where it was clearly a separate dialect. Unlike Irish Gaelic, however, Scottish Gaelic has no official status and is spoken by only 75,000 people, or $1\frac{1}{2}$ percent of the population of Scotland. Scottish Gaelic frequently uses a grave accent where Irish uses an acute.

English words of Gaelic origin include *bard*, *glen*, *bog*, *slogan*, *whiskey*, *blarney*, *shillelagh*, *shamrock*, *colleen*, *brogue*, and *galore*. Specifically Scottish Gaelic are *clan*, *loch*, and *ptarmigan*.

French

Au fond de son âme, cependant, elle attendait un événement. Comme les matelots en détresse, elle promenait sur la solitude de sa vie des yeux désespérés, cherchant au loin quelque voile blanche dans les brumes de l'horizon. Elle ne savait pas quel serait ce hasard, le vent qui le pousserait jusqu'à elle, vers quel rivage il la mènerait, s'il était chaloupe ou vaisseau à trois ponts, chargé d'angoisses ou plein de félicités jusqu'aux sabords. Mais, chaque matin, à son réveil, elle l'espérait pour la journée, et elle écoutait tous les bruits, se levait en sursaut, s'étonnait qu'il ne vînt pas; puis, au coucher du soleil, toujours plus triste, désirait être au lendemain.

At the bottom of her heart, however, she was waiting for something to happen. Like shipwrecked sailors, she turned despairing eyes upon the solitude of her life, seeking afar off some white sail in the mists of the horizon. She did not know what this chance would be, what wind would bring it to her, towards what shore it would drive her, if it would be a shallop or a three-decker, laden with anguish or full of bliss to the portholes. But each morning, as she awoke, she hoped it would come that day; she listened to every sound, sprang up with a start, wondered that it did not come; then at sunset, always more saddened, she longed for the morrow. —GUSTAVE FLAUBERT, *Madame Bovary*

French is one of the world's great languages, rivaled only by English as the language of international society and diplomacy. Besides being spoken in France, it is one of the official languages of Belgium, of Switzerland, and of Canada; it is the official language of Luxembourg, of Haiti, of more than fifteen African countries, and of various French dependencies such as St. Pierre and Miquelon (off the coast of Newfoundland), Guadeloupe and Martinique (in the Caribbean), French Guiana (in South America), Réunion (in the Indian Ocean), and New Caledonia and Tahiti (in the South Pacific). In addition, French is the unofficial second language of a number of countries, including Morocco, Tunisia, Algeria, Lebanon, Syria, Laos, Cambodia, and Vietnam. All told, it is the mother tongue of about 75 million people, with millions more familiar with it, in some degree, as a second language.

French is one of the Romance languages, descended from Latin. The appearance of Latin in France (then called Gaul) dates from Caesar's conquest of the region in the period 58–51 B.C. Gaul became one of the richest and most important provinces of the Roman Empire and Latin superseded the various Celtic (Gaulish) tongues as the language of the domain. A number of dialects emerged but history favored the north; Paris became the capital of France in the 12th century and Parisian French gained ascendancy over the others. In the 17th, 18th, and 19th centuries French was preeminent as an international language, though it has been partially eclipsed by English in the 20th. French was one of the two official languages of the League of Nations and is now one of the six official languages of the United Nations.

The French alphabet is the same as that of English, though the letter *w* appears only in foreign words. Grave (*è*), acute (*é*), and circumflex (*ô*) accents are used (*e.g.*, *père*—father, *été*—summer, *élève*—pupil, *âme*—soul); and the cedilla (*ç*) appears under the letter *c* when preceding *a*, *o*, or *u* to indicate an *s* sound rather than *k* (*leçon*—lesson).

French spelling generally reflects the language as it was spoken four or five centuries ago and is therefore a poor guide to modern pronunciation. Silent letters abound, especially at the ends of words (*hommes* is pronounced *um*; *aiment* pronounced *em*) but a normally silent final consonant is often sounded when it is followed by a word that begins with a vowel. In this process, known as liaison, the consonant becomes part of the first syllable of the following word, so that the sentence *il est assis* (he is seated) is pronounced *ē-lĕ-tă-sē*. Although French pronunciation is governed by fairly consistent rules, the actual sounds of the language are quite difficult for the English speaker, and a good "French accent" is something not easily acquired.

As the two major languages of the Western world, English and French naturally have contributed many words to each other. The enormous impact of Norman French on the English language has already been discussed. More recent French contributions to English—with the French pronunciation retained as closely as possible—include such words and expressions as *hors d'oeuvre*, *à la carte*, *table d'hôte*, *en route*, *en masse*, *rendezvous*, *carte blanche*, *savoir-faire*, *faux pas*, *fait accompli*, *par excellence*, *bon vivant*, *joie de vivre*, *raison d'être*, *coup d'état*, *nouveau riche*, *esprit de corps*, *laissez faire*, *chargé d'affaires*, *pièce de résistance*, and *R.S.V.P.*

In recent years, however, traffic has been mainly in the opposite direction. To the dismay of purists of the language, to say nothing of the French Academy, French has been virtually inundated with English words of all kinds—so much so that the resulting jargon has been dubbed *franglais,* a combination of *français* (French) and *anglais* (English). A few examples among hundreds are *le hamburger, le drugstore, le week-end, le strip-tease, le pull-over, le tee-shirt, le chewing gum, les blue-jeans, le snack-bar,* and *la cover-girl.* Most of these have thus far been denied official status by the Academy, but even here concessions are being made. Recently the Academy approved the adoption into French of *le pipeline* and *le bulldozer*—with the strict proviso, of course, that they be pronounced *peep-LEEN* and *bool-do-ZAIR.*

Breton

Ur wez a oa ur Pesketaër koz, hag a oa dougeres he vroeg. Un abardez ec'h arruas er gèr ha n'hen defoa tapet netra. He vroeg a c'hoantaas debri pesked, hag a renkas retorn d'oc'htu d'ann aod. Teurel a ra he roejo, hag a tigass gant-hanur pesk ar c'haera. Ma oa stad en-han—Brema bepred, a lare d'ehan heunan, am bo peuc'h digant ma groeg. Met setu pa oa o kregi er pesk, heman a em laka da brezeg, hag a làr d'ehan, "Pa vin marw, ro ma c'hig da debri d'as groeg; ma c'halon hag ann dour en pehini a vin bet gwalc'het, d'as kazek, ha ma bouellou ha ma skevend d'as kiez."

Once there was an old fisherman whose wife was pregnant. One evening he returned home having caught nothing. But his wife wanted some fish to eat, so he had to return right away to the shore. He cast his nets and landed a magnificent fish. He was delighted—for the time being at least, he said to himself, my wife will give me a little peace. But just as he was about to bring in the fish, the fish began to speak, saying, "When I am dead, give my flesh to your wife to eat; my heart and the water I will be washed in to your mare; and my entrails and my lungs to your dog."

Breton is spoken in Brittany, the peninsula of westernmost France lying between the English Channel and the Bay of Biscay. It is the only Celtic language spoken on the European continent, having been brought from Cornwall and South Wales in the 5th and 6th centuries by Britons fleeing from Saxon invaders. Today there are fewer than one million speakers of Breton. It has no official status in France and even in Brittany it is not used in the schools.

Provençal

Van parti de Lioun à la primo aubo
Li veiturin que règnon sus lou Rose.
Es uno raço d'ome caloussudo,
Galoio e bravo, li Coundriéulen. Sèmpre
Planta sus li radèu e li sapino,
L'uscle dóu jour e lou rebat de l'aigo
Ié dauron lou carage coume un brounze.
Mai d'aquéu tèms encaro mai, vous dise,
Ié vesias d'oumenas à barbo espesso,
Grand, courpourènt, clapu tau que de chaine,
Boulegant un saumié coume uno busco.

From Lyons at the blush of early dawn
The bargemen, masters of the Rhône, depart,
A robust band and brave, the Condrillots.
Upright upon their crafts of planks of fir,
The tan of sun and glint from glassy wave
Their visages have bronzèd as with gold.
And in that day colossuses they were,
Big, corpulent, and strong as living oaks,
And moving beams about as we would straws.

—FRÉDÉRIC MISTRAL, *The Song of the Rhône*

Provençal is a Romance language spoken in Provence, the historical region of southeastern France, bordering Italy and facing the Mediterranean Sea. In its broader sense it refers to the many similar dialects spoken throughout southern France. In this sense it is often known as *langue d'oc*, in contrast to *langue d'oïl* of the north, *oc* and *oïl* (modern *oui*) being the respective words for "yes" in the two halves of the country.

The high point in the development of Provençal was the period between the 12th and the 14th centuries, when it was the language of the troubadours and the cultured speech of all of southern France. But subsequent encroachments from the north brought this culture to an end, and with it ended troubadour literature and the use of Provençal as the standard idiom of the region. The language split into a number of fragmented dialects, a situation that prevails to the present day.

In the 19th century a movement for the revival and standardization of Provençal was spearheaded by the celebrated poet Frédéric Mistral. In attempting to create a new literary standard for the language, he produced a monumental two-volume dictionary of Provençal plus a collection of epic poems that won him the Nobel Prize in 1904. But despite his efforts, the movement in the long run was not a great success. In the 20th century, with increasing emphasis in France on nationalism and unity, French is slowly but surely reducing Provençal to a regional patois doomed, in the opinion of many, to eventual extinction.

Spanish

En efeto, rematado ya su juicio, vino a dar en el más extraño pensamiento que jamás dió loco en el mundo, y fué que le pareció convenible y necesario, así para el aumento de su honra como para el servicio de su república, hacerse caballero andante, y irse por todo el mundo con sus armas y caballo a buscar las aventuras y a ejercitarse en todo aquello que él había leído que los caballeros andantes se ejercitaban, deshaciendo todo género de agravio, y poniéndose en ocasiones y peligros donde, acabándolos, cobrase eterno nombre y fama.

In short, his wits being quite gone, he hit upon the strangest notion that ever madman in this world hit upon, and that was that he fancied it was right and requisite, as well for the support of his own honor as for the service of his country, that he should make a knight-errant of himself, roaming the world over in full armor and on horseback in quest of adventures, and putting in practice himself all that he had read of as being the usual practices of knights-errant; righting every kind of wrong, and exposing himself to peril and danger from which, in the issue, he was to reap eternal renown and fame.

—MIGUEL DE CERVANTES, *Don Quixote*

Spanish is the most widely spoken of the Romance languages, both in terms of number of speakers and the number of countries in which it is the dominant language. Besides being spoken in Spain, it is the official language of all the South American republics except Brazil and Guyana, of the six republics of Central America, as well as of Mexico, Cuba, the Dominican Republic, and Puerto Rico. Additionally it is spoken in the Balearic and Canary islands, in parts of Morocco and the west coast of Africa, and also in Equatorial Guinea. In the United States it is widely spoken in Texas, New Mexico, Arizona, and California (in New Mexico it is co-official with English), in New York City by the large Puerto Rican population, and more recently in southern Florida by people who have arrived from Cuba. A variety of Spanish known as Ladino is spoken in Turkey and Israel by descendants of Jews who were expelled from Spain in 1492. All told there are about 200 million speakers of Spanish.

Pronunciation and usage of Spanish naturally vary between countries, but regional differences are not so great as to make the language unintelligible to speakers from different areas. The purest form of Spanish is known as Castilian, originally one of the dialects that developed from Latin after the Roman conquest of Hispania in the 3rd century A.D. After the disintegration of the Roman Empire, Spain was overrun by the Visigoths, and in the 8th century the Arabic-speaking Moors conquered all but the northernmost part of the peninsula. In the Christian reconquest, Castile, an independent kingdom, took the initiative and by the time of the unification of Spain in the 15th century, Castilian had become the dominant dialect. In the years that followed, Castilian—now Spanish—became the language of a vast empire in the New World.

Spanish vocabulary is basically of Latin origin, though many of the words differ markedly from their counterparts in French and Italian. Many words beginning with *f* in the other Romance languages begin with *h* in Spanish (*e.g.*, *hijo*—son, *hilo*—thread). The Moorish influence is seen in the many words beginning with *al-* (*algodón*—cotton, *alfombra*—rug, *almohada*—pillow, *alfiler*—pin). As in British and American English, there are differences in vocabulary on the two sides of the ocean—*patata* (potato) is *papa* in Latin America, while *melocotón* (peach) is *durazno*.

Spanish spelling is based on generally consistent phonetic principles, and reflects better than most languages the way a word is pronounced. The consonants *b* and *v* are pronounced alike, the sound falling somewhere between the two sounds in English (*boca*—mouth, *voz*—voice). The letter *z*, and the letter *c* before *e* and *i*, are pronounced as a voiceless *th* in Castilian, but more like *s* in southern Spain and Latin America (*zapato*—shoe, *ciudad*—city). The letter *j*, and the letter *g* before *e* and *i*, are pronounced like the English *h* (*jardín*—garden, *general*—general), though in Spain it is more guttural than in Latin America. The hard *g* sound is represented by *g* before *a*, *o*, and *u* (*gato*—cat), but *gu* before *e* and *i* (*seguir*—to follow). The combination *ch* is pronounced as in English (*muchacho*—boy), but is considered a separate letter of the Spanish alphabet, occurring after *c*. Similarly *ll*, pronounced as in the English "million" in Spain but as *y* in America (*calle*—street), comes after *l* in the alphabet; *ñ*, pronounced *ny* (*pequeño*—small), comes after *n*; and *rr*, a rolled *r* (*correr*—to run), comes after *r*. The *h* is always silent (*hombre*—man).

The stress in Spanish likewise follows a consistent pattern, falling on the next to last syllable in words ending in a vowel, *n*, or *s*, and on the final syllable in words ending in other consonants. Exceptions to this rule are indicated by an acute accent (*árbol*—tree, *corazón*—heart).

English words of Spanish origin include *cargo*, *siesta*, *sombrero*, *mesa*, *hacienda*, *patio*, *armada*, *guerrilla*, *junta*, *plaza*, *canyon*, *rodeo*, *pueblo*, *adobe*, *vanilla*, *armadillo*, *tornado*, *embargo*, and *bonanza*.

Catalan

És el mes de gener. L'aire és sereníssim i glacial, i la lluna guaita, plàcidament, a través de l'emmallat de branques d'una arbreda sense fulles, el mas Cotells de Puigcerdà, el qual la rep amablement, esguardant-la amb l'ullet de groga llum d'una de les seves finestres i saludant-la amb el braç de fum blavís que, com de la curta mànega d'un giponet blanc, surt d'una de les seves xemeneies.

It is the month of January. The air is very clear and frosty, and the moon looks down placidly through the mesh of bare branches at the farmhouse of Cotells de Puigcerdà. It receives her tenderly, watching her with the little eye of yellow light from one of its windows, and greeting her with a wisp of bluish smoke that creeps out of one of its chimneys like an arm out of a short sleeve of a white dress.

—JOAQUIM RUYRA, *Friar Pancraci*

Catalan is spoken in northeastern Spain, in the Balearic Islands, in Andorra, and in a small part of France. Historically it was the language of Catalonia, the region that includes Barcelona, but today its speakers extend down the Spanish coast as far as the province of Valencia. In France it is spoken in the province of Pyrénées-Orientales, formerly known as Roussillon.

There are about 6 million speakers of Catalan. About 500,000 are in the Balearic Islands, 250,000 in France, 20,000 in Andorra, and the rest in Spain. Only in Andorra, where it is the main language spoken, does it have official status. Catalan is of the Romance family, most closely related to Provençal.

Basque

Antxina, bedar txori abere ta patariak euren berbetea aztu baino lentxoago, eŕege bat bizi zan, gizon zintzo, buruargi, biotz-andi, mendekoak maite ebazan eŕege. Seme bat eukan ta bera alper, buru-eritxi, biotz-gogor, mendekoen ardura bagea. Diru baten auŕea ta atzea baino bére banago ziran aita-seme aren izateak. Aitaren ontasun guztien artean agiriena mendekoak seme-alabatzat lez eukitea zan. Semearen gaiztakeri ezagunena baŕiz mendekoak aintzat artu ez eze beste gisaren bateko izakitzat eukitea. Eztago zetan esan aita maite maite ebela eŕi atako lagunak, semea uŕetan bére ez.

Long ago, a short time before the plants, the birds, the animals, and all creeping and crawling things forgot their language, there lived a king, a sincere, frank, generous man, a king who loved his subjects. He had a son who was a good-for-nothing, conceited, hard-hearted, and with no compassion for the subjects. The characters of the father and son were as different as the two sides of a coin. The most outstanding of all the father's good qualities was that he treated his subjects as his own children. In contrast, the son's most obvious failing was that he looked on them as creatures of another world. It goes without saying that the people of the realm had great affection for the father but none at all for the son.

Basque stands alone among the languages of Europe. Despite many efforts, no connection between Basque and any other language has ever been proven. Structural similarities with certain languages in Asia have been noted, but as yet it must be considered a completely isolated and independent language.

Basque is spoken on both sides of the Spanish-French border by about 700,000 people. Of these, about 600,000 are in Spain, living mainly in the provinces of Guipúzcoa, Vizcaya, and Navarra. In France they live in the department of Pyrénées-Atlantiques, in the southwestern corner of the country. Bilbao, the capital of Vizcaya, is the major city of the Basque region. Most Basques are bilingual, speaking Spanish or French (or both) in addition to their own language.

There are a number of widely divergent dialects of Basque. In some the language is known as *Euskara*, in others *Eskuara*. The letter *z* is pronounced *s* (*e.g.*, *zazpi*—seven), while the unusual combination *tx* is pronounced *ch* (*etxe*—house). There is both a soft *r* and a hard *r*, the latter usually spelled *ŕ* (*eŕege*—king). The definite article is merely the suffix *-a* (*gizon*—man, *gizona*—the man), while the plural is formed with the suffix *-k* (*gizonak*—the men).

As the only non-Indo-European language of Western Europe, Basque would appear to be the sole survivor of those languages spoken there before the Indo-Europeans arrived. It was probably part of an extended group that included not only Basque but other languages of southern Europe as well.

The name of the game of jai alai comes from Basque. *Jai* means "festival" in Basque, while *alai* means "joyous."

Portuguese

Falou então de si, com modéstia: reconhecia, quando via na capital tão ilustres parlamentares, oradores tão sublimes, tão consumados estilistas, reconhecia que era um zero!—E com a mão erguida formava no ar, pela junção do polegar e do indicador, um O: um *zero*! proclamou o seu amor à pátria: que amanhã as instituições ou a família real precisassem dele—e o seu corpo, a sua pena, o seu modesto pecúlio, tudo oferecia de bom grado! Queria derramar todo o seu sangue pelo trono!

He spoke modestly of himself. He admitted that he was a mere zero amongst the consummate stylists, the sublime orators and illustrious parliamentarians who swarmed in their capital. In pronouncing the word "zero" he formed an "0" with his index and thumb, raising his hand before him. He proclaimed his love for his country: and said that if its institutions or the Royal Family should ever have need of them—his body, his talent, his pen, and his modest fortune in savings, would all be at their disposal. He would love to pour out his last drop of blood for the throne.

—JOSÉ MARIA EÇA DE QUEIROZ, *Cousin Basilio*

Portuguese is the national language of both Portugal and Brazil. With about 10 million speakers in the former and some 95 million in the latter, coupled with speakers in Portuguese colonies in Africa, in the Atlantic, and in Asia, its total number of speakers is over 100 million. In northwesternmost Spain about 3 million people speak a dialect of Portuguese known as Galician.

Portuguese is a Romance language, closely related to, and yet distinctly different from, Spanish. It is softer and less emphatic than Spanish, with a greater variety of vowel sounds, and contains a number of nasal sounds that are completely unknown in Spanish. Words beginning with *h* in Spanish frequently begin with *f* in Portuguese (*e.g.*, *hijo/filho*—son), while words ending in *-ción* in Spanish generally end in *-ção* in Portuguese (*nación/nação*—nation). There are a number of words from Arabic in both languages (*algodón/algodão*—cotton) plus a few peculiar to Portuguese (*alfaiate*—tailor). Many words are identical in the two languages (*mesa*—table, *flor*—flower, *lago*—lake), but others are completely different (*perro/cão*—dog, *gracias/obrigado*—thank you).

The Portuguese of Brazil is slower and more measured than that of Portugal, but the Brazilians and Portuguese communicate with each other without the slightest difficulty. As in British and American English there are occasional differences in vocabulary. The word for "boy" is *rapaz* in Portugal but *moço* in Brazil; "girl" is *rapariga* in Portugal and *moça* in Brazil. Some Brazilian words are of Indian origin (*e.g.*, *abacaxi*—pineapple).

The Portuguese nasal vowels are indicated by the letters *ã* and *õ*. The *ç* functions as in French, while the combinations *lh* and *nh* correspond to the Spanish *ll* and *ñ* respectively. The letter *j* is pronounced as in French (not as in Spanish), as is the letter *g* before *e* and *i*. The *h* is always silent. Words ending in *a* (but not *ã*), *e*, *o*, *m*, or *s* generally stress the next to last syllable, while those ending in other letters stress the final syllable. Exceptions to this rule are indicated by an acute accent if the vowel has an open sound (*açúcar*—sugar), and by a circumflex if the vowel has a closed sound (*relâmpago*—lightning). The accent marks are also used to distinguish between words that would otherwise have the same spelling, as for example *e*, meaning "and," but *é*, meaning "is," and *por*, meaning "by," but *pôr*, meaning "to put."

Italian

La Pasqua infatti era vicina. Le colline erano tornate a vestirsi di verde, e i fichidindia erano di nuovo in fiore. Le ragazze avevano seminato il basilico alla finestra, e ci venivano a posare le farfalle bianche; fin le povere ginestre della sciara avevano il loro fiorellino pallido. La mattina, sui tetti, fumavano le tegole verdi e gialle, e i passeri vi facevano gazzarra sino al tramonto.

Easter really was near. The hills were clothed in green and the prickly-pear trees were in flower again. The girls had sown basil in the window boxes, and white butterflies came and perched on them. Even the broom on the lava field was covered with poor, pale little flowers. In the morning steam rose from the green and yellow slates on the roofs, where sparrows chattered noisily until sunset.

—GIOVANNI VERGA, *The House by the Medlar Tree*

Italian is considered by many to be the most beautiful of the world's languages. As the transmitter of the great culture of the Renaissance, its influence on the other languages of Western Europe has been profound. Besides being spoken in Italy, it is one of the four official languages of Switzerland, and is also widely spoken in the United States, Canada, Argentina, and Brazil. All told there are about 60 million speakers of Italian.

Italian is one of the Romance languages, and has remained closer to the original Latin than any of the others. Its dialects, however, vary tremendously, often to the point where communication becomes a problem. The literary standard came into being in the 14th century, largely through Dante's *Divine Comedy* and the works of Petrarch and Boccaccio. Since these eminent authors chiefly used the dialect of Tuscany (especially Florentine), modern literary Italian is essentially Tuscan. Since 1870 the dialect of Rome has gained considerable prestige but it has still failed to eclipse the Florentine standard.

The Italian alphabet consists basically of 21 letters—*j*, *k*, *w*, *x*, and *y* appear only in foreign words. The letter *c* is pronounced *k* before *a*, *o*, and *u*, but *ch* before *e* and *i* (*e.g.*, *carcere*—prison). *Ch* and *cch* are also pronounced *k* (*chiave*—key, *bicchiere*—glass). *G* is pronounced as a hard *g* before *a*, *o*, and *u* (*gamba*—leg), but as *j* before *e* and *i* (*giorno*—day). *Gg* before *e* and *i* is also pronounced *j* (*oggi*—today), *gh* before *e* and *i* is a hard *g* (*lunghezza*—length), *gli* followed by a vowel is pronounced *lli* as in "million" (*biglietto*—ticket), *gn* like the *ny* in "canyon" (*ogni*—every), and *gu* followed by a vowel as *gw* (*guerra*—war). *Z* and *zz* are generally pronounced *ts* (*zio*—uncle, *prezzo*—price), but sometimes as *dz* (*pranzo*—dinner, *mezzo*—middle). *Sc* before *e* and *i* is pronounced *sh* (*pesce*—fish).

The stress in Italian generally falls on the next to last or third from last syllable. The only written accent is the grave, which is used whenever a word of more than one syllable stresses the final vowel (*città*—city). It is also used on words of a single syllable to distinguish between two words that would otherwise have the same spelling, as for example *e*, meaning "and," but *è*, meaning "is." And it also appears in a few miscellaneous words such as *più* (more) and *già* (already).

English words of Italian origin include *umbrella*, *spaghetti*, *macaroni*, *broccoli*, *balcony*, *studio*, *casino*, *fresco*, *gusto*, *volcano*, *lava*, *stucco*, *gondola*, *regatta*, *malaria*, *bandit*, *incognito*, *vendetta*, and *inferno*. In the field of music there are *piano*, *viola*, *opera*, *sonata*, *concerto*, *oratorio*, *soprano*, *aria*, *solo*, *trio*, *quartet*, *allegro*, *andante*, *tempo*, *libretto*, *staccato*, *crescendo*, *maestro*, and *virtuoso*.

Latin

Quae potest homini esse polito delectatio, cum aut homo imbecillus a valentissima bestia laniatur aut praeclara bestia venabulo transverberatur? quae tamen, si videnda sunt, saepe vidisti; neque nos, qui haec spectamus, quicquam novi vidimus. Extremus elephantorum dies fuit. In quo admiratio magna vulgi atquae turbae, delectatio nulla exstitit; quin etiam misericordia quaedam consecuta est atque opinio eius modi, esse quamdam illi beluae cum genere humano societatem.

What pleasure can it give a cultivated man to watch some poor fellow being torn to pieces by a powerful beast or a superb beast being pierced with a hunting spear? Even were such things worth looking at, you've seen them many times, and we saw nothing new this time. The last day was devoted to the elephants. The vulgar populace was enthusiastic, but there was no pleasure in it; indeed, the show provoked some sort of compassion, a feeling that there is some kinship between this great beast and humankind.

—CICERO, *Letters to Friends*

Latin, the language of ancient Rome, is the ancestor of the modern Romance languages. Beginning as a local dialect of a small village on the Tiber River, it spread in the course of history over a large portion of the globe. In the Middle Ages Latin served as the international medium of communications, as well as the language of science, philosophy, and theology. Until comparatively recent times a knowledge of Latin was an essential prerequisite to any liberal education; only in this century has the study of Latin declined and emphasis shifted to the modern living languages. The Roman Catholic Church has traditionally used Latin as its official and liturgical language.

Latin was brought to the Italian peninsula by a wave of immigrants from the north about 1000 B.C. Over the centuries the city of Rome rose to a position of prominence and the Latin of Rome became the literary standard of the newly-emerging Roman Empire. Side by side with classical Latin a spoken vernacular developed, which was carried by the Roman army throughout the empire. It completely displaced the pre-Roman tongues of Italy, Gaul, and Spain and was readily accepted by the barbarians who partitioned the Roman Empire in the 5th century A.D. Further divisions led to the eventual emergence of the modern Romance languages—Italian, French, Spanish, Portuguese, and Rumanian.

The Latin, or Roman, alphabet was created in the 7th century B.C. It was based on the Etruscan alphabet, which in turn was derived from the Greek. Of the original twenty-six Etruscan letters the Romans adopted twenty-one. The original Latin alphabet was A, B, C (which stood for both *g* and *k*), D, E, F, I (the Greek *zeta*), H, I (which stood for both *i* and *j*), K, L, M, N, O, P, Q, R (though for a long time this was written P), S, T, V (which stood for *u*, *v*, and *w*), and X. Later the Greek *zeta* (I) was dropped and a new letter G was placed in its position. After the conquest of Greece in the first century B.C. the letters Y and Z were adopted from the contemporary Greek alphabet and placed at the end. Thus the new Latin alphabet contained twenty-three letters. It was not until the Middle Ages that the letter J (to distinguish it from I) and the letters U and W (to distinguish them from V) were added.

Latin lacks somewhat the variety and flexibility of Greek, perhaps reflecting the practical nature of the Roman people, who were more concerned with government and empire than with speculative thought and poetic imagery. Yet in the hands of the great masters of the classical period it was the vehicle for a body of literature and poetry that can bear comparison with any in the world.

German

Pharao's Anblick war wunderbar. Sein Wagen war pures Gold und nichts andres, — er war golden nach seinen Rädern, seinen Wänden und seiner Deichsel und mit getriebenen Bildern bedeckt, die man aber nicht zu unterscheiden vermochte nach dem, was sie darstellten, denn im Prall der Mittagssonne blendete und blitzte der Wagen so gewaltig, daß die Augen es kaum ertrugen; und da seine Räder, wie auch die Hufe der Rosse davor, dichte Staubwolken aufwirbelten, die die Räder umhüllten, so war es, als ob Pharao in Rauch und Feuersgluten daherkäme, schrecklich und herrlich anzusehen.

Pharao's Anblick war wunderbar. Sein Wagen war pures Gold und nichts andres,—er war golden nach seinen Rädern, seinen Wänden und seiner Deichsel und mit getriebenen Bildern bedeckt, die man aber nicht zu unterscheiden vermochte nach dem, was sie darstellten, denn im Prall der Mittagssonne blendete und blitzte der Wagen so gewaltig, daß die Augen es kaum ertrugen; und da seine Räder, wie auch die Hufe der Rosse davor, dichte Staubwolken aufwirbelten, die die Räder umhüllten, so war es, als ob Pharao in Rauch und Feuersgluten daherkäme, schrecklich und herrlich anzusehen.

Pharaoh was wonderful to behold. His chariot was pure gold, naught else—gold wheels, gold sides, gold axles; and covered with embossed pictures, which, however, one could not see because the whole car flashed and glittered so, as it reflected the midday sun, that the eye could scarcely bear it. The wheels and the hoofs of the steeds whirled up thick enveloping clouds of dust so that it was as if Pharaoh came on in flame and smoke, frightful and glorious to behold.

—THOMAS MANN, *Joseph and His Brothers*

German is one of the main cultural languages of the Western world, spoken by approximately 100 million people. It is the national language of both Germany and Austria, and is one of the four official languages of Switzerland. Additionally it is spoken in eastern France, in the region formerly known as Alsace-Lorraine, in northern Italy in the region of Alto Adige, and also in eastern Belgium, Luxembourg, and the principality of Liechtenstein. There are about 6 million speakers of German in the United States, 1½ million in the Soviet Union, and sizable colonies as well in Canada, Argentina, Brazil, and Chile.

Like the other Germanic languages, German is a member of the Indo-European family. Written German is quite uniform but spoken dialects vary considerably, sometimes to the point where communication becomes a problem. The dialects fall within two general divisions: High German (*Hochdeutsch*), spoken in the highlands of the south, and Low German (*Plattdeutsch*), spoken in the lowlands of the north. High German is the standard written language, used almost exclusively in books and newspapers, even in the regions where Low German is more commonly spoken. Low German sounds more like English and Dutch, as may be seen by such words as *Door* (door—High German: *Tür*), and *eten* (to eat—High German: *essen*).

Traditionally German was written in a Gothic style known as *Fraktur*, which dates from the 14th century. In the period following World War II, however, *Fraktur* was largely superseded by the Roman characters used throughout the rest of Western Europe. The Roman script contains only one additional letter, the ß or double *s*, which is used only in the lower case. The letter *j* is pronounced *y* (*e.g.*, *ja*—yes), *v* is pronounced *f* (*vier*—four), and *w* is pronounced *v* (*weiss*—white). Diphthongs include *sch*, pronounced *sh* (*Schnee*—snow); *st*, pronounced *sht* (*Strasse*—street); *sp*, pronounced *shp* (*sprechen*—to speak). The only diacritical mark is the umlaut, which appears over the letters *a*, *o*, and *u* (*Rücken*—back). German is the only language in which all nouns begin with a capital letter.

Since English is a Germanic language, it is not surprising to find a high degree of similarity in the vocabulary of the two languages. *Finger*, *Hand*, *Butter*, *Ring*, *Name*, *warm*, and *blind* are German words meaning exactly what they do in English. Other words that are very similar to their English counterparts are *Vater* (father), *Mutter* (mother), *Freund* (friend), *Gott* (God), *Licht* (light), *Wasser* (water), *Feuer* (fire), *Silber* (silver), *Brot* (bread), *Milch* (milk), *Fisch* (fish), *Apfel* (apple), *Buch* (book), *gut* (good), *alt* (old), *kalt* (cold), and *blau* (blue). More recent German borrowings in English are *schnitzel*, *sauerkraut*, *pumpernickel, kindergarten, dachshund, poodle, yodel, lager, ersatz, edelweiss, meerschaum, wanderlust, hinterland,* and *blitzkrieg.* The words *frankfurter* and *hamburger* come from the German cities of Frankfurt and Hamburg respectively.

The word for German in other languages takes many different forms. In German itself it is *deutsch,* in Spanish *alemán,* in Italian *tedesco,* in the Scandinavian languages *tysk,* and in Russian *nemetsky.*

Dutch

In die nacht wist ik eigenlijk dat ik sterven moest, ik wachtte op de politie, ik was bereid, bereid zoals de soldaten op het slagveld. Ik wou me graag opofferen voor het vaderland, maar nu, nu ik weer gered ben, nu is mijn eerste wens na de oorlog, maak me Nederlander! Ik houd van de Nederlanders, ik houd van ons land, ik houd van de taal, en wil hier werken. En al zou ik aan de Koningin zelf moeten schrijven, ik zal niet wijken vóór mijn doel bereikt is.

During that night I really felt that I had to die, I waited for the police, I was prepared, as the soldier is on the battlefield. I was eager to lay down my life for the country, but now, now I've been saved again, now my first wish after the war is that I may become Dutch! I love the Dutch, I love this country, I love the language and want to work here. And even if I have to write to the Queen myself, I will not give up until I have reached my goal.

—ANNE FRANK, *The Diary of a Young Girl*

Dutch is spoken by the 13 million inhabitants of the Netherlands, and is also the official language of Surinam (Dutch Guiana), in South America, and of the Netherlands Antilles in the Caribbean Sea. It is also spoken in northern Belgium but there the language is generally referred to as Flemish.

Dutch, like English, is one of the Germanic languages, and thus part of the Indo-European family. It stands about midway between English and German and is the closest to English of any of the major languages.

Long a maritime nation, the Dutch have left their imprint on many languages of the world. Many Dutch nautical terms have been adopted into other languages. Dutch idioms and syntax are still evident in present-day Indonesian. English words of Dutch origin include *deck*, *yacht*, *easel*, *freight*, *furlough*, *brandy*, *cookie*, *cruller*, *waffle*, *maelstrom*, *isinglass*, and *Santa Claus*. Many place names in New York City, such as Brooklyn, Flushing, Harlem, Staten Island, and the Bowery, are reminders of the old Dutch colony of New Amsterdam.

Frisian

It hat eigenskip, dat de Fryske bydrage ta de Amerikaenske literatuer tige biskieden is. Der binne einlik mar trije, fjouwer Fryske nammen, dy 't yn de Amerikaenske literaire wrâld nei foaren komd binne. It binne allegearre nammen fan noch libjende Friezen, in biwiis dat de literaire kunst ûnder de Fryske lânforhuzers har net ier ta bloei set hat. Faeks is it lykwols net sûnder bitsjutting en ûnthjit dat de namme dy 't yn tiidsfolchoarder it lêst komt ek de meast forneamde is.

It stands to reason that the Frisian contribution to American literature is a very modest one. There are really only three or four Frisian names that have come to the fore in the American literary world. They are names of Frisian immigrants who are still living, a proof of the fact that literary art among the Frisian immigrants did not come to early fruition. Perhaps, however, it is not without significance or promise that the name which in point of time comes last is also the most noted.

Frisian is spoken in northern Holland, mainly in the province of Friesland, though some speakers are also to be found in the outlying Frisian Islands. A Low German dialect, it is considered closer than any other language to English. Courses in Frisian are offered at a number of Dutch universities. There are about 300,000 speakers.

Flemish

Hij ging buiten, opende duiven- en hoenderkoten en strooide handvollen kempzaad, spaanse terwe, rijst, vitsel, haver en koren. En 't was ineens een geharrewar, gekakel en geslaag van vleugelen. Er waren zwalpers, smieren, hennen, hanen, ganzen, kalkoenen en een overschone pauw. Ze grabbelden met hun rappe bekken gulzig naar het eten, drongen tegen elkander, liepen ondereen en pikten naar de mussen die met grote kladden in den warrelenden hoop neervielen.

He went out of doors, set open the dovecotes and the fowl house, and scattered maize, rice, oats, and corn. There was a flutter, cluttering, cackling, and flapping of wings; all sorts of fowls were there—pouter pigeons and fantails, cocks and hens, geese, turkeys, and a splendid peacock. Greedily they snapped up the food; they pushed and crowded and spread themselves out and pecked at the sparrows that swooped down on the heaving mass in flocks.

—FELIX TIMMERMANS, *Pallieter*

Flemish is one of the two languages of Belgium, the other being French. It is spoken in the northern half of the country by about 5½ million people, or slightly more than half the population. Flemish is actually the same language as Dutch, spoken in the Netherlands, but cultural and religious distinctions over the centuries have led to the use of separate terms for one and the same language. Historically, Flemish was spoken in the region known as Flanders, whose people are called Flemings.

Luxembourgian

Wo' d'Uelzecht durech d'Wisen ze't,
dûrch d'Fielsen d'Sauer brécht,
wo' d'Rief lânscht d'Musel dofteg ble't,
den Himmel Wein ons mécht;
dât ass onst Land, fir dât mer ge'f
heinidden alles wôn,
onst Hémechtsland, dât mir so' de'f
an onsen Hierzer dron.

O Du douewen, dém séng Hand
dûrch d'Welt d'Natio'ne lét,
behitt Du d'Letzebuerger Land
Vru friemem Joch a Léd!
Du hues ons all als Kanner schon
De freie Géscht jo ginn;
Lôss viru blénken d'Freihétssonn,
de' mir so' lâng gesinn!

Where you see the slow Alzette flow,
the Sura play wild pranks,
where lovely vineyards amply grow
on the Moselle's banks,
there lies the land for which our thanks
are owed to God above,
our own, our native land which ranks
well foremost in our love.

Our Father in Heaven whose powerful hand
makes states or lays them low,
protect Thy Luxembourger Land
from foreign foe or woe.
God's golden liberty bestow
On us now as of yore.
Let Freedom's sun in glory glow
for now and evermore.

—*Our Homeland* (Luxembourg National Anthem)

Luxembourgian, more properly Letzeburgesh, is spoken in the Grand Duchy of Luxembourg. It is basically a dialect of German, but since Luxembourg is an independent country, its language is generally thought of as a separate language. There are about 350,000 speakers.

Rhaeto-Romanic

> A Vella, la veglia capitala da Lumnezia e liug distinguiu da purs e pugnieras, tonscha la splendur dil geraun tochen maneivel dallas cases. El ruaus della dumengia damaun fa ei la pareta che vitg e cultira seigien in esser, ch'igl undegiar dils feins madirs seplonti viavon sur seivs e miraglia, encurend in sinzur davos ils veiders glischonts dellas cases. L'empermischun della stad schai ell'aria cun si'odur pesonta da rosas selvatgas e mèl, mo era cugl aspect penibel da spinas e carduns.
>
> In Vella, ancient capital of the Lumnezia Valley, long the domain of breeders of prized cattle, the splendor of the home fields seems to touch the very houses. In the hush of Sunday morning, one gets the feeling that village and nature are fused into one, that the swaying of the ripening alfalfa seems to stretch beyond the boundaries and walls, almost listening for an echo behind the shining windowpanes of the surrounding homes. The promise of summer is in the very air with the sweet perfume of wild roses and honey, but also with the painful sight of thorns and thistles.
>
> —TONI HALTER, *The Herdsman of Greina*

Rhaeto-Romanic is a collective term for three dialects of the Romance family spoken in northeastern Italy and southeastern Switzerland. Of the more than 500,000 speakers of Rhaeto-Romanic, about 90 percent are in Italy, but there the language is considered a mere patois and has no official status. The Swiss dialect on the other hand, known as Romansch, is one of Switzerland's four official languages, despite the fact that it is spoken by only one percent of the population. The passage cited above is in Romansch.

The two Rhaeto-Romanic dialects of Italy are (1) Friulian, with about 500,000 speakers in the region of Friuli, near the border with Austria and Yugoslavia; (2) Ladin, with about 10,000 speakers in Alto Adige to the west. Romansch is spoken by about 50,000 people in the Swiss canton of Graubünden, bordering Austria and Italy. The survival of Rhaeto-Romanic, despite pressures from surrounding languages, is largely due to the isolation of its speakers in extremely mountainous regions.

Icelandic

Þótt þú langförull legðir
sérhvert land undir fót,
bera hugur og hjarta
samt þíns heimalands mót,
frænka eldfjalls og íshafs,
sifji árfoss og hvers,
dóttir langholts og lyngmós,
sonur landvers og skers.

Yfir heim eða himin
hvort sem hugar þín önd,
skreyta fossar og fjallshlíð
öll þín framtíðarlönd.
Fjarst í eilífðar útsæ
vakir eylendan þín:
nóttlaus voraldar veröld,
þar sem víðsýnið skín.

Það er óskaland íslenzkt,
sem að yfir þú býr—
Aðeins blómgróin björgin,
sérhver baldjökull hlýr.
Frænka eldfjalls og íshafs,
sifji árfoss og hvers,
dóttir langholts og lyngmós,
sonur landvers og skers.

Though you wayfaring wander
all the world to explore,
yet your mind has been molded
by your motherland's shore,
kin of ice and volcano,
child of stream and defile,
daught'r of lava and ling-moor,
son of inlet and isle.

Over earth, over heaven,
though your heart may aspire,
yet will cascades and mountains
stud the land you desire.
In the ocean eternal
lies your isle, girt with brine:
nightless world of spring's wonders
where the grand vistas shine.

For the land of your wishes
has an Icelandic form,
but the rocks grow with flowers
and the glaciers are warm,
kin of ice and volcano,
child of stream and defile,
daught'r of lava and ling-moor,
son of inlet and isle.

—STEPHAN G. STEPHANSSON, *From a Speech on Icelanders' Day*

Icelandic is spoken by the 200,000 inhabitants of Iceland. It is one of the Scandinavian languages, which form a branch of the Germanic languages, in turn a part of the Indo-European family.

Icelandic is remarkably similar to Old Norse, the language of the Vikings, which was brought to Iceland from Norway in the 9th century. Whereas the other Scandinavian languages have been strongly influenced by those of neighboring countries, Icelandic, insular and isolated, has retained its pristine character over the centuries. As a result Icelandic schoolchildren today have no difficulty reading the

Eddas and the sagas, the great epics written in Old Norse. Their language is a sort of parent tongue to the other modern Scandinavian languages. It also has many features in common with Old English, the result of the Viking invasions of Britain in the 9th century.

Another factor behind the purity of Icelandic is the absence of international words for modern ideas and inventions. Icelanders avoid such words wherever possible, preferring to coin their own purely Icelandic words instead. Thus "telephone" in Icelandic is *sími*, an old Icelandic word for "thread" or "wire." The word for "radio" is *útvarp* ("broadcast"). "Automobile" is *bíll*, but may also be *bifreið* ("moving ride"). "Electricity" is *rafmagn* ("amber power").

Icelandic's links with Old English are also reflected in the alphabet, which contains the old runic letters *ð* (*eth*), the voiced *th*, and the *þ* (*thorn*), the unvoiced. It also contains the *æ* of Danish and Norwegian.

Faroese

Hammershaimb, ættaður úr Sandavági, gav út í 1854 fyrstu føroysku málløruna og gjørdi ta nýggju rættskrivingina. Tá fór føroyskt at taka danskt mál av ræði. Í fyrstuni vóru nógvir Føroyingar ikki hugaðir fyri tí føroyska málstrevinum, men tjóðskaparhugurin vann sigur, og nú hevur føroyskt fingið somu rættindir sum danskt, og er—formelt—høvuðsmálið. Men nógvir halda at einans føroyskt eigur at verða nýtt í almennum viðurskiftum. Hetta er til dømis støðan hjá loysingarmonnum, t.e. teir, ið vilja hava landið leyst frá Danmark politiskt; soleiðis halda eisini nógv onnur.

It was Hammershaimb, a native of Sandavágur, who in 1854 published the first grammar of Faroese and introduced the modern orthography. From that time on Faroese began to challenge the supremacy of Danish. At first many Faroese were not sympathetic to the Faroese language movement, but the nationally minded won the day and now Faroese has reached a position of equality with Danish and is, formally, the chief language. Many, however, wish Faroese to be the sole official language. This is the standpoint, for example, of the Separatists, *i.e.*, those who wish the country to be politically independent of Denmark, though many others hold it too.

The Faroe Islands are located about 250 miles north of Scotland, midway between Norway and Iceland. They were settled about a thousand years ago by Norwegian Vikings speaking the Old Norse language. Modern Faroese, like Icelandic, strongly resembles Old Norse. It is spoken by most of the islands' 40,000 inhabitants, although the official language is Danish. The alphabet contains the *ð* (but not the *þ*) of Icelandic, and the *ø* of Danish.

Danish

For mange år siden levede en kejser, som holdt så uhyre meget af smukke, nye klæder, at han gav alle sine penge ud for ret at blive pyntet. Han brød sig ikke om sine soldater, brød sig ej om komedie eller om at køre i skoven, uden alene for at vise sine nye klæder. Han havde en kjole for hver time på dagen, og ligesom man siger om en konge, han er i rådet, så sagde man altid her: "Kejseren er i klædeskabet!"

Many years ago there was an Emperor who was so excessively fond of new clothes that he spent all his money on them. He cared nothing about his soldiers, nor for the theater, nor for driving in the woods—except for the sake of showing off his new clothes. He had a costume for every hour of the day. Instead of saying as one does about any other king or emperor, "He is in his council chamber," the people here always said, "The Emperor is in his dressing room."

—HANS CHRISTIAN ANDERSEN, *The Emperor's New Clothes*

Danish is spoken by the 5 million inhabitants of Denmark, and is also the official language of Greenland and the Faroe Islands, which are considered part of Denmark. It is one of the Scandinavian languages, which constitute a branch of the Germanic languages, in turn a part of the Indo-European family.

Danish is most closely related to Norwegian and Swedish. During the centuries that Denmark and Norway were one country, a dialect closer to Danish than Norwegian was spoken in the Norwegian cities. This is still in use today and is sometimes referred to as "Dano-Norwegian."

The Danish alphabet is the same as the Norwegian, consisting of the twenty-six letters of the English alphabet plus *æ*, *ø*, and *å* at the end. Before 1948 the *å* was written *aa*. The spelling reform of that year also abolished the German practice of beginning all nouns with a capital letter.

Norwegian

Påskeøya er verdens ensomste boplass. Nærmeste faste punkt beboerne kan se, er på himmelhvelvet, månen og planetene. De må reise lenger enn noen annen folkegruppe for å få se at det virkelig finnes fastland som ligger nærmere. Derfor lever de stjernene så nær og kan navn på flere av dem enn på byer og land i vår egen verden.

Easter Island is the loneliest inhabited place in the world. The nearest solid land the islanders can see is above, in the firmament, the moon and the planets. They have to travel farther than any other people to see that there really is land yet closer. Therefore, living nearest the stars, they know more names of stars than of towns and countries in our own world.

—THOR HEYERDAHL, *Aku-Aku*

Norwegian is the national language of Norway, spoken by virtually all of the country's 4 million inhabitants. There are also about 600,000 speakers in the United States.

Norwegian is one of the Scandinavian languages, which form a branch of the Germanic languages, in turn a part of the Indo-European family. It is closely related to Danish and Swedish, especially the former. Norway and Denmark were one country for four centuries before 1814, and from then until 1905 Norway was under the Swedish crown. During the years of Danish rule a Danish-influenced "city language" began to develop in Bergen and Oslo, and Danish eventually became the written language of Norway.

Today there are two distinct dialects of Norwegian. The Dano-Norwegian dialect, originally called *riksmål* ("state language"), is now known as *bokmål* ("book language"). Most newspapers and radio and television broadcasts are in *bokmål.* About 1850 a movement for the recognition of Norwegian as a language distinct from Danish led to the establishment of *landsmål* ("country language"), which was based on the dialects of rural Norway. Known today as *nynorsk* ("New Norse"), it was intended to carry on the tradition of Old Norse, interrupted in the 15th century.

At present *bokmål* and *nynorsk* have equal status both in government and in the schools. Attempts to combine the two into *samnorsk* ("Common Norwegian") have thus far been unsuccessful, but most forward-looking Norwegians believe that it is only a matter of time before they are eventually merged.

Both the Norwegian and Danish alphabets contain the additional letters *æ* and *ø*, which in Swedish are *ä* and *ö*. All three contain the letter *å*.

Swedish

Han stod rak—som en snurra sålänge piskan viner. Han var blygsam—i kraft av robusta överlägsenhetskänslor. Han var icke anspråksfull: vad han strävade efter var endast frihet från oro, och andras nederlag gladde honom mer än egna segrar. Han räddade livet genom att aldrig våga det.—Och klagade över att han icke var förstådd!

He stood erect—as a peg top does so long as the whip keeps lashing it. He was modest—thanks to a robust conviction of his own superiority. He was unambitious—all he wanted was a life free from cares, and he took more pleasure in the failures of others than in his own successes. He saved his life by never risking it—and complained that he was misunderstood.

—DAG HAMMARSKJÖLD, *Markings*

Swedish is the most widely spoken of the Scandinavian languages, which constitute a branch of the Germanic languages, in turn a part of the Indo-European family. There are approximately 9 million speakers of Swedish. In addition to the 8 million people of Sweden, about 300,000 speakers live on the southwestern and southern coasts of Finland, and another 600,000 live in the United States.

Swedish is closely related to Norwegian and Danish. Historically it is closer to Danish, but the years of Swedish hegemony over Norway (1814–1905) brought the two languages closer together. A Swedish person today has more difficulty understanding Danish than Norwegian.

The Swedish alphabet consists of twenty-nine letters, the regular twenty-six of the English alphabet, plus *å*, *ä*, and *ö* at the end. The *ä* and *ö* distinguish it from Norwegian and Danish, which use *æ* and *ø*.

During the Middle Ages Swedish borrowed many words from German, while the 18th century witnessed a large infusion of words from the French. In the 19th and 20th centuries English has become by far the largest source of foreign borrowings.

Lappish

Gukken davven Dawgai vuolde
sabma suolgai Same-aednam:
Duoddar laebba duoddar duokken,
jawre saebba jawre lakka,
čokkak čilgiin, čorok čaeroin
allanaddik alme vuostai;
šavvik jogak, šuvvik vuowdek,
cakkik caeggo stalle-njargak
maraidaeggje maeraidi.

Far away in the North, under Charles' Wain,
is Lapland faintly to be seen in the distance.
Mountains lie stretched behind mountains;
lakes full to overflowing lie near each other;
summits with ridges, hills with stony slopes rise toward the sky.
Rivers rush, forests sigh,
steep steel-colored promontories jut into roaring seas.

—Lapp National Anthem

Lappish is the language of the Lapps, or Laplanders, who live in northernmost Scandinavia, Finland, and a small part of the Soviet Union. They number approximately 35,000, distributed roughly as follows: Norway, 20,000; Sweden, 10,000; Finland, 2,500; Soviet Union (Kola Peninsula), 2,000.

Lappish is one of the Finno-Ugric languages, bearing certain similarities to Finnish, but the two languages are actually vastly different. Since the Lapps are of different racial stock than the Finns, it is assumed that about 2,000 years ago they adopted the language of the ancestors of the Finns. Subsequently many words were borrowed from the Scandinavian languages.

Finnish

Sillä minä, Sinuhe, olen ihminen ja ihmisenä olen elänyt jokaisessa ihmisessä, joka on ollut ennen minua, ja ihmisenä elän jokaisessa ihmisessä, joka tulee jälkeeni. Elän ihmisen itkussa ja ilossa, hänen surussaan ja pelossaan elän, hyvyydessään ja pahuudessaan, oikeudessa ja vääryydessä, heikkoudessa ja väkevyydessä. Ihmisenä olen elävä ihmisessä ikuisesti enkä sen tähden kaipaa uhreja hautaani ja kuolemattomuutta nimelleni. Tämän kirjoitti Sinuhe, egyptiläinen, hän, joka eli yksinäisenä kaikki elämänsä päivät.

For I, Sinuhe, am a human being. I have lived in everyone who existed before me and shall live in all who come after me. I shall live in human tears and laughter, in human sorrow and fear, in human goodness and wickedness, in justice and injustice, in weakness and strength. As a human being I shall live eternally in mankind. I desire no offerings at my tomb and no immortality for my name. This was written by Sinuhe, the Egyptian, who lived alone all the days of his life.

—MIKA WALTARI, *The Egyptian*

There are approximately 5 million speakers of Finnish. Besides being the national language of Finland, it is spoken by about 200,000 people in the United States, 135,000 in the northwestern part of the Soviet Union, and 30,000 people in northern Sweden.

Finnish is one of the few languages of Europe not of the Indo-European family. Like Estonian, spoken across the Gulf of Finland, it is one of the Finno-Ugric languages, which constitute the main branch of the Uralic family.

The Finnish alphabet contains only twenty-one letters. There are thirteen consonants (*d, g, h, j, k, l, m, n, p, r, s, t, v*) and eight vowels (*a, e, i, o, u, y, ä, ö*). There is only one sound for every letter, one letter for every sound, and the stress is always on the first syllable. The language makes no distinction as to gender, and has no articles, either definite or indefinite.

Despite these simplifying factors, Finnish is undoubtedly an exceedingly difficult language to learn. Aside from foreign borrowings (mostly from the Germanic languages), the long, often compound words bear no similarity whatever to their counterparts in the Indo-European languages. The Finnish word for "question," for example, is *kysymys*, while the word for "twenty" is *kaksikymmentä.* Even the Finnish names of different countries are often hard to recognize—*e.g.*, *Suomi* (Finland), *Ruotsi* (Sweden), *Tanska* (Denmark), *Saksa* (Germany), *Ranska* (France), and *Venäjä* (Russia). The number of case forms for nouns is staggering—whereas German has four cases, Latin five, and Russian six, Finnish has no fewer than fifteen! In addition to the familiar nominative, genitive, partitive, and ablative, there are also the elative, allative, illative, essive, inessive, adessive, abessive, and several others.

Polish

Mateusz się porwał w ten mig do niego, ale nim mógł zmiarkować co bądź, już Antek skoczył jak ten wilk wściekły, chycił go jedną ręką za orzydle, przydusił aż tamten dech i głos stracił, drugą ujął za pas, wyrwał z miejsca jak kierz, nogą drzwi wywalił na dwór, i poniósł go prędko za tartak, do rzeki ogrodzonej płotem i cisnął z całej mocy, aż cztery żerdki trzasły kiej słomki, a Mateusz niby kloc ciężki padł we wodę.

Matthew sprang instantly at him, but before he knew what happened Antek pounced upon him like a crazed wolf. With one hand he clutched his collar, stifling both his breath and voice, with the other he grabbed his belt and tore him from his place as one roots out a bush. He kicked open the door, rushed with him beyond the sawmill to the river fence, and hurled him with such fury against the fence that four of the posts snapped like straws, and Matthew fell into the water like a heavy log.

—WŁADYSŁAW REYMONT, *The Peasants*

Polish is spoken by almost all of the 33 million inhabitants of Poland, by about 2½ million people in the United States, and by smaller groups in the Soviet Union, Canada, Brazil, and other countries. It is one of the Slavic languages and thus part of the Indo-European family.

Polish is written in the Roman alphabet, with *q*, *v*, and *x* missing, and with *j* pronounced *y*, *w* pronounced *v*, and *c* pronounced *ts*. However, there are a bewildering number of diacritical marks, including acute accents, dots, hooks, and, in the case of the *l*, a bar (*ł*). The letter *ć* is a soft *ch* (*e.g.*, *ćwierć*—quarter); *ś* is a soft *sh* (*śnieg*—snow); *ść* is a soft *shch* (*iść*—to go); *dź* is pronounced like the English *j* (*niedźwiedź*—bear); *ń* is pronounced *ny* as in "canyon" (*jesień*—autumn); *ó* is pronounced *oo* (*góra*—mountain). The letter *ż* is a hard *zh* (*żona*—wife), the letters *ą* and *ę* are nasal vowels (*sąsiad*—neighbor, *pięć*—five), and the barred *ł* is pronounced approximately like a *w* (*głowa*—head). *Ch* is pronounced as in German, but *sz* = *sh* (*szkoła*—school), *cz* = *ch* (*czysty*—clean), *szcz* = *shch* (*szczotka*—brush), and *rz* = *zh* (*grzmot*—thunder). The stress in Polish is always on the next to last syllable.

Polish vocabulary naturally resembles that of the other Slavic languages. Such Polish words as *bez* (without), *most* (bridge), *cena* (price), and *zima* (winter) are identical in Russian, Czech, Bulgarian, and Serbo-Croatian. But "peace," which is *mir* in Russian and *mír* in Czech, in Polish is *pokój*, while "island" (*ostrov* in Russian and Czech) in Polish is *wyspa*. The Polish words for "north," "south," "east," and "west" are respectively *północ* (which also means "midnight"), *południe* (noon), *wschód* (rising), and *zachód* (setting). Some Polish words seem unpronounceable to one who has never studied the language (*e.g.*, *przemysł*—industry, *sześćdziesiąt*—sixty, *wszechświat*—universe, *szczęśliwy*—happy; lucky). Equally formidable are the names of the Polish cities Szczecin, Bydgoszcz, and Świętochłowice.

Władysław Reymont, the Polish novelist and short-story writer, was the winner of the Nobel Prize for Literature in 1924.

Czech

Já vím, ten romantik ve mně, to byla maminka. Maminka zpívala, maminka se někdy zadívala, maminka měla nějaký skrytý a neznámý život; a jak byla krásná tehdy, když podávala dragounovi pít, tak krásná, že mně kloučkovi se srdce svíralo. Říkali vždycky, že jsem po ní. Tehdy jsem chtěl být po tatínkovi, silný jako on, velký a spolehlivý jako tatínek. Asi jsem se nevydařil. To není po něm, ten básník, ten romantik a kdo ví co ještě.

I know that romantic in me, it was my mother. Mother used to sing, mother lost herself in daydreams, mother had had some secret unknown life; and how beautiful she was when she offered the dragoon a drink, so beautiful that my little childish heart stood still. They always said that I took after her. Then I wanted to be like my father, strong like him, big, and reliable like daddy. Perhaps I haven't turned out well. It isn't after him, that poet, that romantic, and who knows what else.

—KAREL ČAPEK, *An Ordinary Life*

Czech is spoken in the western and central two-thirds of Czechoslovakia, in the historical regions of Bohemia and Moravia. It is closely related to Slovak, spoken in Slovakia, the two languages in fact being mutually intelligible. There are 10 million speakers of Czech.

Czech is a Slavic language written in the Roman script. The foundations of the alphabet were laid by the great religious reformer Jan Hus, in the early 15th century. The letters *q*, *w*, and *x* are missing, while *c* is pronounced *ts* (*e.g.*, *cena*—price), *ch* as in German (*kachna*—duck), and *j* as *y* (*jazyk*—language). Acute accents lengthen the vowels (*kámen*—stone), while a circle over the *u* produces a long *oo* sound (*dům*—house). The chevron over *c*, *s*, and *z* produces *ch*, *sh*, and *zh* respectively (*číslo*—number, *koš*—basket, *život*—life). But *ň* is pronounced *ny* as in "canyon" (*daň*—tax), *ě* is pronounced *ye* (*město*—city), and *ř* is pronounced *rzh*, as in the name Dvořák. The letter *r* serves as a vowel, producing such strange-looking words as *krk* (neck), *smrt* (death), and *čtvrt* (quarter). The stress is always on the first syllable.

Slovak

Čím menšie je niečo, tým väčšmi kričí. Taký fafrnok, nevie to ešte ani hovorit', a prekričí celú rodinu, malý úradník urobí viacej štabarcu okolo seba ako desat' ministrov, malý vrabec prečviriká svojho starého otca pokojne skáčúceho po chodníku, malý vozík bude rapotat' na celú dedinu, kým štyridsat' konských síl prebrnkne vedl'a teba, že počuješ iba l'ahké ssst.

The smaller the fry, the bigger the noise. A small brat that cannot say a single word will outscream the whole family, a minor clerk will make more ado than a dozen ministers, a small sparrow will outtwitter its own grandfather hopping about peacefully on the pavement, and a small farm wagon will disturb the whole village with its rattling and creaking while a forty-horsepower vehicle streaks past and you hear only a slight swish.

—JANKO JESENSKÝ, *The Democrats*

Slovak is the second of the two official languages of Czechoslovakia. It is spoken by about 4½ million people in Slovakia, the eastern third of the country, and by another 500,000 in the United States. Slovak is similar enough to Czech to be considered by some as merely a dialect, but the existence of slightly different alphabets, as well as distinct literatures, makes it more convenient to look upon them as separate languages.

The Slovak alphabet is similar to that of Czech, though it lacks three Czech letters (*ě*, *ř*, and *ů*) and contains three of its own. Two are vowels—the *ä*, as in *mäso* (meat), and the *ô*, as in *nôž* (knife), while the *l'* indicates a soft *l* sound (*e.g.*, *učitel'*—teacher). The Slovak word for Slovak is *slovenský*, not to be confused with the word for Slovenian, *slovinský*.

Hungarian

A pokoli komédia még egyre tartott a börzén. A halálra ítélt papírok, a bondavári gyártelep s a bondavári vasút részvényei egyik kézből a másikba repültek. Most már a komikumig vitték a tragédiát, s kezdett humor vegyülni a szerencsétlenségbe. Ez a szó: "Bondavár" csak arra való volt, hogy derültséget idézzen elő a börzeemberek között. Aki az utolsó részvényén túladhatott nagy veszteséggel, nevetett azon, aki megszerezte azt. Kezdték a részvényeket megfoghatlan becsű tárgyakért cserébe kínálgatni. Ráadásul egy új esernyőre egy ócska esernyőért. Használták előfizetési ekvivalensül olyan lapokért, amiket valakinek a szerkesztő a nyakára köt erővel. Ajándékozgatták jótékony célokra.

The devil's comedy was being played daily on the stock exchange. The Bondavara Company's shares, the Bondavara Railway shares were tossed here and there, from one hand to another. The tragedy had turned to comedy—that is, for some people, who found the game very humorous. The very word Bondavara made the stockbrokers laugh. When it happened that some fool bought a share, no one could help laughing. The shares, in fact, were given in exchange for anything of little value—for instance, as make-weight with an old umbrella for a new one. They were also presented to charitable institutions.

—MÓR JÓKAI, *Black Diamonds*

Hungarian is spoken by about 10 million people in Hungary, 1½ million in Rumania, and smaller minorities in Yugoslavia and Czechoslovakia. It is one of the Finno-Ugric languages, which include Finnish, Estonian, and a number of languages spoken in the Soviet Union. Most of these languages, however, belong to the Finnic branch of this group, while Hungarian belongs to the Ugric. The only other existing Ugric languages, and thus the only other languages to which Hungarian is closely related, are the remote Ostyak and Vogul languages of Siberia, spoken in an area more than 2,000 miles from Hungary.

As may be gathered from these facts, the original Hungarian people came from Asia, having long lived a nomadic life on the eastern slopes of the Urals. Forced to migrate westward between the 5th and 9th centuries A.D., they eventually reached the Danube where they settled in 896. In the more than a thousand years that have elapsed since that time the Hungarians have become completely Europeanized, with only their language serving to reveal their Asian origins.

The Hungarians call their language Magyar. It is considered extremely difficult for foreigners to learn, with its vocabulary largely from Asia and its grammar containing a number of complex features not to be found in other Western languages. The alphabet, however, is phonetic, with *s* pronounced *sh* (*e.g.*, *sör*—beer), *c* pronounced *ts* (*ceruza*—pencil), *sz* pronounced *s* (*szó*—word), *cs* pronounced *ch* (*csésze*—cup), *zs* pronounced *zh* (*zseb*—pocket), and *gy* pronounced *dy* (*nagy*—big). The many vowel sounds in spoken Hungarian are indicated by acute accents, umlauts, and the unique double acute accent which appears over *o* and *u* (*bőr*—skin, *fű*—grass). The stress in Hungarian is always on the first syllable.

The most important English word of Hungarian origin is *coach*, after the village of Kocs (remember *cs* = *ch*), where coaches were invented and first used. Others are *goulash* and *paprika*.

Rumanian

Şi scurt şi cuprinzător, sărut mîna mătuşei, luîndu-mi ziua bună, ca un băiet de treabă; ies din casă cu chip că mă duc la scăldat, mă şupuresc pe unde pot şi, cînd colo, mă trezesc în cireşul femeii şi încep a cărăbăni la cireşe în sîn, crude, coapte, cum se găseau. Şi cum eram îngrijit şi mă sileam să fac ce oi face mai degrabă, iaca mătuşa Mărioara c-o jordie în mînă, la tulpina cireşului!

The long and the short of it is that I kissed my aunt's hand and took my leave like a good boy; I went out of the house as if I were going to bathe; I crept stealthily as best I could and, all of a sudden, found myself in my aunt's cherry tree, picking cherries and stuffing them into my shirt bosom, green ones and ripe ones, just as I found them. And just as I was most eager and anxious to get the job done as quickly as possible, up came Aunt Marioara with a stick in her hand, right at the foot of the cherry tree!

—ION CREANGĂ, *Recollections from Childhood*

Rumanian, more correctly spelled Romanian, is, as its name suggests, one of the Romance languages. It is the only such language spoken in Eastern Europe, having descended from the Latin introduced by the Roman Emperor Trajan when he conquered the region in the 2nd century A.D. Rumanian is more archaic than the other Romance languages and has been influenced by the non-Romance languages spoken in nearby countries, especially Hungarian, Albanian, and the various Slavic languages. A variety of Rumanian is spoken in the Moldavian S.S.R of the Soviet Union, where it is known as Moldavian, but there it is written in the Cyrillic alphabet. Rumanian proper is spoken by about 18 million out of the 20 million inhabitants of Rumania.

Rumania switched from the Cyrillic to the Roman script in 1860. The present alphabet contains four special letters: the *ă*, an unstressed vowel (*e.g.*, *vară*—summer); the *î*, a guttural vowel (*gît*—neck); the *ş*, pronounced *sh* (*şase*—six); and the *ţ*, pronounced *ts* (*preţ*—price). The Rumanian definite article, like that of Bulgarian and the Scandinavian languages, is suffixed to the noun (*rege*—king, *regele*—the king). Students of the Romance languages should have no trouble recognizing the Rumanian words *casă*, *arbore*, *legumă*, *ascensor*, *dulce*, and *verde*.

Serbian

То је био афрички слон, још недорастао, млад и бујан; биле су му тек две године. Пре слона стигла је у Травник прича о њему. Све се однекуд сазнавало: како је путовао, како је чуван и негован од пратње, и како је дочекиван, превожен и храњен од народа и власти. И већ су га прозвали «фил», што на турском језику значи слон.

The elephant came from Africa. Young, snappy, and not yet fully grown, he was but two years old. These details, as well as other information, had preceded the elephant into Travnik. Indeed, in Travnik everything was known: how he traveled, how he was looked after by his sizable escort, how he was transported and fed, and how he was received by the authorities along the way. And they referred to him by the Turkish word *fil*, which means elephant.

—IVO ANDRIĆ, *The Vizier's Elephant*

Serbian and Croatian are generally considered one language, combined under the single term Serbo-Croatian. The latter is the most important language of Yugoslavia, where it is spoken by about 15 million people (75 percent of the population), 10 million of them Serbs and 5 million Croats. The Serbs, however, call their language Serbian, and being of Eastern Orthodox religious persuasion, write it in a modified form of the Cyrillic alphabet. The Roman Catholic Croats, on the other hand, call their language Croatian and employ the Roman alphabet. Street signs and other inscriptions in Yugoslavia are generally written in both alphabets.

Serbian is a Slavic language and thus part of the Indo-European family. The Serbian alphabet, though Cyrillic, differs considerably from the Russian. Nine Russian letters are missing from Serbian, but Serbian has six of its own. There is the Roman *j*, pronounced *y*; the џ, pronounced like the English *j*; the љ, pronounced like the *ll* of "million"; the њ, pronounced like the *ny* of "canyon"; the ђ, pronounced *dy* as in "did you"; and the *ћ*, pronounced *ty* as in "hit you." For each Cyrillic letter in the Serbian alphabet there is a corresponding Roman letter in the Croatian alphabet.

Ivo Andrić was the winner of the Nobel Prize for Literature in 1961.

Croatian

Sjedi tako Filip u sutonu, sluša rodu na susjednom dimnjaku kako klepeće kljunom kao kastanjetom, kako jasno odjekuju pastirski glasovi s potoka gdje se napaja blago, kako lastavice proždrljivo kruže oko dimnjaka kao grabilice, i osjeća u sebi prelijevanje tih životnih odraza, živo i zanosno. Kruže slike oko njega kao ptice i oko njegova pogrebnog raspoloženja i unutarnjih potištenosti, i oko vinograda i oranica, i šumskih parcela što gasnu u teškom, baršunastom zelenilu starinskog damasta i nestaju u smeđim tkaninama daljine.

Thus Philip sat in the twilight and listened to a stork clapping its beak like a castanet on a neighboring chimney, to the shepherds' voices echoing from the stream where they watered their beasts, to the swallows greedily circling around the chimney like birds of prey, and vividly and rapturously he felt flowing into him those multitudinous expressions of life. Images circled round him like birds, round his funeral mood and inner depression and round the vineyard and the plowfields, and the tracts of woodland fading in their heavy, velvety green, like old-fashioned damask, and disappearing in the vague brown tissue of the distance.

—MIROSLAV KRLEŽA, *The Return of Philip Latinovicz*

Croatian is that form of Serbo-Croatian spoken by Yugoslavia's Croatian population and written in the Roman alphabet. Except for their scripts, Croatian and Serbian are really the same language, though a slightly different intonation or the use of a certain word will sometimes indicate whether one is a Serb or a Croat. For the word "train" the Serbs generally say *voz* as against Croatian *vlak*, while for "dance" the Serbs prefer *igra* and the Croatians *ples*. For "music" the Serbs say *muzika* as against Croatian *glazba*, while for "theater" there is Serbian *pozorište* and Croatian *kazalište*. In each case, however, both alternatives are understood perfectly well by everyone.

The Croatian alphabet has a Roman letter for each Cyrillic letter of the Serbian alphabet. *Ž*, *č*, and *š* are pronounced *zh*, *ch*, and *sh* respectively (*e.g.*, *nož*—knife, *čovjek*—man, *šešir*—hat). *C*, corresponding to the Serbian ц, is pronounced *ts* (*cipela*—shoe), while *dž*, corresponding to the Serbian џ, is pronounced like the English *j* (*džep*—pocket). *Ć*, corresponding to the Serbian ћ, is pronounced *ty* as in "hit you" (*svijeća*—candle), while *đ*, corresponding to ђ, is pronounced *dy* as in "did you" (*đavo*—devil). The Croatian equivalents of the Serbian љ and њ are *lj* and *nj* respectively.

The Croatian word for Croatian is *hrvatski*, and for Serbian *srpski*. The letter *r* frequently serves as a vowel, as for example in the words *prst* (finger), *vrt* (garden), *krv* (blood), *brz* (fast), *crn* (black), and *trg* (market). The city of Trieste in Yugoslavia is spelled *Trst*.

Slovenian

Mračilo se je, s polja so se vračali kmetje in posli. Takrat se je prikazal petelin na Sitarjevi strehi, rdeč in tenak je švignil visoko proti nebu. Nato se je prikazal petelin na skednju, na hlevu, na šupi, na obeh kozolcih; velik je bil plamen, segal je silen od zemlje do nebes. Goreče treske so padale v kolobarju na zoreče polje, kakor da bi jih metala človeška roka. Tako je prižgal Jernej svojo strašno bakljo.

Night was falling; villagers and farmhands were coming home from the fields. On Sitar's roof the red cock suddenly appeared. A tongue-shaped flame shot up skywards; then another was seen on the stables, and yet another on the barn—and then on both sheds. They were leaping up; they seemed to come out of the earth and to reach up to the sky. Burning beams whirled in the air and fell in a circle on the green fields, as if thrown by a mighty human hand. . . . Yerney had set fire to his terrible torch.

—IVAN CANKAR, *The Bailiff Yerney and His Rights*

Slovenian is another of the three official languages of Yugoslavia. It is spoken primarily in Slovenia, the northwesternmost of the country's six provinces, by about 1½ million people. The principal Slovenian-speaking city is Ljubljana.

Slovenian is a Slavic language written in the Roman alphabet. The letters *q*, *w*, *x*, and *y* are missing while *c* is pronounced *ts* (*e.g.*, *cena*—price), *č* is pronounced *ch* (*črn*—black), *š* is pronounced *sh* (*šola*—school), and *ž* is pronounced *zh* (*življenje*—life). The language is most closely related to Serbo-Croatian but the two are not mutually intelligible.

Macedonian

За нас, како за народ што успеа да го оформи својот литературен јазик дури во последниве децении, ќе биде многу поучно да знаеме какви биле општо основните карактеристики на развојот на литературните јазици во словенскиот свет. Ќе биде поучно особено поради тоа што ќе најдеме во тој развој ред аналогии со тоа што се случувало кај нас и што ќе можеме да забележиме извесни закономерности таму каде што инаку може да ни се чини дека некоја појава произлегува само од нашата посебна ситуација.

For us, a nation which has succeeded in formulating its literary language in the course of the last few decades, it would be very instructive to know the nature of the fundamental characteristics of the development of literary languages in the Slavic world. It would be particularly instructive in that we would find in that development a number of analogies to what has happened in our own case, and we would be able to note certain correspondences, whereas otherwise it might appear that certain phenomena arise solely out of our own particular situation.

Macedonian is the third of the three official languages of Yugoslavia. It is spoken principally in the southernmost province of Macedonia, whose capital is Skopje. Macedonian is closely related to Bulgarian, and is considered by some (especially the Bulgarians) to be merely a dialect of that language. The alphabet contains the unique ѓ and ќ, not to be found in any other language. There are about one million speakers.

Bulgarian

Сутринта Огнянов се упъти към града. Той измина балканското гърло и излезе при манастира. На поляната пред манастира, под големите орехи се разхождаше игуменът, гологлав. Той се възхищаваше от утринната хубост на тия романтични места и приемаше на големи глътки свежия живителен въздух на планината. Есенната природа имаше ново обаяние с тия позлатени листове на дърветата, с тия пожълтели кадифени гърбове на Балкана и с тая сладостнонежна повяхналост и меланхолия.

In the morning Ognyanov set out for town. He went through the gorge which led him out to the monastery. Under the great walnut trees in the meadow in front of the monastery the abbot was walking bareheaded to and fro. He was enjoying the beauty of this romantic spot and drinking in the fresh, bracing air of the mountain. The autumn landscape had a new charm with the golden leaves of the trees, the yellowed velvety hills of the Balkan range, and the atmosphere of sweetly tender decay and melancholy. —IVAN VAZOV, *Under the Yoke*

Bulgarian is spoken by about 90 percent of the population of Bulgaria, or some 8 million people. It is one of the Slavic languages and, in fact, played an important role in the historical development of this family. When the first alphabet for the Slavic languages was devised in the 9th century, it was a dialect of Bulgarian that served as the base. Old Bulgarian, or Old Church Slavonic as it came to be called, long served as the literary vehicle of all the Slavic languages. During the Middle Ages it was one of the three major literary languages of Europe.

The modern Bulgarian alphabet is virtually the same as the Russian, except that the ъ, the little used "hard sign" in Russian, in Bulgarian serves as a vowel. It is pronounced something like the *u* in the English word "fur" and is, in fact, the second letter in the word Bulgaria. Bulgarian also differs from the other Slavic languages in that it makes use of articles, both definite and indefinite, the former being suffixed to the noun. The verb has no infinitive form—like the English infinitive, which is formed by placing the word "to" in front of the verb, the Bulgarian infinitive is formed with the word *da.*

Albanian

Maletë me gurë,	Mountains and stones,
fusha me bar shumë,	Lush meadows unshorn,
aratë me grurë,	A river beyond,
më tutje një lumë.	Fields full of corn.
Fshati përkarshi.	Out yonder, the village,
me kish' e me varre,	Its church and its graves,
rotul ca shtëpi	Cottages here and there,
të vogëla fare.	Low under their eaves.
Ujëtë të ftotë,	Chill water springs.
era punemadhe,	A keen wind blows.
bilbili ia thotë	The nightingale sings.
gratë si zorkadhe.	And the women . . . they're like does!
Burrat nënë hie	Idlers in the shade,
lozën, kuvëndojnë;—	Kept by their wives;
pika që s'u bie.	A plague on them all
se nga gratë rrojnë!	For wasting their lives!

—ANTON ZAKO ÇAJUPI, *My Village*

There are approximately 3 million speakers of Albanian. About 2 million live in Albania, one million in Yugoslavia, and smaller numbers in Italy and Greece. The Albanians call their language *shqip* and their country *Shqipëria.* There are two distinct dialects—Tosk, spoken in the south, and Gheg, spoken in the north.

Albanian is an Indo-European language, constituting a separate and independent branch of this family. Its origin is uncertain and it was not until 1854 that it was conclusively proven to be Indo-European. The vocabulary contains many words not to be found in any other Indo-European language, though there has been considerable borrowing from Latin, Greek, Turkish, and the Slavic languages. Albanian adopted the Roman alphabet in 1908.

Sorbian

UPPER SORBIAN

Hlej! Mócnje twoju sławił swjatu mi sym rolu.
Twój wobraz tkałe su wšě mysle mi a sony,
wěnc twojich hór a twojich honow horde strony,
a chwalił sobu sym će z horami a z holu!

Płač towarš mój je často był, hdyž z dźiwjej bolu
sym z harfy wabił zańdźenosće ćežke stony,
hdyž k njebju wołał sym, su klinčałe kaž zwony
wšě truny. Twój sym z ruku, wutrobu a wołu!

LOWER SORBIAN

Glej! Z mocu som toś twoju swětu rolu sławił.
Twoj wobraz su wše myslenja a sni mě tkali,
wěnk modrych gor' a golow śmojtu zeleń w dali,
a chwalił som śi cełu a śi wěnkow nawił!

Gaž zajšłosć spominach, jo cesto płac mě dawił
a martrow śěžke stukanja su tšuny grali,
gaž k njebju wołach, toś su woni zabrincali
mě ako zwony wše, a wšykno som z nich zjawił!

Look! Strongly have I praised your holy fields.
Your image has woven together all my thoughts and dreams,
the string of blue mountains and vast meadows of proud land,
and I have praised you for these mountains and meadows!

Cries were often my companion, when with a sharp pain
I called with my harp the heavy sighs of the past,
when I shouted to heaven all strings sounded like bells.
I am yours with my hand, heart and will!

—JAKUB BART-ĆIŠINSKI, *Lusatia*

Sorbian, also known by the names of Wendish and Lusatian, is a Slavic language spoken in Lusatia, the southeasternmost part of East Germany bisected by the River Spree. Although surrounded by German speakers for centuries, the Sorbs have preserved their Slavic speech, and the study and propagation of the language is strongly encouraged today by the East German government.

Despite its small number of speakers (about 50,000), and the small area in which it is spoken, Sorbian has two distinct dialects. Upper Sorbian, centered in the city of Bautzen to the south (the word "upper" refers to the *level* rather than the *location* of the land), is closer to Czech. Lower Sorbian, spoken in the vicinity of Cottbus to the north, more closely resembles Polish. The above poem, by the Sorbs' most famous poet, is given in each of the two dialects.

Greek

CLASSICAL GREEK

φίλοι, κακῶν μὲν ὅστις ἔμπειρος κυρεῖ,
ἐπίσταται βροτοῖσιν ὡς ὅταν κλύδων
κακῶν ἐπέλθῃ πάντα δειμαίνειν φιλεῖ·
ὅταν δ' ὁ δαίμων εὐροῇ, πεποιθέναι
τὸν αὐτὸν αἰεὶ δαίμον' οὐριεῖν τύχην.
ἐμοὶ γὰρ ἤδη πάντα μὲν φόβου πλέα
ἐν ὄμμασιν τἀνταῖα φαίνεται θεῶν,
βοᾷ δ' ἐν ὠσὶ κέλαδος οὐ παιώνιος·
τοία κακῶν ἔκπληξις ἐκφοβεῖ φρένας.

My friends, whoever's wise in ways of evil
Knows how, when a flood of evil comes,
Everything we grow to fear; but when
A god our voyage gladdens, we believe
Always that fortune's never-changing wind
Will blow. As my eyes behold all things
As fearful visitations of the gods,
So my ears already ring with cureless songs:
Thus consternation terrifies my sense.

—AESCHYLUS, *The Persians*

Greek, the first great language of Western civilization, is considered by many to be the most effective and admirable means of communication ever devised. Its lucidity of structure and concept, together with its seemingly infinite variety of modes of expression, render it equally suitable to the needs of the rigorous thinker and the inspired poet. We can only surmise how classical Greek must have sounded to the ear,

MODERN GREEK

Κι ὁ νοῦς του ἀγκάλιασε πονετικὰ τὴν Κρήτη. Τὴν ἀγαποῦσε σὰν ἕνα πράμα ζωντανό, ζεστό, πού 'χε στόμα καὶ φώναζε, καὶ μάτια κι ἔκλαιγε, καὶ δὲν ἦταν καμωμένη ἀπὸ πέτρες καὶ χώματα κι ἀπὸ ρίζες δεντρῶν, παρὰ ἀπὸ χιλιάδες χιλιάδες παπποῦδες καὶ μάνες, ποὺ δὲν πεθαίνουν ποτέ τους, παρὰ ζοῦν καὶ μαζεύουνται κάθε Κυριακὴ στὶς ἐκκλησιὲς κι ἀγριεύουν κάθε τόσο, ξετυλίγουν μέσα ἀπὸ τὰ μνήματα μιὰ θεόρατη σημαία καὶ πιάνουν τὰ βουνά. Κι ἀπάνω στὴ σημαία ἐτούτη, χρόνια σκυμμένες οἱ ἀθάνατες μάνες, ἔχουν κεντήσει μὲ τὰ κορακάτα καὶ γκρίζα καὶ κάτασπρα μαλλιά τους τὰ τρία ἀθάνατα λόγια: ΕΛΕΥΤΕΡΙΑ Ἢ ΘΑΝΑΤΟΣ.

Full of pity, his spirit embraced Crete. Crete was to him a living, warm creature with a speaking mouth and weeping eyes; a Crete that consisted not of rocks and clods and roots, but of thousands of forefathers who never died and who gathered, every Sunday, in the churches. Again and again they were filled with wrath, and in their graves they unfolded a proud banner and rushed with it into the mountains. And on the banner the undying Mother, bowed over it for years, had embroidered with their black and gray and snow-white hair the three undying words: FREEDOM OR DEATH.

—NIKOS KAZANTZAKIS, *Freedom or Death*

but the spoken word was probably no less beautiful than the written.

Greek-speaking people moved into the Greek Peninsula and adjacent areas from the Balkan Peninsula in the second millennium B.C. In time four distinct dialects evolved: Aeolic, Ionic, Arcado-Cyprian, and Doric. It was in the Ionic dialect that the epic poems of Homer, the *Iliad* and the *Odyssey*, appeared, perhaps in the 9th century B.C. With the rise of Athens in succeeding centuries, a dialect of Ionic known as Attic began to produce the great literature of the classical period. Attic became the dominant form of the language and the basis of the *Koine*, or common language, whose use passed far beyond the borders of present-day Greece. After the conquests of Alexander the Great it was spoken as far east as India, and later was adopted as a second language by the Roman Empire. The New Testament was written in the *Koine* and it is used by the Eastern Orthodox Church through the present day.

The Greek alphabet, an adaptation of the Phoenician, dates from about 1000 B.C. It was the first alphabet in which letters stood for vowels as well as for consonants, in contrast to the Semitic alphabets, which had only consonants. Like the Semitic alphabets, it was at first written from right to left, but then shifted to a style in which lines alternated from right-to-left and left-to-right, and then shifted again to the present left-to-right direction. An earlier form of Greek writing, known as Linear B and dating from 1500 B.C., was deciphered in 1952, but this was largely abandoned by 1200 B.C.

Greek was the official language of the Byzantine Empire from the 4th to the 15th century and thereafter continued to be spoken by Greeks under Turkish rule. Modern Greek began to take shape about the 9th century, and became the official language of the kingdom of Greece in the 19th. Today Greek is spoken by about 10 million people, including some 500,000 on the island of Cyprus. In addition to the common speech, known as Demotic, an imitation of classical Greek, known as Pure, has been revived for literary purposes.

The impact of Greek upon the vocabulary of all languages, including English, has been enormous. Such prefixes as *poly-* (much, many), *micro-* (small), *anti-* (against), *auto-* (self), *hemi-* (half), *hetero-* (different), *chrono-* (time), *tele-* (distance), *geo-* (earth), *physio-* (nature), *photo-* (light), *hydro-* (water), *litho-* (stone), *phono-* (sound), *anthropo-* (man), *psycho-* (mind), and *philo-* (love), each generate dozens of vital words in scientific, technical, and other fields. Equally important Greek suffixes are *-meter* (measure), *-gram* (letter), *-graph* (write), *-scope* (see), *-phone* (sound), and *-phobia* (fear).

Romany

So me tumenge 'kana rospxenava, ada živd'ape varikicy Romenge. Me somas išče tykny čxajori berša efta — oxto. Ame samas terde kakesa Pxuroronkosa ade smolensko veš. Tele b'el'v'el bolype azurestar sa butydyr i butydyr kerd'ape molyvitko. Syge lyja tetamas'ol i syr kontrast sa pašidyr i pašidyr jek jekxeste jagune zygzagi p'erečšingirde bolype. Pe bax, ame čxavore, zalyžijam kašta xoc' pe kurko, pxenesas, variso žakiri.

What I am going to tell you now has been experienced by many Gypsies. I was only a little girl of seven or eight. We camped with our uncle Pxuroronko in the forest of Smolensk. Towards evening the blue sky gradually assumed a lead color. Soon it grew dark and as a contrast the zigzags of fire cut across the sky close to each other. Fortunately, we children had gathered such a heap of firewood that it would have been sufficient for a whole week—maybe we had a presentiment.

—*The Ghosts*

Romany is the language of the Gypsies. The origin of the Gypsies was long a matter of speculation. The English word "Gypsy" stems from an early belief that they came from Egypt. This has now been disproved.

The question was resolved by the science of linguistics. Detailed study of the Gypsy language has shown that the Gypsies originally came from India. The common features it shares with Sanskrit and later Indian languages can lead to no other conclusion.

The Gypsies are believed to have begun their migration westward about 1000 A.D. Loanwords in their language from Persian, Armenian, and Greek provide some indication of the general course of their travels. Today Gypsies are to be found in many countries of both Eastern and Western Europe as well as in the United States. A rough estimate of their numbers would be in the neighborhood of 5–6 million.

The name Romany is derived from the Gypsy word *rom*, which means "man." Dialects vary considerably, each strongly influenced by the language of the country in which it is spoken. The English word "pal" is of Gypsy origin, coming from the Romany word *phral*, which means "brother."

Yiddish

אין טורבין איז געווען אַ מאָל אַ טרעגער, האָט ער געהייסן
טובֿיה און איז געווען אַ גרויסער אָרעמאַן. איין מאָל, דאָנערשטיק,
שטייט ער אַזוי אין מאַרק, און קוקט אויס, פֿון וואַנעט וועט קומען
זײַן הילף, ער זאָל פֿאַרדינען עפּעס אויף שבת. און דאָ שטייען די גע־
וועלבן אָרום און אָרום ליידיק, מע זעט ניט, עס זאָל עמעצער קומען
סחורה קויפֿן, עס זאָל זײַן וואָס אָפּצוטראָגן. הייבט ער נעבעך אויף
די אויגן צום הימל מיט אַ געבעט, ער זאָל חלילה קיין פֿאַרשטערטן
שבת ניט האָבן, און זײַן ווײַב סערל מיט די קינדער זאָלן ניט הונגערן
אום שבת.

Once upon a time there lived in Turbin a porter named Tevye, who was poor beyond description. On a Thursday he was standing in the marketplace, his coattail rolled up under the rope about his hips, and looking about for a possible turn of fortune that would enable him to earn something for the Sabbath. But the stores all about him were empty and void, with nobody going in or coming out, with not a single customer in sight who was likely to need help in carrying bundles. Tevye lifted up his eyes to heaven with a prayer that the Sabbath might pass without sadness, that at least on the Sabbath his dear Sarah and the children might be spared the pangs of hunger.

—ISAAC LOEB PERETZ, *Seven Years of Plenty*

Yiddish until recent times was the language spoken by the majority of the Jews of the world. Prior to World War II more than 10 million people, about two-thirds of world Jewry, spoke or at least understood Yiddish.

Yiddish originated nearly a thousand years ago among Jewish emigrants from northern France who settled in a number of cities along the Rhine and adopted the German dialects of the area. Their speech, however, was strongly influenced by Hebrew, which remained for Jews everywhere the language of religion and scholarship. In the 14th and 15th centuries Yiddish was carried eastward into Poland, Lithuania, and Russia, where it absorbed elements from the various

Slavic languages. Thus it is the result of the fusion of a number of linguistic elements, to which it added many unique characteristics of its own.

Yiddish is written in Hebrew characters with the important difference that it uses letters for vowels. German is the dominant element in the language, accounting for about 80 percent of the vocabulary as against 10 percent each for Hebrew and the Slavic languages. Yiddish is exceptionally idiomatic, with many words and expressions that are virtually untranslatable. Many Yiddish words have entered the English language and are now to be found in standard English dictionaries. A few of the best known are *chutzpah* (effrontery), *schlemiel* (dolt), *schmaltz* (sentimentality), and the expression *mazel tov* (good luck).

The destruction of European Jewry in World War II reduced the number of Yiddish speakers by half. Since that time the number has decreased even further as the younger generation of Jews in America, the Soviet Union, and Israel are abandoning Yiddish for the language of their homelands. As Jews continue to emerge from their isolation of past centuries, and assimilate into the modern societies of which they are now a part, the use of Yiddish can only decline even further. It is generally agreed that under these circumstances the long-range future for spoken Yiddish is not bright.

LANGUAGES OF THE SOVIET UNION

Russian

«Что это? я падаю? у меня ноги подкашиваются», подумал он и упал на спину. Он раскрыл глаза, надеясь увидать, чем кончилась борьба французов с артиллеристами, и желая знать, убит или нет рыжий артиллерист, взяты или спасены пушки. Но он ничего не видал. Над ним не было ничего уже, кроме неба — высокого неба, не ясного, но все-таки неизмеримо высокого, с тихо ползущими по нем серыми облаками.

"What's this? am I falling? my legs are giving way under me," he thought, and fell on his back. He opened his eyes, hoping to see how the struggle of the French soldiers with the artillerymen was ending, and eager to know whether the red-haired artilleryman was killed or not, whether the cannons had been taken or saved. But he saw nothing of all that. Above him there was nothing but the sky—the lofty sky, not clear, but still immeasurably lofty, with gray clouds creeping quietly over it.

—LEO TOLSTOY, *War and Peace*

Russian is the most important of the Slavic languages and now one of the major languages of the world. The emergence of the Soviet Union in the postwar period as a major world power, coupled with impressive achievements in science and technology, has significantly increased the interest in and the study of Russian in recent years. With English, French, Spanish, Chinese, and Arabic, Russian is one of the six official languages of the United Nations.

In the most recent Soviet census, taken in 1970, 142 million people listed Russian as their mother tongue, and another 42 million indicated that they spoke it fluently as a second language. If we add to these figures the many Russians living in Western Europe and the United States, the number of speakers of Russian would be in the neighborhood of 190 million.

Russian is written in the Cyrillic alphabet, whose origin dates from the 9th century. Its creators were two missionaries from Greece, the brothers Cyril and Methodius, who based it largely on the Greek. Though appearing formidable to one who has never studied it, the Russian alphabet is not difficult to learn. A number of letters are written and pronounced approximately as in English (*A*, К, *M*, *O*, *T*), while others, though written as in English, are pronounced differently (*B* = *V*, *E* = *YE*, *Ë* = *YO*, *H* = *N*, *P* = *R*, *C* = *S*, *X* = *KH*). The Greek influence is clearly visible in Г (*G*), Д (*D*), Л (*L*), П (*P*), and Ф (*F*). Other letters are Б (*B*), З (*Z*), У (*U*), Ж (*ZH*), И (*I*), Ц (*TS*), Ч (*CH*), Ш (*SH*), Щ (*SHCH*), Э (*E*), Ю (*YU*), and Я (*YA*). The Ы is a vowel pronounced something like the *i* in "bit," the Й is used in forming diphthongs, while the Ъ and the Ь are the so-called hard and soft signs respectively.

If learning the Russian alphabet is not especially difficult, learning to speak the language is something else again. Russian is notorious for its long personal and place names (*e.g.*, Nepomnyashchiy, Dnepropetrovsk), for its long words (*upotreblenie*—use, *dostoprimechatelnosti*—sights, *zhenonenavistnichestvo*—misogyny), and for its unusual consonant clusters (*vzvod*—platoon, *tknut'*—to poke, *vstrecha*—meeting). Nouns, pronouns, adjectives, and numbers are declined in six cases: nominative, genitive, dative, accusative, instrumental, and prepositional or locative. The Russian verb has two aspects, each represented by a separate infinitive—the imperfective to indicate a continuing action, and the perfective to indicate an action already completed or to be completed. The genders number three, masculine, feminine, and neuter, with a different declensional pattern for each (though the neuter is similar to the masculine), and a fourth one for the plural. The stress in Russian is particularly difficult, impossible to predict in an unfamiliar word, and frequently shifting in the course of declensions or conjugations.

Yet despite these difficulties, Russian is being mastered by an increasing number of students in many different countries. They have found it worth the effort for many reasons, not the least of which is the great body of Russian literature which ranks among the most brilliant in the world.

English words of Russian origin include *vodka*, *tsar*, *samovar*, *ruble*, *pogrom*, *troika*, *steppe*, and *tundra*. The word *sputnik* entered the language in 1957.

Belorussian

Партызаны падхапіліся, як па камандзе, калі маці падышла. Пастарэлая, ссутуленая, у чорнай хустцы — помню, бачу яе і цяпер — Марына падоўгу стаяла каля кожнай труны, узіраючыся ў твары забітых. Не, яна не плакала. Зрэдку варушыліся засмяглыя вусны. Што яна казала? Чытала малітву? Ці слала праклёны забойцам? Я баяўся: ці не памутнеў ад гора яе розум?

The partisans jumped aside, as if by command, when the mother approached. Aged, bent over, in a black kerchief—I remember, I can see her even now—Marina stood for a long time beside each grave, staring into the faces of the dead. No, she did not cry. Now and then her parched lips moved. What was she saying? Was she reciting a prayer? Or cursing the killers? I was worried: had her mind become clouded from grief?

—IVAN SHAMYAKIN, *Snowy Winters*

Belorussian is the language of the Belorussian republic of the Soviet Union, which borders Poland and whose capital is Minsk. Though similar to Russian—so much so that some consider it merely a dialect of Russian—it has been given official status by the Soviet government, and official documents, books, and periodicals are published in it. There are about 7 million speakers. The alphabet contains the non-Russian letters *i* and *ў*.

Latvian

Reiz, sensenos laikos, aiz trejdeviņām jūram un trejdeviņiem kalniem dzīvoja kāds tēvs, kam bija trīs dēli—divi gudri un tas trešais es. Bet kaimiņos dzīvoja divi briesmīgi sumpurņi—katrs savā pusē tai zemītei. Viņi nemitīgi kāvās savā starpā, bet visvairāk cieta cilvēki, kas dzīvoja vidū. Tad reiz tēvs sasauca savus dēlus kopā un teica: "Ejiet pasaulē un mācieties, kā sumpurņus pievārēt. Tad nāciet atpakaļ un rādiet, ko protat. Kurš būs tēvu zemes cienīgs, tam tā paliks."

Once upon a time, in a faraway land, beyond many seas and mountains, there lived a man who had three sons. The first two were smart, the third was—I. But on each side of my father's land there were two monsters who constantly fought each other, and the innocent people in the middle always suffered. One day my father called his sons to him and said: "Go into the world and learn how to slay the monsters. Then come back and show me what you have learned. The one who is worthy of his father's land will inherit it."

—MARTINS ZIVERTS, *Kurrpurru*

Latvian, also known as Lettish, is spoken by about 1½ million people, most of them in the Latvian S.S.R. of the Soviet Union. Together with its closest relative, Lithuanian, it constitutes the Baltic language group, a part of the Indo-European family.

Latvian employs the Roman script with a number of diacritical marks to indicate special sounds. A macron (horizontal line) indicates a long vowel (*e.g.*, *māte*—mother, *tēvs*—father), while *č*, *š*, and *ž* are pronounced *ch*, *sh*, and *zh* respectively (*četri*—four, *seši*—six). A cedilla under certain consonants adds a *y* sound (*nedēļa*—week). The stress in Latvian is always on the first syllable.

Lithuanian

Keistas, nesuprantamas disonansas tarp šios vargų ir tamsumo jūros atrodė nauja brangi bažnyčia. Aišku buvo, kad ji, tokia daili ir didelė, pakliuvo čion kažin kaip, kažkokiu fatališku žmonių nesusipratimu, padariusi jiems didelę nuoskaudą, iščiulpusi jų visas sultis, palikusi jiems tik skurdą—bent šimtmečiui. Žiūrėdamas į ją, jauti, kad ji pati gėdinasi savo puikybės, gėdinasi žmonių tamsumo, jų neturto ir, rodos, turėtų kojas, tuoj pabėgtų iš to miestelio.

The elaborate new church seemed a strange and incomprehensible anomaly amidst this sea of misery and ignorance. It was clear that the church, so elegant and grand, had turned up here in some way by some fatal misunderstanding of the people and had brought great offense to them. It had drained their last ounce of strength and left them only poverty—for a century at least. Looking at it, one senses that it is ashamed of its splendor, ashamed of human ignorance and poverty, and that, if it had legs, it would quickly flee this town.

—ANTANAS VIENUOLIS, *The Last Place*

Lithuanian is spoken principally in the Lithuanian S.S.R. of the Soviet Union. About $2\frac{1}{2}$ million speakers are located here, while perhaps another 500,000 live in other countries. Lithuanian is one of the two Baltic languages, which form a branch of the Indo-European family.

Lithuanian is perhaps the oldest of all the modern Indo-European languages. It has been said that the speech of a Lithuanian peasant is the closest thing existing today to the speech of the original Indo-Europeans. Lithuanian also bears certain remarkable similarities to Sanskrit, the progenitor of the modern Indic languages. The Lithuanian words *sūnus* (son) and *avis* (sheep) are identical to the Sanskrit, while many others such as *dūmas* (smoke, Sanskrit: *dhūmas*), *vilkas* (wolf, Sanskrit: *vrkas*), and *antras* (second, Sanskrit: *antaras*) differ only by a letter or two. Some Lithuanian words are thought to be even older than their Sanskrit counterparts—*i.e.*, they may have disappeared from Sanskrit before the latter was committed to writing.

The Lithuanian alphabet contains thirty-two letters with a number of diacritical marks to indicate special sounds. The letters *č*, *š*, and *ž* are pronounced *ch*, *sh*, and *zh* respectively (*e.g.*, *čia*—here, *širdis*—heart, *žmogus*—man), while vowels include *ą*, *ę*, *į*, *ų*, *ė*, and *ū* (*į*—to, *abėcėlė*—alphabet, and *jūra*—sea).

Estonian

Oma kõvad käed mu pihku anna,
hoian sind, mu vaprat sõjameest.
Pea mul omad jälle risti panna
sinu ja su relvavende eest.

Nõnda mehine on nüüd su pale—
kui sa läksid, olid alles poiss . . .
Tule, tule aga lähemale—
tõsinend sa metsades ja sois.

Lapsesilmad! . . . aga nagu teaksid
nad nii mõndagi, mis ränk ja võik;
teaksid vahest rohkem kui nad peaksid,
nagu teaksid—nagu teaksid kõik.

Ära seisa nõnda kaua tummalt!
Mis su pilgu taga—koormab suud . . .
Kahelt suurelt—Elult, Surmalt—kummalt
oled, ainumane, märgitud?

Let me hold your hands in resignation,
Soldier, whom this mortal strife must take.
Soon my hands will fold in supplication
For your own and all your comrades' sake.

Now your changing face is even dearer.
I recall you as a schoolboy when
You first left me. Come, dear child, come nearer!
You have grown mature in wood and fen.

Yet your vivid eyes are still ingenuous,
Though they must have witnessed what is vile—
Things that men will do when life is strenuous
And resorts to cruelty and guile.

Do not stand there rigid and unspeaking;
In your glance are things that cry for breath.
Which of those two lords of man is seeking
To command your valor, Life or Death?

—MARIE UNDER, *Soldier's Mother*

There are about one million speakers of Estonian, the vast majority living in the Estonian S.S.R. of the Soviet Union.

Estonian is one of the Finno-Ugric languages, which constitute a branch of the Uralic language family. Its closest relative is Finnish, spoken across the Gulf of Finland. The two languages are sufficiently similar to be mutually intelligible, at least for those Estonians who speak the dialect of the north. Estonian is not, as is sometimes thought, in any way related to its nearest geographic neighbors, Latvian and Lithuanian.

Like Latvian and Lithuanian, Estonian employs the Roman script, the three languages being the only ones in the Soviet Union to do so. The alphabet lacks the letters *c*, *q*, *w*, *x*, *y*, *z*, but contains the letter *õ*, found in no other language of eastern Europe. Umlauts may appear over the letters *a*, *o*, and *u*.

Ukrainian

Тече вода в синє море,
Та не витікає;
Шука козак свою долю,
А долі немає.
Пішов козак світ за очі;
Грає синє море,
Грає серце козацькеє,
А думка говорить:
«Куди ти йдеш, не спитавшись?
На кого покинув
Батька, неньку старенькую,
Молоду дівчину?
На чужині не ті люде,—
Тяжко з ними жити!
Ні з ким буде поплакати,
Ні поговорити».

Сидить козак на тім боці,—
Грає синє море.
Думав, доля зустрінеться,—
Спіткалося горе.
А журавлі летять собі
Додому ключами.
Плаче козак—шляхи биті
Заросли тернами.

The river to the blue sea flows
But flows not back again.
The Cossack seeks his fortune too,
But all his search is vain.
Wide in the world the Cossack goes,
And there the blue sea roars,
The Cossack's heart is boisterous too,
This question it explores:
"Where have you gone without farewell?
To whom has all been left
Of father and old mother now

And of your maid bereft?
These alien folk have alien hearts;
It's hard with them to live!
No one is here to share one's tears
Or gentle words to give."

The Cossack haunts the farther coast,—
And still the blue seas roar.
He hoped to find his fortune there,
But met with sorrow sore.
And while the cranes in coveys seek
The ocean's farther bournes,
The Cossack weeps—the beaten paths
Are overgrown with thorns.

—TARAS SHEVCHENKO, *Kobzar*

Ukrainian is, after Russian, the most widely spoken language in the Soviet Union. Its 35 million speakers live mainly in the Ukrainian S.S.R., with its capital at Kiev. There are also about 500,000 Ukrainians in the United States and Canada.

Like Russian, to which it is closely related, Ukrainian is written in the Cyrillic alphabet. Three Ukrainian letters not to be found in Russian are: the є, pronounced *ye* as in "yet," the *i*, pronounced *ee* as in "meet," and the *ï*, pronounced *ye* as in "year."

Moldavian

Тотул с'а ынчепут азь ла ревэрсатул зорилор де зи . . . Орь, поате, ку ун вяк ын урмэ . . . Гындул ынарипат с'а фэкут нэдежде ши вис. Дорул мистуитор пентру ун сэлаш луминос, пентру скутиря фемеий де мунчиле греле дин касэ, пентру штержеря дистанцей суфлетешть ши сочиале динтре сат ши ораш—се черя ынфэптуит. Аштептаря ышь иросисе ултимул строп ал рэбдэрий.

It all began at break of day . . . Or perhaps a century ago . . . The winged thought turned to hope and dream. The consuming desire for a bright place to live, for the freeing of women from burdensome household chores, for eliminating the spiritual and social gulf between village and town—demanded fulfillment. The waiting had dissipated the last ounce of patience.

—EMILIAN BUKOV, *The Last Paling*

Moldavian is spoken in the Moldavian S.S.R., the area traditionally known as Bessarabia. A part of Rumania before World War II, it was incorporated into the Soviet Union in 1940. Moldavian is merely a dialect of Rumanian, but since the creation of the Moldavian S.S.R. and the adoption of the Cyrillic alphabet it is generally thought of as a separate language. It is the only Romance language of the Soviet Union. There are about 2½ million speakers.

Azerbaijani

Мејдана јығылан чамаат көзүнү даш булагдан чыхан нова зилләмишди.

Бирдән су сәсләнди, шән бир курулту илә ахмаға башлады. Узун илләр су һәсрәтиндә олан әһали һәјәчанла бахыр, сусурду. Сүкуту сујун шаграг сәси позурду. Инсанлар гурумуш сәһрада илкин су көрмүш јолчулар кими мәфтунлугла бахыр, динмир, санки сујун сәраба чевриләчәјиндән горхурдулар. Лакин көрдүкләри һәгигәт иди. Шаирә Натәван доғма елинә Шушаја булаг чәкдирмишди. Бирдән һамы чошду, су һәсрәтилә јанан синәләр галхыб енди:

—Јашасын Натәван.

—Вар олсун Хан гызы.

The crowd that had gathered in the square gazed at the stone fount.

Suddenly a great noise was heard and the water burst forth with a happy sound. The people, having dreamed of water for many a year, watched in anxious silence. Only the gay murmur of the stream could be heard. Like travelers in the desert coming upon water for the first time, the people watched with delight, but remained silent, as if afraid the water would suddenly disappear like a mirage. But what they were seeing was real. The poetess Natavan had laid a pipe into her native land of Shushu. Suddenly everyone cried out, their chests heaving with the oppressive thirst:

"Long live Natavan!"

"Glory to Khan Gyzy!"

—AZIZA JAFARZADE, *Tales of Natavan*

Azerbaijani is spoken both in the Soviet Union and Iran, on the west bank of the Caspian Sea. In the Soviet Union its 4 million speakers live mainly in the Azerbaidzhan S.S.R., whose capital is Baku. In Iran it is spoken by another 4 million people in the northwesternmost part of the country, an area also known as Azerbaijan.

Azerbaijani is a Turkic language and thus part of the Altaic family. Traditionally it was written in the Arabic script but in 1924 the Soviet government introduced the Roman script, and in 1940 the Cyrillic. The present alphabet contains eight special characters: ғ, ә, *j*, ҝ, ө, ү, *h*, and ч. The *j* is a more recent addition, not introduced until 1958.

Georgian

„ღმერთსა შემვედრე, ნუთუ კვლა დამხსნას სოფლისა შრომასა,
ცეცხლსა, წყალსა და მიწასა, ჰაერთა თანა ძრომასა;
მომცნეს ფრთენი და აღვფრინდე, მივჰხვდე მას ჩემსა ნდომასა,
დღისით და ღამით ვჰხედვიდე მზისა ელვათა კრთომასა.

„მზე უშენოდ ვერ იქმნების, რათგან შენ ხარ მისი წილი,
განაღამცა მას ეახელ მისი ეტლი, არ თუ წბილი!
მუნა გნახო, მადვე გსახო, განმინათლო გული ჩრდილი,
თუ სიცოცხლე მწარე მქონდა, სიკვდილიმცა მქონდა ტკბილი!

"Entreat God for me; it may be He will deliver me from the travail of the world and from union with fire, water, earth and air. Let Him give me wings and I shall fly up, I shall attain my desire—day and night I shall gaze on the sun's rays flashing in splendor.

"The sun cannot be without thee, for thou art an atom of it; of a surety thou shalt adhere to it as its zodiac, and not as one rejected. There shall I seek thee; I shall liken thee to it, thou shalt enlighten my darkened heart. If my life was bitter, let my death be sweet!

—SHOTA RUSTAVELI, *The Knight in the Tiger's Skin*

Georgian is spoken primarily in the Georgian S.S.R. of the Soviet Union, situated in Transcaucasia and bordering Turkey and the Black Sea. Its speakers number over 3 million, or about two-thirds of the republic's population. Georgian belongs to the Caucasian family, but since these languages have been grouped more on the basis of geography than linguistics, it is questionable whether any of the other Caucasian languages are actually related to it. In any event, it is the most widely spoken of these languages, and the only one with an ancient literary tradition.

The origin of the Georgian alphabet is obscure, but it is known to have been invented in the 5th century A.D. It is written from left to right. The present script, called Mkhedruli ("secular writing"), replaced the original Khutsuri ("church writing") in the 11th century. There are thirty-three letters, without distinction between upper and lower case, and with one letter for each sound and one sound for each letter.

The Georgians call themselves *Kartvelebi* and their land *Sakartvelo*. The language contains some formidable consonant clusters, as may be seen in the names of such Georgian cities as Tbilisi, Mtskheta, Tkvarcheli, and Tskhinvali. Many Georgian surnames end in *-idze*, *-adze*, *-dali*, and *-vili*. Joseph Stalin's original Georgian name was Dzhugashvili.

The Knight in the Tiger's Skin, the great epic of Georgian literature, was composed about the year 1200. It consists of more than 1,600 four-line stanzas, two of which are shown above. Virtually nothing is known of the author other than his name.

Armenian

Անցնեի իմ լավ ուղին լավաբար,
Կյանքս չտայի կասկածի մեգին...
Այնպես կուզեի մեկն ինձ հավատար,
Այնպես կուզեի հավատալ մեկին:

Շահեի կռիվն այս անհավասար,
Սիրո՛վ շահեի փոքրին ու մեծին..
Այնպես կուզեի մեկն ինձ հավատար,
Այնպես կուզեի հավատալ մեկին:

Թող լռությունը ահեղ որոտար,
Եվ լռեր հավետ աղմուկն անմեկին...
Այնպես կուզեի մեկն ինձ հավատար,
Այնպես կուզեի հավատալ մեկին:

Oh to walk my way with kindness,
And not betray my life to a cloud of suspicions . . .
How I wish that someone would believe me,
How I wish that I could believe someone.

To triumph in an unequal battle,
To embrace with love both small and big,
How I wish that someone would believe me,
How I wish that I could believe someone.

Let the silence burst forth with fury,
And the eternal noise die down for good . . .
How I wish that someone would believe me,
How I wish that I could believe someone.

—HAMO SAHYAN

There are approximately 4 million speakers of Armenian. About 2.2 million live in the Armenian S.S.R. of the Soviet Union, and about one million in the Georgian, Azerbaidzhan, and Russian republics. There are also sizable Armenian communities in Lebanon (150,000), Syria (150,000), Iran (100,000), and Turkey (50,000). About 250,000 Armenians reside in the United States, though in general only the older generation is able to speak the language.

The Armenians are an ancient people whose history dates back about 2,500 years. The Armenian alphabet was invented by Mesrop Mashtots, a missionary, about the year 400 A.D. Originally it consisted of thirty-six letters—six vowels and thirty consonants—to which two letters were added in the 12th century.

Armenian constitutes a separate and independent branch of the Indo-European family. The Armenians call their country *Hayastan* and their language *Hayaren*. During many centuries of Persian domination so many Iranian words entered the language that even in the 19th century many linguists thought it a dialect of Persian. It was not until 1875 that it was established as an independent language. Much of the Armenian vocabulary is not to be found in any other Indo-European language. Undoubtedly many words were derived from languages that are now extinct.

Ossetian

Фæззæг

Æхсæлы ызгъæлы,
Лæджирттæг фæбур . . .
Мигъ бады цæгаты,
Нæ йæ тавы хур . . .

Æркарстам, æрластам
Нæ хортæ, нæ хос . . .
Чи кусы йæ мусы,
Чи'лвыны йæ фос . . .

Хор бирæ, фос бирæ
Хуыцауы фæрцы . . .
Нæ хæхбæсты бæркад,
Цы диссаг дæ цы!

Зымæг

Хъызт зымæг, тыхст зымæг,
Нæ катай, нæ мæт!
Йæ бонтæ—фыдбонтæ,
Йæ бахсæв—мæлæт.

Нæ хъæутæ—лæгæттæ,
Нæ фезмæлд—зæйуат.
Фыдæлтæй нын баззад
Зæйы сæфтæн рад.

Нæ мæгуыр, нæ сидзæр,
Æнæ хай куыстæй,
Хуыцаумæ дзыназынц
Ыстонгæй, сыдæй . . .

Autumn

The juniper sheds its foliage,
The buckwheat has turned yellow . . .
The fog has settled on the northern slope,
Which is not warmed by the sun . . .

We have mown and carted away
Our grain, our hay . . .
Some work at threshing,
While others shear their sheep . . .

There is much grain and cattle
With the help of God . . .
The abundance of our mountain land,
What a wonder you are!

Winter

Cruel winter, oppressive winter,
Our despair, our sorrow!
Its days are bitter,
Its nights like death.

Our villages are caves,
Our homes are scenes of avalanches.
Our ancestors have ordained that we
Perish in turn under an avalanche.

Our poor ones, our orphans,
Without a drop of work,
To God cry out
Hungry, frozen . . .

—KOSTA KHETAGUROV

Ossetian is spoken on the slopes of the Caucasus Mountains, which divide the Russian Republic from the Georgian S.S.R. The area in the Russian Republic is known as the North Ossetian A.S.S.R. (capital: Ordzhonikidze), while the area in the Georgian S.S.R. is called the South Ossetian Autonomous Region (capital: Tskhinvali). Ossetian speakers number about 400,000, 60 percent of whom live in the North Ossetian Republic, and 15 percent in the South Ossetian Autonomous Region.

Ossetian is an Iranian language—the only one of any consequence spoken in the Caucasus. There are two important dialects—Iron and Digor—the former, shown above, being the more widely spoken. Written Ossetian may be immediately recognized by its use of the *æ*, a letter to be found in no other language using the Cyrillic alphabet.

Kabardian

ДамэшхуитIыр ишэщIарэ зэзэмызэ ар игъэхъейуэ бгъэшхуэ гуэри уафэгум щесырт, мэкъупIэр къиуфэрэзыхьу. Хуэмурэ хьэуам ар щесырт, къищэкIун гуэрхэр къилъыхъуэу. Зыхуейр и нэм къыщыпэщIэмыхуэм, дамэшхуитIыр зыплIытхурэ иудынынщIри, мэщ хьэсэбгъум зритауэ, бгъэр елъэтэкIырт. Мыхъейуэ икIи дахэ дыдэу ар зэресыр хьэлэмэт щыхъуат Бэрокъуэми, и нэр тенауэ абы кIэлъыплъырт. Зы напIэзыпIэ закъуэкIэ бгъэр къызэтеувыIэ хуэдэ хъуащ, итIанэ и дамитI шещIар зришэлIэжщ, и щхьэр егъэзыхауэ зыкъритIупщхьэхри, мэшым зыхидзащ. Дакъикъэ ныкъуи дэмыкIауэ, бгъэжьым зыкъиIэтыжащ, дамэшхуитIыр хьэлъэу иудынынщIэурэ. Лъэбжьанэ жанхэмкIэ тхьэкIумэкIыхьыр бгъэм зэщIиубыдауэ и лъэныкъуэмкIэ къихьу щилъагъум, Бэрокъуэм и плIэм илъ фочыр къипхъуэтащ.

Spreading its two tremendous wings and occasionally flapping them, a great eagle soared through the sky, circling over the meadow. It glided slowly through the air, seeking some prey. Not spotting what it was looking for, it flapped its great wings about five times and, coming to a millet patch, began to circle the perimeter. Baroko was delighted that the bird glided gracefully without flapping its wings and kept his eyes riveted on it. In an instant the bird seemed to stop, then, folding its wings, swept down headfirst and dove into the millet. Not a half-minute later it flew up again, violently flapping its wings. Seeing that the eagle's sharp claws were clutching a hare and that it was flying directly toward him, Baroko grabbed the gun on his shoulder.

—KHACHIM TEUNOV, *The Shadzhamokov Family*

Kabardian is spoken in the Caucasus region of the Soviet Union, principally in the Kabardin-Balkar A.S.S.R. (capital: Nalchik) and the Karachai-Cherkess Autonomous Region (capital: Cherkessk). It is spoken by two peoples—the Kabardians, who number about 280,000, and the Circassians (Russian: *cherkesy*), who number about 40,000. The language is thus sometimes referred to as Kabardin-Cherkess.

The Kabardians, Circassians, and a third people, the Adygeis, who speak the closely related Adygei language, are sometimes referred to collectively as Circassians. Historically, the Circassians date back to ancient times, and until the middle of the 19th century occupied almost the entire region between the Caucasus Mountains, the Kuban River, and the Black Sea. Following the annexation of the region by Russia in 1864, several hundred thousand Circassians migrated south and some are still to be found today in Turkey and Syria.

Kabardian belongs to the Western branch of the Caucasian family of languages. The alphabet is Cyrillic with only one additional letter—the I—which is common to many of the Caucasian languages.

Chechen

Ламанах духдуьйлу шал шийла шовданаш
Шиэн бекъачу кийрана Iаббалца ца молуш,
Iин кIоргиэ буьйлуш, мела муж муьйлуш,
Варшан йистиэ йолу маргIал сийна буц
Шиэн оьздачу зоьрхана буззалца ца юуш,
Орцал лахабуьйлуш, сема ладуьйгIуш,
Иччархочун тоьпуо лацарна, кхоьруш,
Дехачу диэгIана буткъа мотт хьоькхуш,
Мокхазан бердах куьран га хьоькхуш,
Попан орамах торгIала тIа детташ,
Лергаш дуьхьал туьйсуш, кур аркъал туьйсуш,
Гу лекха буьйлуш, гIелашка ва гIергIаш,
Масаниэ сай лиэла гIелашца ва боцуш!
Вай биэн дац, ва кIентий, аьллар ца хуьлуш?

From the depths of the mountains gush the ice-cold springs,
But he doesn't fill his lean stomach there.
Rather he descends to the depths of the ravine and drinks from a warm puddle.
The wooded slope is bordered by rising fresh blue grass,
But he doesn't fill his noble belly there.
Coming out below the wooded hills, he listens carefully,
Anxious to avoid the dreaded hunter's gun.
Licking his long body with his slender tongue,
Sharpening his branched antlers on the flinty shore,
Striking his spotted hind leg on the plane tree's root,
Pointing his ears forward, tossing his antlers onto his back,
Climbing high on the hill, bellowing to the does,
How many stags walk without their mates?
And are there not many lads besides us of whom the same is true?

—*The Stag* (Chechen folk song)

Chechen is spoken in the Chechen-Ingush A.S.S.R. of the Soviet Union, located in the Caucasus with its capital at Grozny. Together with the closely related Ingush language (the two are for the most part mutually intelligible), it constitutes the Eastern branch of the Caucasian family of languages. There are about 600,000 speakers. As in Kabardian and other Caucasian languages, the alphabet contains the additional letter I.

Avar

Зодоса цIер гIадин гулла балелъул
Гуллий кьураб керен кьуризабичIо.
Кьвагьулаго чабхъен тIаде кIанцIидал
Кодоб бирданги ккун тIаде вахъана.
ЦохIо кьвагьун аралъ кIиго вегана,
КIиго кьвагьаралъги лъабго лъукъана.
Вакка-ваккаравго ккезе гьавуна.
Боял тIуризарун, тIаде гулла бан
ТIаде чи виччачIо цохIо гIадамцин.

The bullets fly like hail from the sky,
But he doesn't turn his breast away from them.
And when they set upon him with guns ablaze
He stood up tall with rifle in hand.
One shot and two men fell,
A second shot wounded three more.
Whoever appeared met his death.
He scattered the army with a hail of bullets,
Not a single soul could get near.
—*Zelimkhan* (Avar song of heroism)

Avar is spoken in the Dagestan A.S.S.R. of the Soviet Union (capital: Makhachkala), situated in the Caucasus on the west bank of the Caspian Sea. In this single republic, smaller than West Virginia, some thirty different languages are spoken, most of them falling within a single subdivision of the Caucasian family known as the Dagestan languages. Avar, spoken in the southwestern part of the republic, ranks first in number of speakers with about 400,000. Like the other Caucasian languages, it contains the special letter I. The Avars of today (Russian: *avartsy*) bear no relationship to the ancient Avars (Russian: *avary*), a powerful Turkic-speaking people of the 6th and 7th centuries.

Kalmyk

Бахта ил нәр болад, күргн үзгдәд хуурв. Гиичин улс мөрләд, нәәрин нөөрмү улс тарлhнла, Булhн гертән тесҗ сууҗ ядад, Киштә талан гүүhәд күрәд ирв. —Нүдңчн хавдад җе болад бәәҗч, мә эн киитн усар уhаҗ ав,—гиҗ келәд Киштә бор ааhар, бутхачсн, шаврта ус утхҗ авад Булhнд өгв. —Нә болв. Хавдрнь бийнь хәрх. —Шулун кел, ямаран бәәдлтә, кениг дурасн юмн бәәҗ?—гиҗ сурад, Булhн, торад ямаран хәрү өкән медҗ ядҗ бәәсн Киштән өвдг түшәд суув.

The noisy party was over, at last the bridegroom had appeared. When the groom's family had left and the last sleepy guests had gone their way, Bulgan could not sit home and raced to see her girlfriend Kishtya. "Your eyes are awfully swollen, wash your face with some cold water," said Kishtya, taking a cup of cloudy water and handing it to her. "It's all right. The swelling will subside on its own. I'd rather you tell me what you think of my fiancé, whom he reminds you of," asked Bulgan, resting her elbows on Kishtya's knees. Kishtya sat silently, not knowing how to answer her questions.

—BAATAR BASANGOV, *The Truth of the Past*

Kalmyk, or Kalmuck, is spoken in the Kalmyk A.S.S.R. of the Soviet Union (capital: Elista), located just to the west of the Volga River delta, northwest of the Caspian Sea. Its speakers, the Kalmyks, who number about 125,000, are descendants of a Mongol people who migrated to this region from central Asia in the 17th century. The language is thus most closely related to modern Mongolian, as well as to Buryat, of southern Siberia, the three belonging to the Mongolian branch of the Altaic family. The Kalmyk alphabet is based on the Cyrillic, with the non-Russian letters, ә, *h*, җ, ң, ө, and ү.

Turkmen

Ашгабат Совет Союзының республикаларының пайтагтларының иң гүнортада ерлешйәнидир. Шәхериң бир тарапыны Көпетдаг эрңеклэп отуран болса, бейлеки бир тарапыны Гарагумуң чәгелери голтуклап ятыр.

Совет хәкимиети йылларында Ашгабат чалт өсди ве кешбини таналмаз ялы өзгертди. 1948-нҗи йылың ер титремесинден озалам Ашгабат Орта Азиядакы иң гөзел шәхерлериң бири хасапланярды.

Тебигы бетбагтчылык пайтагты вес-вейран этди. Совет хөкүметиниң ве юрдумызың әхли халкларының көмеги билен өрән гысга мөхлетиң ичинде бүтинлей тәзе, өңкүсинденем хас овадан шәхер бина эдилди. Ашгабат бу ере гелип-гидйән мыхманларда улы гуванч дуйгусыны дөредйәр.

Ashkhabad is the southernmost of the republic capitals of the Soviet Union. On one side of the city lie the foothills of the Kopet-Dag; just on the other side the sands of the Kara-Kum Desert.

Under Soviet rule Ashkhabad grew rapidly and became a new city. Before the earthquake of 1948 Ashkhabad was deservedly considered one of the most beautiful cities of Central Asia.

The calamity reduced the city to rubble. With the help of the Soviet government, and all the brotherly peoples of the country, a completely new city arose out of the ruins. Today Ashkhabad is a delight to everyone visiting it.

Turkmen, also known as Turkoman, is spoken principally in the Turkmen S.S.R. of the Soviet Union (capital: Ashkhabad), lying on the eastern shore of the Caspian Sea and bordering Iran and Afghanistan. There are about 1½ million speakers here plus another 400,000 in Afghanistan. Closely related to Turkish, Turkmen is a member of the Turkic branch of the Altaic family of languages. The alphabet, based on the Cyrillic, contains the additional letters җ, ң, ө, ү, and ә.

Kazakh

Бойдақ жылқының бәрі жайылысты тастап, сонау биік адырдың басына шығып ап үйездеп тур. Өрістен қайтқан қоралы қой да су маңына шубырып, баурын сызға төсеп, бүйірін соғып жатыр. Жайылысты ойлар емес. Қумаса су қасынан турар емес. Сиыр атаулы Бақанас суынан бөлінген қара су, шалшық суларға кіріп, көлбей-көлбей жатып апты. Бірен-саран оқшау шыққан тайынша, қунажын болса, сәйгелдің қуғынына ушырап, қутырғандай жосып жүр. Қуйрығын шаншып алып, қос танауы делдиіп, екі көзі дәл бір сойғалы жатқандай аларып, ежірейіп ап, жынданғандай жүйткиді.

The flocks had left the pastures and were herded together on the bleak crest of a distant hill, whence they had been driven by the tireless and vicious gadflies. The sheep returning from the meadows wallowed limply in the mud at the side of the river. The cows had waded into the water and stood dozing, only their heads showing above the water. The few calves left on the bank were rushing frantically to and fro, trying to shake off the gadflies. With lashing tails, distended nostrils, and bulging eyes, they dashed about, as if to escape slaughter.

—MUKHTAR AUEZOV, *Abai*

Kazakh is spoken principally in the Kazakh S.S.R. of the Soviet Union, which stretches from the Chinese border to the Caspian Sea, and whose capital is Alma-Ata. There it is spoken by about 4 million people, with another one million in the rest of the Soviet Union, about 500,000 across the border in China, and some 50,000 in Mongolia. Kazakh is one of the Turkic languages for which the Cyrillic alphabet was introduced just prior to World War II. There are a number of special characters, including ә, ғ, қ, ң, ө, ү, ұ, *h*, and *і*.

Uzbek

—Хайр, биз бу дағдағаларни ўртадан кўтаришга ҳаракат қилурмиз, —деди Навоий қатъий оҳанг билан. —Гарчи бу мазҳабларнинг бирини ўзгасидан афзал кўрмасак ҳам, улуснинг бирлигини эътиборга олурмиз. Иним, дунёда китоб ўқимоқдан, тафаккурдан, шеър айтмоқдан ўзга завқбахш машғулот йўқдир. Табиатим кўпроқ бу томонга мойил эди. Сокин бир масканда яшаб, бу завқ дарёсида сузмоқчи эдим. Лекин, менга, маълумингиз, давлатда вазифа бердилар . . . Ёлғиз эл ва улус манфаатини назарга олиб, мансабни қабул этдим. Бу муборак юртда қилинадиган ишлар бениҳоят кўпдир. Бу ишларнинг ҳар бирига элимиз асрлардан бери ташнадир.

"Then let us try to prevent such dissension," said Navoi firmly. "We must not show preference for any one religious doctrine. Brother, there is no pleasanter occupation in this world than just reading books, contemplating and writing verses. By nature I am cut out for just such a life. I should like to live in some quiet place and float lazily on the sea of enjoyment but, as you know, I have been given a court appointment. I accepted it for the sake of the people and the country. There is an endless number of things to be done in this land and the people have awaited each one of them for centuries."

—AIBEK, *Navoi*

Uzbek is the most widely spoken of the non-Slavic languages of the Soviet Union. There are about 9 million speakers, most of whom live in the Uzbek S.S.R. with its capital at Tashkent. There are also about one million Uzbek speakers in Afghanistan.

Uzbek is one of the Turkic languages, which form a branch of the Altaic family. At the time of the Russian Revolution it was written in the Arabic script, but this was replaced by the Roman in 1927, and the Cyrillic in 1940. The alphabet contains the special letters ў, қ, ғ, and ҳ.

Aibek is the pseudonym of Musa Tashmukhamedov, whose historical novel *Navoi* was published in 1945. Its title is the name of a famous Uzbek poet and statesman of the 15th century.

Tadzhik

Аз тирезаҳои фарохи троллейбус иморатҳои зебои се-чор ошьёна, дарахтони баланд-баланди хиёбон ва гурӯҳ-гурӯҳ одамон, лентаи кино барин, як-як аз мадди назар мегузаштанд. Қодирҷон ба берун нигоҳ карда ҳайрон мешуд, ки Душанбеи дилкушо чи қадар тез ободу васеъ шуда истодааст. Дирӯзакак дар ҷои ана он бинои сербари Унвермаги Марказӣ қатор-қатор дӯкончаҳои молфурӯшии тахтагӣ меистоданд. Вай аз дил гузаронд, ки шаш моҳ боз дар ҳамин шаҳр таҳсили илм мекунаду аммо ҳанӯз на ҳамаи растаю хиёбонҳои онро дидааст.

Through the wide windows of the trolleybus there flashed by, as if in a motion picture, the attractive three- and four-story buildings, the immensely tall trees, the avenues, and the endless stream of people. Kadirzhan looked out and marveled at how fast Dushanbe was being built up. On the spot where there now stood the tall building of the Central Department Store it seemed that only yesterday there were rows of wooden trading benches. He reflected that although he had been studying in the city for six months, he had still not gotten around to seeing all the avenues and squares.

—ABDUMALIK BAKHORI, *A Window Without Light*

Tadzhik is spoken principally in the Tadzhik S.S.R. of the Soviet Union (capital: Dushanbe), which borders Afghanistan and China. Over 1½ million of its total of 2 million speakers are located here, the rest mainly in the Uzbek republic.

Tadzhik is an Iranian language and thus part of the Indo-European family. It is, for all practical purposes, the same language as Persian, the Cyrillic alphabet being its main distinguishing feature. There are six letters not to be found in the Russian alphabet: ӣ, *ӯ*, ғ, қ, ҳ, and ҷ.

Kirgiz

Сүрөттүн тээ ички тереңинде – күзгү асмандын ала-бүркөк чет жакасы. Шамал бирин-серин булуттарды бир жакка бет алдырып, алыста кылтайган чокуларга жандатып, кыялата айдап бара жатат. Андан берки көрүнүштө – бозоргон сары талаа, кең өзөн. Чет-четтен чийлер ыкташып, жаан – чачындан кийин топурагы борпоң тоборсуп карайган жолдо, катарлаш баскан эки жолоочунун изи тигинден бери чубайт. Жолоочулар улам жакындаган сайын алардын издери жерге даана түшүп, өздөрү азыр дагы бир-эки кадам шилтешсе, рамканын сыртына аттап, ушундан ары кетип калчудай сезилет.

The background of the picture is a patch of bleak autumn sky with the wind chasing scattered clouds along the highest mountain tops in sight. A broad valley with a steppe of golden bronze color and two wayfarers walking side by side on the road black and damp from recent rains, with waving clusters of needle grass on both its sides, form its foreground. In the course of coming to the fore the footprints gradually become clearer and it seems that they will disappear behind the frame if they take one step more.

—CHINGIS AITMATOV, *Jamila*

Kirgiz is spoken principally in the Kirgiz republic of the Soviet Union, which borders China and whose capital is Frunze. Like Turkmen, Uzbek, and Kazakh, it is one of the Turkic languages, and is spoken by about $1\frac{1}{2}$ million people. Kirgiz was written in the Arabic script until 1928 when the Latin alphabet was introduced, which in turn was replaced by the Cyrillic in 1940. The alphabet contains three additional letters, the ү, ө, and ң.

Bashkir

Ятаҡхана тып-тын булып ҡала. Көндөң күп өлөшөндә гөрләп торған ятаҡханаға бындай тынлыҡ килешмәй. Мәктәптә уҡыусы «художниктәр» тарафынан стенаға күмер, карандаш ҡәләмдәр менән эшләнгән рәсемдәр ҙә ятаҡхана өҫтөнә моңайып ҡарап ҡалған һымаҡ була.

Уның урынына был минутта ашханала көслө шау-шыу, йәнлелек башлана. Уҡыусылар ҡыҙарып янған тоноҡ нурлы электрик лампаһы яктыһында, кухняләге киң төплө бәләкәй тәҙрәнән ҡалай һауыттарға һалдырып аш алалар.

All is quiet in the dormitory. For a place usually bustling with activity all day, such quiet is unusual. Even the charcoal and pencil drawings on the walls done by the school "artists" look down somehow dejectedly.

At that moment there is a commotion in the mess hall. In the dim reddish light of an electric lamp the students are served tin bowls of soup through a small window.

—SAGIT AGISH, *The Foundation*

Bashkir is spoken principally in the Bashkir A.S.S.R. of the Soviet Union (capital: Ufa), which lies to the west of the southern slopes of the Ural Mountains. It is another of the many Turkic languages of the Soviet Union, and has about one million speakers. The Bashkir alphabet is based on the Cyrillic, with the additional letters ғ, ҙ, ҡ, ң, ө, ҫ, ү, *h*, and *ə*.

Chuvash

Çулçă сарса тикĕсленнĕ йывăçсем пархатарлă сывлăмпа çăвăннă хыççăн çăмăллăн вăшлатса иртекен çилпе шăлăнса тасалнă та йăлтăркка ешĕл курăнаççĕ. Темле йывăç та ӳсет çĕр çинче, пурин валли те вырăн çитет, темелле: хăшĕ пахчара саркаланса савăнать, хăшĕ çурт умĕнче юри тăратнă хурал пек ларать, ял урлă каçакан тарăн çырмара та йăмрасем таçта çӳле кармашаççĕ. Çырма варринче çеç, лутра карлăклă кĕпер тĕлĕнче, иртен-çӳрен валли ятарласа çавра хапха касса хăварнă пек, уçлăх юлнă. Çав патвар йăмрасем çырмана пĕтĕмпе хупăрласа илнĕ, хĕвел çути аяла кăнтăр варринче те хĕсĕнсе кăна сăрхăнать.

The leafy trees, bathed in pure morning dew and dried in the soft wind, make a beautiful scene. They catch your eye wherever you look. The trees are everywhere. All sorts grow on the earth, there is plenty of room here for every kind of plant. You can see some in the orchards where they enjoy the grassy fertile soil. Others you can see lined up in front of the houses like guards. Even the ravine dividing the village is crowded with tall willow trees. Only down at the bottom a tiny bridge with low railings makes a gate in the wall of them. The trees and bushes seem to have conquered the whole ravine. Even at noon the rays of the sun struggle fiercely to get through the thick branches to the shaded roots.

—NIKOLAI ILBEKOV, *Brown Bread*

Chuvash is spoken in the middle Volga region of the Soviet Union, especially in the Chuvash republic whose capital is Cheboksary. Though it is one of the Turkic languages, it differs markedly from the other members of this family, and the question of its affiliation was long a matter of dispute. There are about 1½ million speakers. The alphabet is based on the Cyrillic, with the additional letters *ă*, *ĕ*, *ç*, and *ӳ*.

Tatar

Өстенә искерә төшкән язгы пальто, аягына тула оек белән резина галош кигән Газинур, Миңнурыйның ике беләгеннән тотып, соңгы мәртәбә аның кадерле күзләренә текәлеп карады. Миңнурый гаҗәеп зур түземлелек күрсәтә иде. Йокысыз үткән төн аның матур йөзенә тирән кайгы эзен салса да, анда: «Син киткәч, ике кечкенә бала белән мин берүзем нишләрмен, көнемне ничек үткәрермен?»—дип аптырап, өметсезлеккә төшү дә, тетрәү дә юк иде. Ул бер генә тапкыр да еламады. Тик менә хәзер, китәр минутта, Газинур аның ике беләгеннән тотып, күзләренә текәлгәч кенә, аның озын керфекләре дерелдәп китте.

Wearing a shabby spring coat, country-style overshoes, and woolen stockings, Gazinur held Minnuri's hand in his, and looked into her dear eyes for the last time. Although the sleepless agonizing night had left a trace of sadness on her pretty face, she showed no signs of despair or confusion. In her loving look there was no suggestion of the usual question in such situations: "What will I do without you, alone, with two small children? How will I live?" Only now, at the moment of saying goodbye, when Gazinur took Minnuri in his arms, did her long eyelashes begin to quiver.

—ABDURAKHMAN ABSALYAMOV, *Gazinur*

Tatar, also spelled Tartar, is a widely dispersed language of the Soviet Union, spoken both in European Russia and in Siberia. Its 5 million speakers are divided into a number of branches, the most important being the Volga Tatars, who inhabit the lands drained by the Volga River and its tributaries. The greatest concentrations of Volga Tatars are in the Tatar A.S.S.R. (capital: Kazan), where they number about $1\frac{1}{2}$ million, and in the Bashkir A.S.S.R. (capital: Ufa), where they number about one million. A second branch of the Tatars consists of the Siberian Tatars, who number about 75,000 and live in western Siberia.

Tatar is a Turkic language belonging to the Altaic family. The

Tatars first appear in Russian history in the 13th century when, as the Mongols, they overran most of the country and settled down to rule. The new state was known as the Golden Horde, with its capital at Sarai, near the modern city of Astrakhan. But its distance from the capital of the Mongol Empire, coupled with the small number of governing Mongols in the Horde itself, led to its ultimate absorption by Turkic elements. When the Golden Horde began to crumble in the 15th century, a number of new Tatar kingdoms were formed—Kazan, Astrakhan, Crimean, and Siberian. These in turn fell to Russia a century later.

Originally written in the Arabic script, Tatar now uses the Cyrillic. The alphabet contains the additional letters *ә*, ө, ү, җ, ң, and *h*.

Mordvin

Теде мейле Чурьканов эсензэ ёжос сась а ёвтавикс якшамодо. Пеензэ калцкаевсть вейс, рунгованзо прок ульнесть сялгонезь кельме эрень салмукскеть. Сорнось рунгозо, эзть кунсоло кедтне ды пильгтне. Сон панжинзе сельмензэ ды несь кодамо-бути тусто сув ёнов молиця валдо, кона совась решоткасо пирязь сэрей вальматнева. Куватьс эзь чарькодеве капитанонтень, косо сон ашти.

Later Churkanov regained consciousness from the indescribable cold. His teeth were chattering, his body felt as if it were being pricked with needles of cold ice. His body shivered, his hands and feet were numb. He opened his eyes and glimpsed a sort of hazy light coming in through the high grated windows. For a long time the captain had no idea where he was.

—A. SHCHEGLOV, *Happiness*

Mordvin is spoken over a broad area of European Russia, lying generally in the middle Volga region and extending as far as the Ural Mountains. There are about one million speakers, about one-third of whom live in the Mordvinian A.S.S.R. with its capital at Saransk.

Mordvin belongs to the Finnic branch of the Finno-Ugric languages, which form the main subgroup of the Uralic family. There are really two Mordvin languages—Erzya and Moksha—the two being sufficiently different that communication sometimes becomes a problem. The basic word "no" for example is *aras'* in Erzya, but *ash* in Moksha. The passage above is in Erzya.

Within the Mordvinian A.S.S.R. Erzya is generally spoken in the east, while Moksha is spoken in the west. Speakers of the former outnumber those of the latter by about two to one. The Mordvin alphabet contains exactly the same letters as the Russian.

Udmurt

Дёми армие мынонзэ уно уйёсты изьылытэк витиз. Таманлы умме усьылыкуз но пöртэм вöтъёсын курадӟылйз. Тушмонъёсын ожмаськылйз.

Гожтэт басьтэм бераз Дёми кык нунал ӵоже военкоматысь öз кошкылы ни. Туннэ солы военкомат ивортйз:

—Ну, Демян Платонович, дасяськы! Армие мыныны туннэ ик быгатйськод.

—Мон дась!—шумпотыса, мултэс квараен черектйз Дёми.

Dyoma had not slept for several nights awaiting his induction into the army. And when he did doze off for a bit he had all kinds of dreams. He was fighting the enemy.

After receiving his orders Dyoma did not leave the induction center for two days. Today the induction center told him:

"Well, Demyan Platonovich, get ready! Today is the day you may enter the army."

"I am ready!" cried Dyoma in a loud voice.

—PYOTR BLINOV, *I Want to Live*

Udmurt, formerly known as Votyak, is spoken by about 600,000 people living mainly in the Udmurt A.S.S.R. of the Soviet Union, whose capital is Izhevsk. Another of the Finno-Ugric languages, it is most closely related to Komi, the two forming the so-called Permian branch of this family. The Udmurt alphabet is based on the Cyrillic with the additional non-Russian letters ö, ӥ, ӝ, ӟ, and ӵ. The last four of these are not to be found in any other language.

Komi

Олiс-вылiс Öньö-макö. Сылöн вöлi вит монь: сёй монь, сюмöд-тупыль-монь, турун-кöрöб-монь, рос монь да гадь монь. Öньö-макö ачыс век педзö. Сёй моньöс вала ыстас. Зэрмас дай сёй монь нильзяс. Сюмöд-тупыль-моньöс ыстас пывсян ломтыны. Сiйö истöг тувсö öзтас, а бияс бöжас кутчысяс, дай сотчас. Турун-кöрöб-моньöс ыстас мöслы турун сетны. Тöв пöльыштас да турун-кöрöб-моньöс мöслы вомас нуас. Мöс сiйöс сёяс. Рос моньöс ыстас сарай чышкыны да джодж плака костö сибдас. Гадь монь сералас, сералас дай потö. А Öньö-макö век педзö.

Once upon a time there lived a man named Önyö-makö. He had five daughters-in-law: one made of clay, another of birch bark, another of hay, another who was a broom, another a bubble. Önyö-makö himself just stood around. The daughter-in-law of clay he sent to fetch water. It began to rain and she was washed away. The daughter-in-law of birch bark he sent to light the fire in the bath. She struck a match, her tail caught fire, and she burned up. The daughter-in-law of hay he sent to feed hay to the cow. The wind began to blow and swept her into the mouth of the cow. The cow ate her up. The daughter-in-law who was a broom he sent to sweep the shed but she got caught between the floorboards. The daughter-in-law who was a bubble laughed and laughed until she burst. And Önyö-makö just stood around.

Komi is another of the Finno-Ugric languages spoken in north-eastern European Russia. It is closely related to Udmurt (Votyak), spoken to the south, the two constituting the so-called Permian branch of this family.

There are two dialects of Komi. Traditionally they were known as Zyrian and Permyak, but in the Soviet era the former has been designated Komi-Zyrian or simply Komi, the latter Komi-Permyak. Komi-Zyrian is spoken by about 275,000 people in what is now the Komi A.S.S.R. (capital: Syktyvkar), which extends over a large area (the size of California) eastward to the North Ural Mountains and north past the Arctic Circle. Komi-Permyak is spoken by about 125,000 people in the much smaller Komi-Permyak National District (capital: Kudymkar), bordering the Komi A.S.S.R. on the south.

Komi is written in the Cyrillic alphabet with two non-Russian letters, the *i* and *ö*.

Mari

Марий элысе моло йогын вӱд дене таҥастарымаште Элнетыште шолым волташат, пырням покташат йӧсӧ. Элнет пеш талын йога. Йогышыжла, осал янлыкла сержым пурын каткала. Серыште кокшӱдӧ ияш пӱнчӧ шога гынат, тудымат вожге вӱдышкӧ шуҥгалтара. Элнет ик сержым пуреш, вес веланже ошмам шава, тӱрлӧ-тӱрлӧ тӱрлем дене сылнештараш тӧча. Тиде ок сите гын, Элнет южо вере ожнысыла кадырген каяш ӧркана да, гоч пӱчкын, корныжым угыч виктарен, ӧрдыжкӧ каен колта, а тошто корнешыже икса лийын кодеш. Южгунам тыгай икса ятырак кугу, келге лиеш да тыгай иксаште кол пеш чот тӱла.

Floating logs and rolling timber is more difficult on the Ilet than on other rivers of the Mari region. The Ilet is very turbulent. As it flows along, like a ferocious animal, it gnaws and eats away its own shores. If a two-hundred-year-old pine tree should be standing on the shore, the river pushes it—roots and all—into the water. The Ilet gnaws at one shore, but on the other it deposits sand as if trying to decorate it with various designs. And as if this were not enough, if the river is too lazy to flow as before—wriggling along, then cutting straight across, correcting its bed—it strikes out in another direction, while bays are formed over the old bed. Sometimes such a bay is rather large and deep, and various fishes spawn there.

—SERGEI CHAVAIN, *The Ilet*

Mari, also known as Cheremis, is spoken principally in the Mari A.S.S.R. of the Soviet Union (capital: Ioshkar-Ola), located in central European Russia directly north of the Chuvash and Tatar republics. About 300,000 speakers live here, with another 100,000 in the Bashkir A.S.S.R. to the east, and another 100,000 scattered about in neighboring regions.

Mari is one of the Finno-Ugric languages. There are two main dialects—Meadow and Hill—the former spoken by about 80 percent of the total. The Mari alphabet contains the non-Russian letters *ӓ*, ҥ, *ӧ*, *ӱ*, and ӹ.

Nenets

Тецьда нгэрм' нянгы яха'на ханярина варк' тамна нгокаць. Харевдавэй' сармикэця' нись пин' Арктика' латдувна сарвырнгаць, пыдо' сынггоси' Северной Ледовитой океан' нгохо'на илець. Вадмбои' варк' Сибирь еси' ня'авха'на нгадиберцеты'. Салабаха'на варк' Берингов ямд ереберцеты', сян по' тяхана нгани' ханена' Охотской ямгана сэр' варкм хадаць.

In the northern polar countries there were bears everywhere. The fearless animals bravely roamed the great expanses of the Arctic or lived placidly on the islands of the Arctic Ocean. Occasionally bears were discovered at the mouths of the Siberian rivers. By floating on ice floes they reached the Bering Sea, and a few years ago trappers caught a white bear in the Sea of Okhotsk.

Nenets, formerly known as Yurak, is spoken in the northernmost part of the Soviet Union, in an area extending from the White Sea on the west to the Yenisei River on the east, a distance of about 1,500 miles. Its speakers, who are known as Nentsy, number about 25,000. Most of them live in the Yamal-Nenets National District, with its capital at Salekhard; about 3,500 live in the Nenets National District, whose capital is Naryan Mar. Nenets is the most widely spoken of the Samoyed languages, one of the two branches of the Uralic family.

Ostyak

Этӛр, ватләг котәл вәлгал. Мӛрӛм пајл̣ывтәт ч̣ымәл н'өгагасәт. Т'и котәлнә мä т'ӛкäјӛглäмнä ула мәнгäлӛм. Мӛӈ рытна мәнгäлӧг.

Воронтнә јӛм вәлгал. Мӛӈ пӱт'кäл'и лулпәнытә тәгы коләнтәгалөг.

Т'и алнә воронтнә äрки ул вәлгал.

Кунтәнә киллӧг ула ван'галөг тәлӛп, мӛӈӛн лӛгӛ ӛл̣л̣ӛ југ канӈа амәгалөг. Мәӈтӧг ул литä äр пәл̣ӛкпä нӧрӛгтӛгäлӧг. Мäпөн̣кäмөг вäл'онтог кӧт'ӛрки нуг-лӧккäл.

It was a bright and calm day. Only the leaves of the birch tree rustled softly. That day I went with my younger sisters to pluck berries. We went by boat.

It was good in the forest. We listened to the singing of the little birds.

In that year there were a lot of berries in the forest.

When we had plucked our pots full, we put them beside a big tree. We ran far and wide to eat berries. Before me, out of the bushes leaped a streaked squirrel.

Ostyak, now officially known as Khanty, is spoken in western Siberia, along the banks of the Ob River and its numerous tributaries. Ostyak and Vogul (Mansi), spoken just to the west, are known as the Ob-Ugric languages, which together with Hungarian constitute the Ugric branch of the Finno-Ugric languages. The area in which Ostyak and Vogul are spoken is known as the Khanty-Mansi (formerly Ostyak-Vogul) National District. Its capital, Khanty-Mansiisk, stands near the confluence of the Ob and Irtysh rivers. Speakers of Ostyak number about 15,000. There are several dialects and subdialects.

Evenki

Энӣм хуюкэ̄ндӯв бӯчэ̄н. Амӣндӯй 1933 анӈанӣла̄ инчэ̄в. Тадук учичилча̄в байкитскайдӯ школадӯ. Учитчача̄в 1935 анӈанӣла̄. Манача̄в тар школадӯ дыгинмэ классил. Тадук Турулэ̄ суручэ̄в. Хавалилча̄в Турудӯ типографиядӯ. Типография эвэдывэ газетава ю̄вдеӈкин. Тар газета гэрбӣн «О̄макта Ин.» Хавалча̄в тадӯ иланма анӈанӣл. Тадук Илимпийскай Райком комсомол минэ Игаркала̄ алагувда̄в уӈчэ̄н.

My mother died when I was small. Until 1933 I lived with my father. Then I began studying at the Baikit school. I studied until 1935. I finished the fourth grade in that school. Then I went to Tura. I began working at a printing plant in Tura. The printing plant put out an Evenki newspaper. The name of the newspaper was "New Life." I worked there for three years. Then the Ilimpea regional committee of the Komsomol sent me to study in Igarka.

Evenki, also known as Tungus, is spoken over a vast expanse of territory extending from central Siberia to the Pacific Ocean. Its speakers number only 15,000, about one-fifth of whom live in the Evenki National District, an area of some 286,000 square miles astride the Lower Tunguska and Stony Tunguska rivers. The remainder live in scattered settlements to the east, a few even as far as Sakhalin Island.

The Evenki live by hunting, fishing, and reindeer-herding. Their language is of the Tungusic group, which forms a branch of the Altaic family. The alphabet, which is based on the Cyrillic, contains the additional letter ӈ.

Buryat

Доржо утаатай бүрүүлхэн гэрээ һанана. Эгээ түрүүнээ эхэеэ энхэрүү дулаанаар үгылбэ. Дэлхэй дээрэхи эгээл һайн һайхан, эгээл сэсэн эхэ хадаа Доржын өөрынь эхэ гээшэл! Мүнөө баһал унтангүй хэбтэжэ болоо. Ууургайгаа орхижо ниидэһэн дальбараагаа үгылжэл һууна хаш даа. Юугээ хэжэ, юугээ оёжо һууна хаб? Эхэнь мүнөө үнеэгээ һаажа байгаа бэзэ. Үбэл болохоһоо урид Доржодоо эльгээхэеэ дулаахан оймһо оёжо һууна гү? Аханарайнь самсада халааһа табихаяа зүү һабагшалхаяа байжа болоо. Инагхан Доржынь шарай эхэдэнь тэрэ зүүнэйнь һүбэ соогуур харагдан байжашье болоо юм аалам?

Dorzho missed his smoky, dimly lit yurt. For the first time he felt a tender nagging loneliness for his mother. She was the loveliest, smartest mother in the world, Dorzho's mother! Perhaps she too was lying awake at this moment. She probably missed her little bird who had left his nest. What was she doing and what was she sewing? At that moment she was probably milking a cow. Or perhaps knitting warm stockings to send to Dorzho before winter? Perhaps she was making the payments for her brother's shirts. And perhaps through the eye of the needle she seemed to see the face of her dear Dorzho?

—CHIMIT TSYDENDAMBAYEV, *Dorzho, Son of Banzar*

Buryat is spoken in southern Siberia, in the area surrounding Lake Baikal. The great majority of its speakers live in the Buryat A.S.S.R. (capital: Ulan-Ude), while others are to be found in the nearby Aginsk Buryat and Ust-Ordynsk Buryat national districts.

Buryat is one of the Mongolian languages and is closely related to Mongolian proper, spoken across the border in Outer Mongolia. It is written in the Cyrillic alphabet, with the additional letters ө, ү, and *h*. There are about 300,000 speakers.

Yakut

Кыра, «антон» дэнэр самолетунан көтөн кэлэн, үоһэттэн көрдөххө, — хотугу өрүс хаҥас биэрэгэр баар Суокурдаах боһүөлэк маҥан таба тириитигэр уонча хас испиискэни мээнэ бырахпыт кэриэтэ. Дьиэлэр ол курдук ойом-сойом тураллар, олбуор, уулусса эҥин диэн суох.

Мин Суокурдаахха үс хоннум. Өрүс уҥуор хараалга — таба турар сиригэр, элбэх табаны өлөрдүлэр, ону ыйаан туттараллар — ити табаһыттар үлэлэрин биир түмүгэ. Мин бастыҥ табаһыттары кытта кэпсэттим, уочарка суруйаары «матырыйаал» хомуйдум. Үһүс күммэр — субуота этэ. Суокурдаахха кэлэн, били «антон» почта аҕаларын, күүтэбин — ол самолетунан төннуһээри.

If you fly on an AN-2, or "Anton" as they call the plane out here, and view from on high the village of Suokurdaakh on the left bank of the northern river, it seems to resemble ten small matchsticks tossed onto a white reindeer skin. The houses stand every which way—there are neither yards nor streets.

I spent three nights in Suokurdaakh. On the far side of the river, in the corral, many reindeer had been slaughtered. The carcasses were hung up—a way of measuring the work of the herders. I talked with the leading herders and collected some "material" for an article. On the third day of my stay in Suokurdaakh—it was a Saturday—I waited for the same "Anton," which was scheduled to arrive with the mail and on which I was to return home.

—NIKOLAI GABYSHEV

Yakut is spoken in the Yakut A.S.S.R. (capital: Yakutsk) of the Soviet Union, a vast expanse of over one million square miles in northeastern Siberia. A Turkic language, it represents the easternmost extension of this group, having been brought here by settlers from Central Asia some 500–800 years ago. Today there are about 300,000 speakers of Yakut. The alphabet, based on the Cyrillic, contains the additional letters ө, ү, ҕ, нг, and *h*.

Chukchi

Игыр вай ӈэлвыл пъоӈгэлеркын. Ӈотқэн йъилгын рэплыткугъэ=ым, ӈэлвыл ратаӈпаагъа пъоӈгэлек.

Ы'летык ӈэлвыл наранлеӈӈоӈын алялқэты, чама=ым чинит ӈэнри ратагъяӈыӈогъа. Амватапванвэты наранлеӈӈоӈын, лыгэн=ым тэӈыскыгйит. Прикатира рэгитэркынин ватапъян, ынкыри лыгэн нэрэнлеркын. Ынӈин ымльаляӈэт.

Гырокы=ым нэрэльуркын алялқыян, рыратылқыян, нивқинэт: «Ӈутку тымгылқык ныгръоркын ӈэлвыл.» Ынкы лыгэн ныгръоқэн ӈэлвыл. Гыръольыт рэквытти чаакаеты нытақэнат, каляйӈатыльыт нынватқэнат.

At the present time the herd is searching for mushrooms. When the month is over the herd will stop searching for mushrooms.

When the snow begins to fall the herd will be driven to places where there is no longer any snow, or it may head there on its own. They will be driven to places with an abundance of Iceland moss, in general to nice places. The leader will find places with Iceland moss and will drive them there. Thus it shall be all winter.

In the spring they will seek places free from snow, flat country, saying, "Here, where there is no wind, the herd can bear their young." It is here that they bear their young. Those who give birth are kept in one place, those who run away are brought back.

Chukchi is spoken in northeasternmost Siberia, principally in the Chukchi National District, whose capital is Anadyr. With only 12,000 speakers it is nonetheless the most important member of the Paleo-Asiatic family of languages.

The Chukchi alphabet, based on the Cyrillic, contains the additional letters қ and ӈ. A curious feature of the language is that the letter *k* is pronounced *k* by men but *ts* by women, while the combination *rk* is pronounced *rk* by men but *tsts* by women. Thus the Chukchi word for "walrus" is pronounced *kyrky* by men but *tsytstsy* by women.

LANGUAGES OF THE MIDDLE EAST

Turkish

Yeryüzü kendi kendine bir toprak.
Yurt bir toprak üstünde var olduğumuz.
Ta dev atalardan beri, ta dev çocuklara dek,
Ekmek, tuz.

Peki nasıl ayak basmıştır onlar,
Yurda, benim at koşturduğum yere?
Kavak uykusunda, yer türküsünde kocaman
Süt üzre büyüdüğüm köylere.

Peki nasıl ayak basmıştır onlar,
Yurda, benim bayrak diktiğim yere?
Bu ekin serinliğine gündüzün,
Geceleyin bu çınar gölgelere.

Yeryüzü kendi kendine bir toprak.
Yurt bir toprak üstünde yaşadığımız.
Yurt ormanlarıyla yeşil, yurt dağbaşlarıyla mavi
Ölsek bile içimizde kalan hız.

The world is just the soil by itself.
Homeland is the ground which our lives exalt.
From giant forefathers to giant children,
Bread and salt.

How then did they ever set foot,
Where my horses gallop, on my homeland?
Or on the villages where I grew up on milk
In the poplar's sleep, in the soil's song, grand?

How then did they ever set foot,
Where I raised my flag, in my country?
By day, on the coolness of the crops . . .
By night, on the shades of the sycamore tree . . .

The world is just the soil by itself.
Homeland is the ground which our lives exalt.
Green with our land's forests, blue with her hills,
Even if we die its speed never comes to a halt.

—FAZIL HÜSNÜ DAĞLARCA, *Homeland*

Turkish is the national language of Turkey, and is also spoken by minority groups in Bulgaria, Greece, Cyprus, and other countries. It is the most important member of the Turkic group of languages which form a branch of the Altaic family. There are about 40 million speakers.

Turkish was originally written in the Arabic script which, though poorly suited to the language, had been in use since the conversion of the Turks to Islam. In 1928 President Mustafa Kemal Atatürk decreed the introduction of a slightly modified version of the Roman alphabet, consisting of twenty-one consonants and eight vowels. In Turkish the letters *q*, *w*, and *x* are absent, while the letter *c* is pronounced like the English *j* (*e.g.*, *cep*—pocket), *j* like the French *j* (*jale*—dew), *ç* is pronounced *ch* (*çiçek*—flower), and *ş* is pronounced *sh* (*şişe*—bottle). The letter *ğ* merely serves to lengthen slightly the preceding vowel (*dağ*—mountain).

The Turkish vowels are divided into the so-called front vowels, *e*, *i*, *ö*, *ü*, and the back vowels *a*, *ı* (undotted *i*), *o*, *u*. The dotted *i* retains the dot even when capitalized, as in İstanbul. As in all the Altaic languages, most Turkish words adhere to the principle of vowel harmony—that is, all the vowels in a given word belong to the same class (front or back), and any suffixes added generally contain vowels of the same class. Thus the plural of a noun with a front vowel or vowels is formed with the suffix *-ler* (*e.g.*, *ev*—house, *evler*—houses), while the plural of a noun with a back vowel or vowels is formed with the suffix *-lar* (*at*—horse, *atlar*—horses). In the accompanying poem notice the word *uykusunda* ("in its sleep"), with the vowel *u* appearing throughout, as against *türküsünde* ("in its song"), *büyüdüğüm* ("where I grew up"), and *gündüzün* ("by day"), with the vowel *ü* throughout. As an agglutinative language, Turkish frequently adds on suffix after suffix, thus producing words that may be the equivalent of a whole phrase or sentence in English.

The English words *caviar*, *yogurt*, and *shish kebab* are of Turkish origin. The word *tulip* comes from a Turkish word for *turban*, because its flower was thought to resemble a turban. The word *meander* comes from the ancient name of the Menderes River of western Turkey which was noted for its winding course.

Arabic

بِسْمِ ٱللَّهِ ٱلرَّحْمَٰنِ ٱلرَّحِيمِ ﴿١﴾

ٱلْحَمْدُ لِلَّهِ رَبِّ ٱلْعَٰلَمِينَ ﴿٢﴾ ٱلرَّحْمَٰنِ ٱلرَّحِيمِ ﴿٣﴾

مَٰلِكِ يَوْمِ ٱلدِّينِ ﴿٤﴾ إِيَّاكَ نَعْبُدُ وَإِيَّاكَ

نَسْتَعِينُ ﴿٥﴾ ٱهْدِنَا ٱلصِّرَٰطَ ٱلْمُسْتَقِيمَ ﴿٦﴾

صِرَٰطَ ٱلَّذِينَ أَنْعَمْتَ عَلَيْهِمْ غَيْرِ ٱلْمَغْضُوبِ

عَلَيْهِمْ وَلَا ٱلضَّآلِّينَ ﴿٧﴾

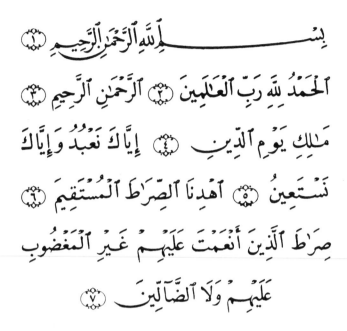

1. In the name of Allah, the Beneficent, the Merciful.
2. Praise be to Allah, the Lord of the Worlds.
3. The Beneficent, the Merciful.
4. Master of the Day of Judgment.
5. Thee (alone) do we worship, and Thee (alone) we ask for help.
6. Show us the straight path.
7. The path of those whom Thou hast favored; not (the path) of those who earn Thy anger nor of those who go astray.

—Opening *sura* (chapter) of the Koran

Arabic is one of the world's major languages, spoken in a broad belt extending from the Arabian Peninsula across the Fertile Crescent and on to the Atlantic Ocean. It is the official language of Saudi Arabia, Yemen, Southern Yemen, Oman, Kuwait, Bahrain, Qatar, Iraq, Syria, Jordan, Lebanon, Egypt, Sudan, Libya, Tunisia, Algeria, and Morocco, making it the mother tongue of about 115 million people. In addition many millions of Moslems in other countries have some knowledge of

Arabic, it being the language of the Moslem religion and of the sacred Koran. In 1974 Arabic was made the sixth official language of the United Nations.

Great languages spring from great empires, and Arabic is no exception. A Semitic language closely related to Hebrew, its use was confined to the Arabian Peninsula until the 7th century A.D. But the spectacular Islamic conquests of that century carried the language far beyond its original borders, and it supplanted almost all the previous languages of Iraq, Syria, Egypt, and North Africa. After further conquest in succeeding centuries Arabic was spoken as far east as Afghanistan and as far west as Spain.

The Arabic alphabet is believed to have evolved from that of an ancient people known as the Nabateans, but how, when, and where exactly it originated is still a matter of controversy. By the early Mohammedan period two scripts were in use—the Naskhi, the ordinary cursive form used in books and correspondence, and the Kufic, an angular script used mainly for decorative purposes. The present alphabet of twenty-eight letters consists basically of consonants, the vowel signs being indicated by marks above or below the letters. While these marks are generally omitted, they do appear in elementary school books and in all editions of the Koran. Like the other Semitic languages, Arabic is written from right to left. (In the text above the numbers appear at the end, rather than the beginning, of each verse.) The script is employed in many other languages, such as Persian, Pashto, Urdu, and Sindhi.

Spoken Arabic naturally varies from country to country, but classical Arabic, the language of the Koran, has remained largely unchanged since the 7th century. It has served as a great unifying force in the development and standardization of the language. When educated Arabs from different countries meet, they generally converse in classical Arabic. On the southern coast of the Arabian Peninsula the people speak a number of dialects known collectively as South Arabic, but these differ so greatly from the Arabic of the north that South Arabic is often considered a separate language.

Arabic has contributed many words to the English language, many of them beginning with the Arabic definite article *al-*. These include *algebra*, *alcohol*, *alchemy*, *alkali*, *alcove*, *alfalfa*, and *albatross*. Others are *mosque*, *minaret*, *sultan*, *elixir*, *harem*, *giraffe*, *gazelle*, *cotton*, *amber*, *sofa*, *mattress*, *tariff*, *magazine*, *arsenal*, *syrup*, *sherbet*, and *artichoke*. *Coffee* is also an Arabic word which entered English by way of Turkish and Italian. The word *assassin* comes from a similar Arabic word meaning "hashish addicts."

Coptic

ⲁⲓ̈ϭⲱϣⲧ ⲉϫⲙ̄ ⲡⲕⲁϩ ·
ⲁⲩⲱ ⲉⲓ̈ⲥϩⲏ̄ⲏⲧⲉ ⲙⲙⲛ
ⲗⲁⲁⲩ ⲉϩⲣⲁⲓ̈ ⲉⲧⲡⲉ · ⲁⲩⲱ
ⲛⲉⲩϣⲟⲟⲡ ⲁⲛ̄ ⲛϭⲓ ⲛⲉⲥ
ⲟⲩⲟⲉⲓⲛ · ⲁⲓ̈ⲛⲁⲩ ⲉⲛⲧⲟⲩⲉⲓ̈ⲏ
ⲁⲩⲱ ⲛⲉⲩⲥⲧⲱⲧ ⲡⲉ
ⲁⲩⲱ ⲛⲧⲁⲗ ⲧⲏⲣⲟⲩ ⲛⲉⲩ
ϣⲧⲣⲧⲱⲣ · ⲁⲓ̈ϭⲱϣⲧ
ⲁⲩⲱ ⲉⲓ̈ⲥϩⲏⲏⲧⲉ ⲛⲉ ⲙⲛ̄ ⲣⲱ
ⲙⲉ ⲡⲉ · ⲁⲩⲱ ⲛϩⲁⲗⲁⲁ
ⲧⲉ ⲧⲏⲣⲟⲩ ⲛⲧⲡⲉ ⲛⲉⲩϩⲓ̈
ⲛⲉⲩⲉⲣⲏⲩ ⲡⲉ · ⲁⲓ̈ⲛⲁⲩ
ⲁⲩⲱ ⲉⲓ̈ⲥ ⲡⲕⲁⲣⲙⲏⲗⲟⲥ ⲁϥ
ⲣϫⲁⲉⲓ̈ⲉ · ⲁⲩⲱ ⲙⲡⲟⲗⲓ̈ⲥ
ⲧⲏⲣⲟⲩ ⲁⲩⲣⲟⲕϩⲟⲩ ⲙ
ⲡⲉⲙⲧⲟ ⲉⲃⲟⲗ ⲙⲡϫⲟⲉⲓ̈ⲥ
ⲁⲩⲱ ⲁⲩⲧⲁⲕⲟ̄ ⲙⲡⲉⲙⲧⲟ̄ ⲉ
ⲃⲟⲗ ⲛⲧⲟⲣⲅⲏ ⲙⲡⲉϥϭⲱⲛⲧ ·

I beheld the earth, and, lo, it was without form and void; and the heavens, and they had no light. I beheld the mountains, and, lo, they trembled, and all the hills are moved. I beheld, and, lo, there was no man, and all the birds of the heavens were fled. I beheld, and, lo, the fruitful place was a wilderness, and all the cities thereof were broken down at the presence of the Lord, and by his fierce anger.

—Jeremiah iv. 23–26

Coptic represents the final stage of the ancient Egyptian language, whose familiar hieroglyphic writing dates as far back as 3000 B.C. The word "Copt" is derived from the Greek, and later the Arabic, word for "Egyptian." Coptic is a Hamitic language, constituting one of the branches of the Afro-Asiatic (Hamito-Semitic) family.

The transition from Egyptian to Coptic in Egypt may be said to have coincided with the introduction of Christianity. The language was profoundly affected by the translation of the Bible. By the 3rd century A.D. Coptic was the prevailing language of Christian Egypt, though the upper classes generally preferred speaking Greek. In the 5th century a schism occurred in the Egyptian Christian church, with the branch known as the Monophysites coming to be known as the Coptic Church. After the Moslem conquest of Egypt in 642 Coptic began to give way slowly to Arabic, but it was another thousand years before it died out completely as a spoken language. Today it remains the liturgical language of the Coptic Church, whose headquarters are in Cairo. Its present membership is over one million.

The Coptic alphabet consists of thirty-two letters, twenty-five borrowed from the Greek, and seven from Demotic, a later simplified form of the ancient Egyptian hieroglyphs. The latter signs were adopted to represent sounds lacking in Greek, such as *sh* and *f*.

Hebrew

וְהָיָה ׀ בְּאַחֲרִית הַיָּמִים נָכוֹן יִהְיֶה הַר בֵּית־יְהוָה בְּרֹאשׁ
הֶהָרִים וְנִשָּׂא מִגְּבָעוֹת וְנָהֲרוּ אֵלָיו כָּל־הַגּוֹיִם׃ וְהָלְכוּ
עַמִּים רַבִּים וְאָמְרוּ לְכוּ ׀ וְנַעֲלֶה אֶל־הַר־יְהוָה אֶל־בֵּית
אֱלֹהֵי יַעֲקֹב וְיֹרֵנוּ מִדְּרָכָיו וְנֵלְכָה בְּאֹרְחֹתָיו כִּי מִצִּיּוֹן
תֵּצֵא תוֹרָה וּדְבַר־יְהוָה מִירוּשָׁלָֽם׃ וְשָׁפַט בֵּין הַגּוֹיִם
וְהוֹכִיחַ לְעַמִּים רַבִּים וְכִתְּתוּ חַרְבוֹתָם לְאִתִּים וַחֲנִיתוֹתֵיהֶם
לְמַזְמֵרוֹת לֹא־יִשָּׂא גוֹי אֶל־גּוֹי חֶרֶב וְלֹא־יִלְמְדוּ עוֹד
מִלְחָמָה׃

And it shall come to pass in the end of days, that the mountain of the Lord's house shall be established as the top of the mountains, and shall be exalted above the hills; and all nations shall flow unto it. And many peoples shall go and say: "Come ye, and let us go up to the mountain of the Lord, to the house of the God of Jacob; and He will teach us of His ways, and we will walk in His paths." For out of Zion shall go forth the law, and the word of God from Jerusalem. And he shall judge between the nations, and shall decide for many peoples; and they shall beat their swords into plowshares, and their spears into pruning hooks; nation shall not lift up sword against nation; neither shall they learn war any more.

—Isaiah ii. 2–4

Hebrew is one of the world's oldest languages, spoken and written today in much the same way as it was more than two thousand years ago. After ceasing to exist as a spoken language about 250 B.C., it was reborn as a modern language in the 19th century, and today it is the principal language of the State of Israel. Books, newspapers, and magazines published in Israel today are written in a Hebrew that is much the same as the language of the Bible.

For over three millennia Hebrew has been the religious, and often the literary and secular, language of the Jewish people. A Semitic tongue, it was spoken during the period of the migration of the Patriarchs into Palestine and remained the language of the Jews throughout the Old Testament period. In the postbiblical period Hebrew gradually gave way to Aramaic as the spoken language, but continued throughout the centuries to serve as the language of ritual and prayer.

The renaissance of Hebrew as a spoken language in the 19th century may be ascribed almost entirely to the efforts of one man: Eliezer ben Yehudah, who devoted his life to the revival of the language, and at the same time adapted it for modern use through the introduction of thousands of modern terms. Hebrew gradually came into use among the Jewish settlers in Palestine and became the official language of the State of Israel when that nation was created in 1948. Today about 3 million people speak Hebrew either as their maternal, adopted, or religious tongue.

The Hebrew alphabet of twenty-two letters (five of which have a different form when they appear at the end of a word) consists entirely of consonants. The language is written from right to left without vowels. Thus the word *kelev* (dog) appears as the Hebrew equivalents of, from right to left, *k*, *l*, and *v*. It is therefore impossible for one not familiar with the language to know how to pronounce a word from the way it is written. About the 8th century a system developed for indicating vowels through the use of small dots and dashes placed above and below the consonants. These signs are still in use today, but they are confined to school books, prayer books, and textbooks for foreigners, and are not to be seen in newspapers, magazines, or books of general use. The text above contains the vowel signs as well as a series of marks called the trope, which indicates the notes to be used when the passage is chanted in the synagogue.

English words of Hebrew origin include *amen*, *hallelujah*, *sabbath*, *rabbi*, *cherub*, *seraph*, *Satan*, *kosher*, *manna*, *shibboleth*, and *behemoth*. More recent contributions are *kibbutz* and *sabra*.

Syriac

ܕܡܪܝܐ ܗܝ ܐܪܥܐ ܒܡܠܐܗ̇. ܬܒܝܠ ܘܟܠܗܘܢ ܕܥܡܪܝܢ ܒܗ̇. ܡܛܠ ܕܗܘ ܒܝܡܡܐ
ܫܬܐܣܗ̇. ܘܒܢܗܪܘܬܐ ܐܬܩܢܗ̇. ܡܢܘ ܢܣܩ ܠܛܘܪܗ ܕܡܪܝܐ.
ܘܡܢܘ ܢܩܘܡ ܒܛܘܪܗ ܩܕܝܫܐ. ܐܝܢܐ ܕܕܟܝܢ ܐܝܕܘܗܝ ܘܕܟܐ ܠܒܗ.
ܘܠܐ ܢܣܒ ܒܣܪܝܩܘܬܐ ܢܦܫܗ ܘܠܐ ܝܡܐ ܒܢܟܠܐ. ܗܢܐ ܢܩܒܠ ܒܘܪܟܬܐ
ܡܢ ܡܪܝܐ. ܘܙܕܝܩܘܬܐ ܡܢ ܐܠܗܐ ܦܪܘܩܗ. ܗܢܘ ܕܪܐ ܕܒܥܘܗܝ ܘܡܫܟܚܝܢ
ܦܪ̈ܨܘܦܝܟ ܕܐܠܗܗ ܕܝܥܩܘܒ. ܐܪܝܡܘ ܬܪ̈ܥܐ ܪ̈ܝܫܝܟܘܢ. ܐܬܬܪܝܡܘ
ܬܪ̈ܥܐ ܕܡܢ ܥܠܡ. ܢܥܘܠ ܡܠܟܐ ܕܫܘܒܚܐ. ܡܢܘ ܗܢܐ ܡܠܟܐ ܕܫܘܒܚܐ.
ܡܪܝܐ ܚܣܝܢܐ ܘܓܢܒܪܐ ܡܪܝܐ ܓܢܒܪܐ ܘܡܩܪܒܢܐ. ܐܪܝܡܘ ܬܪ̈ܥܐ ܪ̈ܝܫܝܟܘܢ.
ܐܬܬܪܝܡܘ ܬܪ̈ܥܐ ܕܡܢ ܥܠܡ. ܢܥܘܠ ܡܠܟܐ ܕܫܘܒܚܐ. ܡܢܘ ܗܢܐ ܡܠܟܐ
ܕܫܘܒܚܐ. ܡܪܝܐ ܚܝܠܬܢܐ ܗܘܝܘ ܡܠܟܐ ܡܫܒܚܐ ܠܥܠܡܝܢ.

The earth is the Lord's, and the fullness thereof; the world, and they that dwell therein.

For he hath founded it upon the seas, and established it upon the floods.

Who shall ascend unto the mountain of the Lord? or who shall stand in His holy place?

He that hath clean hands, and a pure heart; who hath not lifted up his soul unto vanity, nor sworn deceitfully.

He shall receive the blessing from the Lord, and righteousness from the God of his salvation.

This is the generation of them that seek Him, that seek thy face, O Jacob.

Lift up your heads, O ye gates; and be ye lifted up, ye everlasting doors; that the King of glory may enter.

Who then is the King of glory? The Lord strong and mighty, the Lord mighty in battle.

Lift up your heads, O ye gates; yea, lift them up, ye everlasting doors; that the King of glory may enter.

Who then is the King of glory? The Lord of hosts, He is the king of glory.

—Twenty-fourth Psalm

Syriac grew out of Aramaic, the dominant language in the Near East from about the 4th century B.C. through the 6th century A.D. Syriac developed around the city of Edessa (now Urfa, in southeastern Turkey), the leading center of Christianity after about 200 A.D. It eventually became the most important of the Aramaic dialects and, after Greek, the most important language in the eastern Roman Empire. Syriac (or Aramaic) continued to be spoken until the rise of Islam, when it quickly gave way to the dominant influence of Arabic. By the 8th century the language remained in use mainly for liturgical purposes.

In modern usage the term Syriac generally refers to the liturgical language of the Maronite Catholic Church, the Syrian Catholic Church, the Syrian Jacobite Church, the Nestorian (or sometimes Assyrian) Church, and a number of others. The term Aramaic refers to the language as it is still spoken in small communities in Syria (in and around the village of Malula, north of Damascus) and in Turkey (near the town of Mardin, east of Urfa). Another dialect of Aramaic, generally referred to as Assyrian, is spoken by about 75,000 people in northeastern Syria, Lebanon, Iraq, Iran, and the Soviet Union.

Aramaic was originally written in the Hebrew alphabet. The first Syriac alphabet developed from a later form of Aramaic used at Palmyra in Syria. This gradually evolved into the script known as Estrangelo, which was used almost exclusively until the 5th century. At that time the Eastern Church split into a number of factions, with each producing a modified version of its own. Three scripts are in use today: Estrangelo, Jacobite (or Serto), and Nestorian. The text above is in Nestorian.

Persian

یارم چو قدح بدست گیرد   بازار بتان شکست گیرد
هر کس که بدید چشم او گفت   کو محتسبی که مست گیرد
در بحر فتاده‌ام چو ماهی   تا یار مرا بشست گیرد
در پاش فتاده‌ام بزاری   آیا بود آنکه دست گیرد
خرّم دل آنکه همچو حافظ   جامی ز می الست گیرد

When my Beloved the cup in hand taketh
The market of lovely ones slack demand taketh.

Every one saith, who her tipsy eye seëth
"Where is a shrieve, that this fair firebrand taketh?"

I, like a fish, in the ocean am fallen,
Till me with the hook yonder Friend to land taketh.

Lo, at her feet in lament am I fallen,
Till the Beloved me by the hand taketh.

Happy his heart who, like Hafiz, a goblet
Of wine of the Prime Fore-eternal's brand taketh.

—HAFIZ, *Cup in Hand*

Persian is one of the world's oldest languages, a standard and well-recognized tongue as early as the 6th century B.C. It is one of the Iranian languages which form a branch of the Indo-European family. To native speakers Persian is known as Farsi.

Old Persian was the language of the great Persian Empire which at one time extended from the Mediterranean to the Indus River in India.

The language was written in Cuneiform, the wedge-shaped characters used throughout much of the ancient world. In the 2nd century B.C. the Persians created their own alphabet, known as Pahlavi, which remained in use until the Islamic conquest of the 7th century. Since that time Persian has been written in the Arabic script with a number of additional characters to accommodate special sounds.

Modern Persian is spoken by over 20 million people in Iran and another 5 million in Afghanistan. A variety of Persian called Tadzhik is spoken in the Tadzhik republic of the Soviet Union, but there it is written in the Cyrillic alphabet. English words of Persian origin include *shawl*, *pajama*, *taffeta*, *khaki*, *kiosk*, *divan*, *lilac*, *jasmine*, *julep*, *jackal*, *caravan*, *bazaar*, *checkmate*, *dervish*, and *satrap*.

Shams ud-Din Mohammed, or Hafiz, who lived in the 14th century, is considered Persia's greatest lyric poet.

Pashto

دواړه شونډې کړه په بيارته   در ريزي و کړه خپل يار ته
زۀ چه ستا و مخ ته ګورم   زړۀ مې نۀ کيږي ګلزار ته
ګل له شرمه خولې پرېږدي   چه نظر کا ستا رخسار ته
که مې وار درباندې جوړ شي   منتظر يم و خپل وار ته
ګله دا در باندې بنائي   چه ځير ځير ګورې و خار ته
آئينې و ته نظر کړه   که دې مينه شي بهار ته

زار و چا ته کړې خوشحاله
چه دې نه ګوري څوک زار ته

When her petall'd lips are parting,
  Whitest pearls do lose their lustre;
When her glance to me is darting.
  Fades the fairest flower cluster;
Roses shamed, forget to blossom
  Brighter radiance to discover
In the budding of a bosom
  Flaunting as to bee the clover;
She the rose, her grace bestowing
  On the thorn that waits her pleasure,
I the fountain, faintly glowing,
  Mirror of a garden's treasure,
Lover, loved, together knowing
  Rapture passing dream or measure.

—KHUSHHAL KHAN KHATAK, *Love in a Garden*

Pashto, also known as Pushtu, is one of the two major languages of Afghanistan. It is spoken by about 10 million people there—about 60 percent of the population—mostly in the eastern half of the country. It is also spoken in northwestern Pakistan by about 6 million people.

Pashto is the language of the Pathans, the indigenous inhabitants of Afghanistan. Like Persian, it is one of the Iranian languages, and thus part of the Indo-European family. It is written in the Perso-Arabic script, but the alphabet contains a number of letters not to be found in either Persian or Arabic. The term "Pashto" actually refers to the more important of the two dialects—the so-called soft dialect of Afghanistan which preserves the ancient *sh* and *zh* sounds. For those parts of Pakistan where the "hard" *kh* and *gh* prevail, the language is generally referred to as Pakhto.

Kurdish

ئەگەر جوانی نەمامێکی سەوزی پاراو بێ ، چاو جووتێ
گوڵی گەشە بە تەوقەسەرەکەیەوە ،
چاو جووتێک شائەستێرەیە بە بەرزایی ئاسمانەوە
چریسکەچریسک ئەدرەوشێتەوە ، جووتێک گەوهەری
پرشنگدارە تاجی عەشقو جوانی ئەرازێنێتەوە ،
جووتێک پەنجەرەی رووناکە ئەنوارێ بە سەر باخچەی
رۆحا ،
چاو دوو پەڕەیە لە کتێبێکی مقدس ، پڕە لە ئایەتی
حسن ! حقیقەتەکانی رۆح ، سڕرەکانی دڵ ، رازەکانی
دەروونی بە حەرفی نوور تیا نووسراوە !
ئاخۆ لە چاو بەلیغ تر ، لە چاو پڕ معناتر ، لە چاو
سحراوی تر چیی ئەثەرێکی رۆحی ، چیی کتێبێکی
ئاسمانیی هەیە ؟
یەکێک لە معجزەکانی چاو ئەوەیە ، وەک بەردی بە
قیمەت بە هەموو رەنگێکەوە مەقبووڵە : هەندێ چاو
وەک شەوە رەشن ، هەندێکییش چەشنی پیرۆزە شینن ،
هەندێ چاوی تریش هەن ئەڵێی چاوی هەڵۆن ،
چەشنی یاقووت ئاگریان لێ ئەبێتەوە .
لای من وایە چاوی رەش بە جلوەی حزن و دڵۆپی
فرمێسکەوە قەرالیچەی هەموو چاوەکانە ، ئەوەندە
شیرین ، ئەوەندە بێوێنەیە !

> If beauty is a tender succulent plant, then eyes are two bright flowers crowning it. Eyes are a pair of kingly stars glittering through the deep heavens; two precious stones that adorn the crown of love and beauty; two bright windows overlooking the garden of the soul.
>
> Eyes are two pages from a sacred book, full of words of excellence, and written into them with words of light are the realities of life, the secret of the heart, and the inner mysteries of the conscience.
>
> I wonder what other vestiges of the soul, what other heavenly books there are, which are more expressive, more beautiful, and more enchanting than eyes.
>
> One of eyes' wonders is that, like gems, they go with every color. Some are black like jet; some blue like turquoise; others resemble the eyes of an eagle shining like rubies.
>
> —ABDULLAH GORAN, *Eyes*

There are about 5 million speakers of Kurdish, scattered over five countries. There are about $1\frac{1}{2}$ million each in Turkey, Iraq, and Iran, about 250,000 in Syria, and 80,000 in the Soviet Union. The general area in which they live is often referred to as Kurdistan.

The Kurds are an ancient people who have always had a strong sense of ethnic identity. Their language belongs to the Iranian branch of the Indo-European family. It is generally written in a variation of the Arabic script, though the Cyrillic alphabet has been introduced in the Soviet Union, and a Roman script exists in Iraq and Syria.

Maltese

L-Arċipelagu Malti huwa magħmul mill-Gżejjer ta' Malta, Għawdex, Kemmuna u żewġ gżejjer oħra, Kemmunett u Filfla li mhumiex abitati. Il-Maltin jitkellmu lingwa antika ħafna li hi ta' nteress kbir għallingwisti. Bażikament Semetika, maż-żmien assimilat għadd kbir ta' kliem rumanz, sakemm illum hi tirrappreżenta l-għaqda ta' żewġ friegħi lingwistiċi. Dan il-fatt jirrifletti l-qagħda ta' Malta fil-Baħar Mediterran, nofs triq bejn l-Ewropa t'Isfel u l-Afrika ta' Fuq.

The Maltese Archipelago consists of the islands of Malta, Gozo, and Comino and two other uninhabited islands, Cominotto and Filfla. The Maltese speak a very ancient language which is of great interest to linguists. Basically Semitic, it assimilated a large number of Romance words over the years, with the result that today it represents the fusion of two linguistic branches. This fact reflects the position of Malta in the Mediterranean Sea, halfway between southern Europe and North Africa.

Maltese is spoken on the island of Malta, in the Mediterranean Sea. Its basis is Arabic, which was brought to the island by Moslem conquerors in the 9th century. In the year 1090 the Arabs were driven out by Normans from Sicily, who introduced a large number of Romance words into the vocabulary.

The Maltese alphabet contains the additional letters *ħ*, pronounced like the English *h* but comparatively stronger, and the *għ*, which, like the *h* (without a bar), serves only to lengthen the preceding or succeeding vowel. Other letters are *ċ*, pronounced *ch*; *ġ*, pronounced like the English *j*; and *ż*, pronounced like the English *z* (the letter *z*, without the dot, being pronounced *ts*). *J* is pronounced *y*, *x* as *sh*, and the letter *q* is a glottal stop, a sound not to be found in English. There are about 300,000 speakers of Maltese.

LANGUAGES OF ASIA

Sanskrit

अस्ति हस्तिनापुरे कर्पूरविलासो नाम रजकः। तस्य गर्द-
भो ऽतिभारवाहनाद्दुर्बलो मुमूर्षुरिवाभवत्। ततस्तेन रज-
केनासौ व्याघ्रचर्मणा प्रच्छाद्यारण्यसमीपे सस्यक्षेत्रे मोचितः।
ततो दूरादवलोक्य व्याघ्रबुद्ध्या क्षेत्रपतयः सत्वरं पलायन्ते। स
च सुखेन सस्यं चरति। अथैकदा केनापि सस्यरक्षकेण धूसर-
कम्बलकृततनुत्राणेन धनुष्काण्डं सज्जीकृत्यावनतकायेनैकान्ते
स्थितम्। तं च दूरे दृष्ट्वा गर्दभः पुष्टाङ्गो गर्दभीयमिति मत्वा
शब्दं कुर्वाणस्तदभिमुखं धावितः। ततस्तेन सस्यरक्षकेण गर्द-
भो ऽयमिति ज्ञात्वा लीलयैव व्यापादितः।

In Hastinapura there was a washerman named Vilasa. His donkey was near death, having become weak from carrying excessive burdens. So the washerman covered him with a tiger-skin and turned him loose in a cornfield near a forest. The owners of the field, seeing him from a distance, fled away in haste, under the notion that he was a tiger. Then a certain corn guard, having covered his body with a gray blanket, and having made ready his bow and arrows, crouched down in a secluded spot. Then the donkey, having grown plump from eating, spied him at a distance, and supposing him to be a she-donkey, trotted up to him braying. The corn guard, discovering him to be only a donkey, killed him with ease.

—*The Donkey in the Tiger-Skin*, from the *Hitopadeśa*

Sanskrit is the ancient literary and classical language of India, the sacred language of the Hindu religion. Brought to India from the northwest about the middle of the second millennium B.C., Sanskrit (which means "refined," "perfected," or "elaborated") eventually gave rise to the Prakrit ("natural" or "common") languages. These in turn gave rise to the modern Indian languages such as Hindi, Bengali, Marathi, and Gujarati, as well as Nepali, spoken in Nepal, and Sinhalese, spoken in Ceylon (now Sri Lanka).

The oldest form of Sanskrit is known as Vedic Sanskrit, after the Vedas, the ancient hymns of the sacred Hindu scriptures. The later stage is known as classical Sanskrit, whose writings deal chiefly with secular subjects. For over three millennia Sanskrit continued to flourish as the language of learning in India, and the output of literary works continued without diminution until well into the 19th century. Although the competition of English as the language of government and science, coupled with the rising influence of the modern Indian languages, has undercut much of Sanskrit's former preeminence, it is still widely studied and, in fact, is even spoken by a number of Indian scholars.

Sanskrit is an Indo-European language, whose entry into the Indian subcontinent marked a new frontier for this widely dispersed family. Its Indo-European origin was, of course, unknown to the ancient and even to the medieval world. It was only in the 18th century that the striking similarity of Sanskrit to Latin and Greek was first noted in detail. Thus were set in motion the investigations that led to the discovery of the interrelationship of all the Indo-European languages, which in turn laid the foundation of the science of modern comparative and historical linguistics.

Sanskrit is written in an alphabet known as Devanagari. To trace its origin is to trace the development of writing in India. The source of most of the Indian alphabets is an ancient script known as Brahmi which, in the opinion of most scholars, is of Semitic origin, probably Aramaic. One of its many offshoots was the Gupta script, used throughout the powerful Gupta empire in the 4th–6th centuries A.D. The Devanagari characters developed from a variety of Gupta, the earliest inscriptions appearing in the 7th century. The alphabet, which is written from left to right, consists of forty-eight signs, of which thirty-four are consonants and fourteen are vowels or diphthongs. It is considered one of the most perfect systems of writing ever devised.

Hindi

गोबर ने और कुछ न कहा। लाठी कन्धे पर रखी और चल दिया। होरी उसे जाते देखता हुआ अपना कलेजा ठंढा करता रहा। अब लड़के की सगाई में देर न करनी चाहिए। सत्रहवाँ लग गया; मगर करें कैसे? कहीं पैसे के भी दरसन हों। जब से तीनों भाइयों में अलगौझा हो गया, घर की साख जाती रही। महतो लड़का देखने आते हैं, पर घर की दशा देखकर मुँह फीका करके चले जाते हैं। दो-एक राजी भी हुए, तो रुपए माँगते हैं। दो-तीन सौ लड़की का दाम चुकाये और इतना ही ऊपर से खर्च करे, तब जाकर ब्याह हो। कहाँ से आवें इतने रुपए। रास खलिहान में तुल जाती है। खाने-भर को भी नहीं बचता। ब्याह कहाँ से हो? और अब तो सोना ब्याहने योग्य हो गयी। लड़के का ब्याह न हुआ, न सही। लड़की का ब्याह न हुआ, तो सारी बिरादरी में हँसी होगी।

Gobar said nothing more. He put his staff on his shoulder and walked away. Hori looked with pride at the receding figure of his son. He was growing into a fine young man. Time he married. But Hori had no money for the marriage. With the division in the family they had fallen on evil days. People did come to see Gobar and approved of him. But when they saw the family down and out, they washed their hands of the idea. Those who agreed pitched the demand for bride money so high that Hori was helpless. He had to marry off Sona too. It was bad enough if a son did not marry, but for a grown-up girl to remain unmarried was sacrilege. How could he look his friends in the face with an unmarried girl in the house?

—PREMCHAND, *Godan*

Hindi is the most widely spoken language of the Republic of India, centered principally in the states of Uttar Pradesh and Madhya Pradesh in the north-central part of the country. Its 180 million speakers rank it as one of the leading languages of the world but it is, nevertheless, understood by only about one-third of India's population. When independence was achieved in 1947, Hindi was chosen as India's national language, but its failure to win acceptance among speakers of other languages has forced it to share the title of official language with English.

Speakers of Hindi are also to be found in many scattered parts of the world. In the newly independent countries of Mauritius, in the Indian Ocean, and Fiji, in the Pacific, it is spoken by about a third of the population. There are also sizable bodies of speakers in Trinidad, Guyana, and Surinam.

Like most of the languages of northern India, Hindi is descended from Sanskrit. Hindi and Urdu, the official language of Pakistan, are virtually the same language, though the former is written in the Sanskrit characters and the latter in the Perso-Arabic script. Pure Hindi derives most of its vocabulary from Sanskrit, while Urdu contains many words from Persian and Arabic. The basis of both languages is actually Hindustani, the colloquial form of speech that served as the lingua franca of much of India for more than four centuries.

Hindi was originally a variety of Hindustani spoken in the area of New Delhi. Its development into a national language had its beginnings in the colonial period, when the British began to cultivate it as a standard among government officials. Later it was used for literary purposes and has since become the vehicle for some excellent prose and poetry.

English words of Hindi origin include *cot*, *loot*, *thug*, *chintz*, *bandanna*, *dungaree*, *rajah*, *pundit*, *coolie*, *tom-tom*, and *juggernaut*.

Urdu

ستاروں سے آگے جہاں اُور بھی ہیں — ابھی عشق کے امتحاں اُور بھی ہیں
تہی زندگی سے نہیں یہ فضائیں — یہاں سینکڑوں کارواں اُور بھی ہیں
قناعت نہ کر عالمِ رنگ و بُو پر — چمن اُور بھی آشیاں اُور بھی ہیں
اگر کھو گیا اِک نشیمن تو کیا غم — مقاماتِ آہ و فغاں اُور بھی ہیں
تُو شاہیں ہے پرواز ہے کام تیرا — ترے سامنے آسماں اُور بھی ہیں
اِسی روز و شب میں اُلجھ کر نہ رہ جا — کہ تیرے زمان و مکاں اُور بھی ہیں

Beyond the stars there are still other worlds;
There are other fields to test man's indomitable spirit.

Not devoid of life are those open spaces of heaven;
There are hundreds of other caravans in them as well.

Do not remain contented with this sensible world;
Beyond it there are other gardens and nests as well.

If thou hast lost one nest, what then?
There are other places for sighing and wailing as well.

Thou art an eagle; thy business is to soar in the empyrean;
Thou hast other skies in which thou canst range as well.

Be not entangled in this world of days and nights;
Thou hast another time and space as well.

—MUHAMMAD IQBAL, *Bal-e-Jibril*

Urdu is the official language of Pakistan and is also widely spoken in India. In Pakistan it is the mother tongue of about 5 million people and is spoken fluently as a second language by perhaps 40 million more. In India, where it is spoken by some 30 million Moslems, it is one of the official languages recognized by the constitution.

Urdu is very similar to Hindi, the most important difference between them being that the former is written in the Perso-Arabic script, while the latter is written in the Sanskrit characters. Urdu also contains many words from Arabic and Persian, while Hindi makes a conscious effort to preserve the older Indian words.

Urdu by origin is a dialect of Hindi spoken for centuries in the neighborhood of Delhi. In the 16th century, when India fell under Moslem domination, a large number of Persian, Arabic, and Turkish words entered the language via the military camps and the marketplaces of Delhi. Eventually a separate dialect evolved, written in Arabic characters with additional letters supplied for sounds peculiar to Indian and Persian words. In time it came to be called Urdu ("camp language") and after further Moslem conquest became the lingua franca over much of the Indian subcontinent.

After the partition of India in 1947, Hindi became the principal language of India, and Urdu of West Pakistan. The older term Hindustani, embracing both languages, has fallen into general disuse since partition.

Punjabi

ਜੈ ਘਰਿ ਕੀਰਤਿ ਆਖੀਐ
ਕਰਤੇ ਕਾ ਹੋਇ ਬੀਚਾਰੋ ॥ ਤਿਤੁ
ਘਰਿ ਗਾਵਹੁ ਸੋਹਿਲਾ ਸਿਵਰਿਹੁ
ਸਿਰਜਨਹਾਰੋ॥੧॥ ਤੁਮ ਗਾਵਹੁ ਮੇਰੇ
ਨਿਰਭਉ ਕਾ ਸੋਹਿਲਾ ॥ ਹਉਵਾਰੀ
ਜਿਤੁ ਸੋਹਿਲੈ ਸਦਾ ਸੁਖੁ ਹੋਇ ॥੧॥
ਰਹਾਉ ॥ਨਿਤ ਨਿਤ ਜੀਅੜੇ ਸਮਾ-
ਲੀਅਨਿ ਦੇਖੈਗਾ ਦੇਵਣਹਾਰੁ ॥
ਤੇਰੇ ਦਾਨੈ ਕੀਮਤਿ ਨਾ ਪਵੈ ਤਿਸੁ
ਦਾਤੇਕਵਣੁਸੁਮਾਰੁ॥੨॥ਸੰਬਤਿਸਾਹਾ
ਲਿਖਿਆ ਮਿਲਿ ਕਰਿ ਪਾਵਹੁ ਤੇਲੁ
॥ ਦੇਹੁ ਸਜਣ ਅਸੀਸੜੀਆ ਜਿਉ
ਹੋਵੈ ਸਾਹਿਬ ਸਿਉ ਮੇਲੁ ॥੩॥ ਘਰਿ
ਘਰਿ ਏਹੋ ਪਾਹੁਚਾ ਸਦੜੇ ਨਿਤ
ਪਵੰਨਿ ॥ ਸਦਣਹਾਰਾ ਸਿਮਰੀਐ
ਨਾਨਕ ਸੇ ਦਿਹ ਆਵੰਨਿ ॥੪॥੧॥

Sing ye, my comrades, now my wedding song!
In the Temple House where saints sing His Name, where saintly hearts glow all day and night with His Love,
Sing ye, my comrades, now the song of His Praise!
Sing the song my Creator!
I fain would be a sacrifice for the harmony divine that giveth everlasting peace!
My Lord careth for the smallest life,
The Bounteous Giver meets the needs of each,
No arithmetic can count His gifts,
Naught is it that we can render unto Him.
The Auspicious Day has dawned!
The Hour is fixed for my wedding with my Lord!
Come, comrades! Assemble and make rejoicings,
Anoint the Bride with oil and pour on her your blessings!
Comrades! Pray, the Bride may meet her Lord!
This message to every human being!
This call is for all.
O Man! Remember Him who calls!

—*Adi Granth* (Holy Book of Sikhism)

Punjabi, often spelled Panjabi, is spoken in the Punjab, the historic region now divided between India and Pakistan. The variety spoken in India is similar to Hindi, but dialects vary considerably as one moves westward. In Pakistan one variety, Lahnda, is sufficiently different to be considered by some a separate language. There are approximately 45 million speakers of Punjabi in Pakistan and about 15 million in India.

The Punjabi language is closely associated with the Sikh religion. It was the vehicle for recording the teachings of the gurus, the ten great founders of Sikhism. The Punjabi alphabet was invented by the second of the gurus in the 16th century. It is known as the Gurmukhi script, Gurmukhi meaning "proceeding from the mouth of the guru."

In modern India and Pakistan, however, Punjabi is rapidly passing out of use as a written language. In everyday life most literate Punjabi speakers do their reading and writing in Hindi and Urdu.

Sindhi

مونکي اکڙين، وڏا ڏورا لاتيا؛ تہ پڻ پسن، کڻان جي کر سامهون.

اکڙيون پرين ري، جي ڪي ٻيو پسن؛ تہ ڪڍي ڪي ڪانگن، نيرالا نيڻ ڏيان.

نن نيڻن ڪئي نيران، جن ساجر سيڻ سانڀيا؛ جي، جسي ۽ جان، ڪر حضوري حج ڪيو.

ڏسن ڏهاڙي، توءِ نہ رسن او ڏهين؛ آيا سڃاڻي، نيڻ نهاري پرين کي.

اکين کي آهين، عجب جهڙيون عادتون؛ سور پرائي سات جا وڃيو وهائين،

آئي لنئو لائين، جت حاجت ناهہ هٿيار جي.

These paltry eyes of mine
Have brought me favor's grace.
If evil but before them be,
They see Love in its place.
If paltry eyes of mine
Did aught but Love disclose
I'd pluck them out to cast
As morsels for the crows.
Mine eyes have made a feast
Where kin and friends engage.
It is as if life, body, soul
Had gone on pilgrimage.
All day they look and yet
They halt out there to see.
They saw and recognized Love
And have returned to me.
Strange habits have mine eyes
To trade with others' pain.
Love's conquest they have made
Where weapon brings no gain.

—SHAH ABDUL LATIF BHITAI, *Risalo*

Sindhi is spoken in Pakistan and is also one of the constitutional languages of India. It is spoken by about 7 million people in the province of Sind, southern Pakistan, and by about 1½ million more across the border in India. The largest Sindhi-speaking city is Hyderabad, Pakistan.

Sindhi is an Indo-European language, related to Urdu and the languages of northern India. In Pakistan it is written in the Arabic script with several additional letters to accommodate special sounds.

Kashmiri

राधा राधा राधा राधा कृष्णु जी । ... ॥
रास-मंडुलिस च़्यन प्रेमुक मस ।
मासु-वज मनु गांमनु नऱनम ॥
अक-अकिस अछु-वासु लायान आस नादा । राधा ॥

तुंन आमुत्य् तंत्य् मंत्य् गांमुत्य् ।
न्याय अंज़ुरित पागम प्रेमुत्य् ॥
नारुद सुदाम शुकदेव ध्रुव तु प्रह्लादा । ... ॥

कुल्य् कन तु कनि मुजि मुचुरावित ।
सीनु मंज़ मागुकय् गीर भांवित ॥
गोक़लुकय् मुक्त गांमुत्य दादा पर्दादा । ... ॥

अक्रुय सु कृष्णु ज़ुव सारिनुय सूत्य् ।
ज़ीव-गण कवु ज़ानु तति आंस्य् कृत्य् ॥
कृष्णाय अवाधि-मान तस-रुस्त सांरुय राधा । .... ॥

परमानंदु च़ेति लजिनय अंद ।
पूशिनय पुथुय प्रेम अंदय-वंद ॥
राधा-सरस्वतियि कंरुनन प्रसादा । .... ॥

In the rasa circle, drunk with the wine of love, thousands of Gopis were absorbed in dancing. Holding one another's hand they shouted (repeating, Radha-Krishna! Radha-Krishna!)

Bhaktas like Narada, Sudama, Shuka, Dhruva, and Prahlada were there, mad with joy—their doubts dissolved, their minds having found the truth.

Trees, plants, stones opened their eyes and revealed the secrets of their innermost hearts. All in Gokal felt liberated (from bondage of earthly existence) with their grandfathers and great-grandfathers.

One Krishna was with each and every soul. The species of souls present there were so many that I cannot tell their number. Among them all Krishna alone is eternal, all else is subject to disappearance (to be eliminated as not true and real).

May you too, Paramananda, attain the goal! May such love continue to bless you all along! (Rejoice that) Radha as Sarasvati (Goddess of Poetry and Eloquence) has bestowed on you her grace.

—PARMANAND, *The Dance of the Gopis*

Kashmiri is the principal language of the state of Kashmir, long disputed between India and Pakistan. In India it is one of the official languages recognized by the constitution. Though generally considered to belong to the Indic group of Indo-European languages, Kashmiri's exact affiliation is still uncertain, and it is thought by some to constitute a separate subgroup. Latest figures show about 3 million speakers.

Kashmiri is written in both the Devanagari (Hindi) and the Arabic script, each with additional diacritical marks for special sounds in the language. The former is generally used by Hindus, the latter by Moslems. Moslem speakers of Kashmiri also tend to use many words of Persian and Arabic origin.

Burushaski

Pfʌqir Ali sɛnʌs hin hirʌnɛ čʌγa ɛčʌm.

I·nɛ i·ɛn bʌm, i·ik Dərbɛ·šo bilʊm. Šišpərɛ te·rɛ hʊru·tʌm bʌm. Hʌn guntsʌnʊlo huyɛ·s Hʌnumʌn Mu·n yʌkʌlʌtɛ uyərčər tsu·mi. Huyɛ·s ru·ŋʊlo fʌt no gučʌmi. Gučaiyʌsər e·yɛnʊmtsɛ qau mʌnimi: "Dərbɛ·šo! Dərbɛ·šo!" nʊsɛn. Di·tʌlimi. Di·tʌl bəre·ɪmi kɛ hin bu·t pa·ki·za dʌsi·nʌn ɛ·škitsər dumobo.

I·nɛ sɛnʊmo: "Mi bʌb'a go·r qau ɛčai" ɛsʊmo. Sɛnʌsər i·nɛ dʌsin mʊtsi nʊltʌn i·sɛ Hʌnumʌn Mu·n ya·rər ni·mi. Ni·ʌsər i·sɛ çišɛ hʌn hiŋʌn sɪka manimi. Ulo niči kɛ hin γɛnišɛ sʌlʌtʌŋɛ hirʌn hʊru·tʊm bai; bu·t mariŋ mariŋ tʌlo gʊšiŋʌnts sita·riŋ nʊka hʊručʌm ba·n. Dərbɛ·šo ni·n sʌla·m ɛtimi. Inɛ hi·rɛ sʌlamɛ juwa·b du·mərimi. Duməri·n yugʊšʌntser o·simi: "Dərbɛ·šu.ər hʌn həri·pʌn sita·rɛtɛ 'ɛ·γərin." U·ɛ tʌlo·wɛ sita·riŋ nʊka bu·t uyʌm učəreka həri·pʌn 'ɛ·γərumʌn.

I shall tell the story of a man called Faqir Ali.

He had a son, his name was Derbesho. He was staying at the Shishper grazing ground. One day he took the goats off to graze in the direction of Hunumun Mun. Leaving the goats in the pasture, he laid himself down. When he had lain down and had gone to sleep, a call came: "Derbesho! Derbesho!" He woke up. On waking up he saw that a beautiful maiden had come up to his head.

She said to him: "My father is calling you." When she said this he followed the girl and came to the foot of Hunumun Mun. On approaching it, a door opened in the mountain. When he went in a man with a golden mustache was sitting there, and seven beautiful women were sitting there with sitars. Derbesho entered and salaamed. The man responded to his salaam. Having done so he said to his daughters: "Play a tune for Derbesho on the sitar." The seven took their sitars and while singing with sweet voices played a tune.

Burushaski is spoken by a mere 40,000 people living in the mountainous regions of northwestern Kashmir. It is of special interest to philologists in that it appears to be completely unrelated to any other language of the area, or for that matter to any other language of the world. It is probably a remnant of some prehistoric language community, all but obliterated by successive Dravidian and Indo-European invasions. Burushaski has never been committed to writing. The text above is merely a phonetic transcription of the spoken language.

Gujarati

માનવીનું હૈયું

માનવીના હૈયાને નંદવામાં વાર શી?
અધબોલ્યા બોલડે,
થોડે અબોલડે,
પોચાશા હૈયાને પીંજવામાં વાર શી?

સ્મિતની જ્યાં વીજળી,
જરીશી ફરી વળી,
એના એ હૈયાને રંજવામાં વાર શી?
એવા તે હૈયાને નંદવામાં વાર શી?

માનવીના હૈયાને રંજવામાં વાર શી?
એના એ હૈયાને નંદવામાં વાર શી?

THE HUMAN HEART

How little it takes to break the human heart!
A word half spoken;
A word unspoken;
How little it takes to bleed the heart!

The lightning flash of a teeny smile;
How little it takes to please that heart!
And how little it takes to break it!

How little it takes to please the human heart!
And how little it takes to break it!

—UMASHANKAR JOSHI

Gujarati is spoken principally in the state of Gujarat, westernmost India, bordering Pakistan and the Arabian Sea. Like the other languages of the northern two-thirds of India, it is descended from Sanskrit, and is thus a member of the Indo-European family. Gujarati is written in an alphabet similar to that used by Sanskrit and Hindi, but without the continuous horizontal line running along the top. With about 25 million speakers, it is one of the official provincial languages recognized by the Indian constitution.

Marathi

मला उगीच अंधुक अंधुक अशा गोष्टी आठवतात. परंतु त्या जशा आठवतात तशाच खरोखर झाल्या, कीं, त्यांच्या-संबंधीं आठवणींत माझ्या चपल कल्पनेनें त्यांत आपलें चापल्य बरें-च योजिलें आहे, तें कांहीं सांगतां येत नाही.तरी पण आतां अधिक चर्पटपंजरी न लावतां जी म्हणून अगदीं जुनी आठवण मला होते आहे तिथून मी आपलें चरित्र सांगण्यास प्रारंभ करतों आणि अशा तऱ्हेनें माझ्या आठवणीपासून प्रारंभ करून मग आधींच्या गोष्टी जसजशा मला कळल्या (अर्थातच लोकांच्या तोंडून) तसतशा सांगेन.

I have a sort of hazy recollection of certain events, but I am unable to state for a certainty whether they really happened as I remember them, or whether these memories are greatly embellished by my fertile imagination. However, enough of these tiresome reflections. Let us begin the story of my life with the earliest recollection that comes to mind. Having thus begun, I shall recount later on what I know of earlier events (as told, of course, by those around me).

—HARINARAYAN APTE, *I*

Marathi is spoken in western India, principally in the state of Maharashtra, which includes the city of Bombay. Speakers of Marathi extend down the coast as far as Goa, though there a special dialect called Konkani is spoken, different enough from Marathi to be considered by some linguists as a separate language. Marathi, like Hindi, is one of the Indic languages, and the alphabet is the same as that used in Hindi. With about 42 million speakers, it ranks as one of the major languages of India.

Bengali

কত অজানারে জানাইলে তুমি.
    কত ঘরে দিলে ঠাঁই—
দূরকে করিলে নিকট বন্ধু.
    পরকে করিলে ভাই।
        পুরানো আবাস ছেড়ে যাই যবে
        মনে ভেবে মরি কী জানি কী হবে.
        নূতনের মাঝে তুমি পুরাতন
            সে কথা যে ভুলে যাই
        দূরকে করিলে নিকট বন্ধু,
            পরকে করিলে ভাই

জীবনে মরণে নিখিল ভুবনে
    যখনি যেখানে লবে.
চিরজনমের পরিচিত ওহে.
    তুমিই চিনাবে সবে।
        তোমারে জানিলে নাহি কেহ পর.
        নাহি কোনো মানা. নাহি কোনো ডর
        সবারে মিলায়ে তুমি জাগিতেছ,
            দেখা যেন সদা পাই
        দূরকে করিলে নিকট বন্ধু.
            পরকে করিলে ভাই

Thou hast made me known to friends whom I knew not. Thou hast given me seats in homes not my own. Thou hast brought the distant near and made a brother of the stranger.

I am uneasy at heart when I have to leave my accustomed shelter; I forget that there abides the old in the new, and that there also thou abideth.

Through birth and death, in this world or in others, wherever thou leadest me it is thou, the same, the one companion of my endless life who ever linkest my heart with bonds of joy to the unfamiliar.

When one knows thee, then alien there is none, then no door is shut. Oh, grant me my prayer that I may never lose the bliss of the touch of the one in the play of the many.

—RABINDRANATH TAGORE, *Gitanjali*

Bengali is spoken in the region known as Bengal, lying both in India and in the new nation of Bangladesh. In the latter it is spoken by virtually the entire population of 75 million; in India it is spoken by about 45 million people in the province known as West Bengal. Only five other languages in the world can claim as many as 120 million speakers.

Bengali, like Hindi, is descended from Sanskrit, and is thus of the Indo-European family. It is written in a variety of the Sanskrit Devanagari alphabet, from which it began to diverge about the 11th century. Bengali literature is dominated by the towering figure of Rabindranath Tagore (1861–1941), who won the Nobel Prize for Literature in 1913.

Oriya

ଦକ୍ଷିଣ ଦେଶରେ ସିନ୍ଧୁ ନାମକ ଏକ ରାଜ୍ୟ ଥିଲା । ସେଠାରେ ବୀରବାହୁ ବୋଲି ଜଣେ ରାଜା ଥିଲେ । ତାଙ୍କର ଦୁଇଟି ରାଣୀ ଥାନ୍ତି । ବଡ଼ରାଣୀର ନାମ ପ୍ରେମଶୀଳା, ସାନ ରାଣୀର ନାମ କନକମଞ୍ଜରୀ । ସାନ ରାଣୀଟି ବଡ଼ ସୁନ୍ଦରୀ । ତାଠାରେ ରାଜା ବଡ଼ ସ୍ନେହ କରୁଥାନ୍ତି । ବଡ଼ ରାଣୀଟିକୁ ଦେଖି ପାରନ୍ତି ନାହିଁ । କେତେ ଦିନ ଗଲାପରେ ଦୈବଯୋଗେ ବଡ଼ ରାଣୀର ଗୋଟିଏ ପୁଅ ଜନ୍ମ ହେଲା । ବଡ଼ ରାଣୀର ପୁଅ ହେବା ଦେଖି ସାନରାଣୀ ମନେ ମନେ ଚିନ୍ତାକରି ବସିଲା, ତାର ତ ପୁଅ ହେଲାଣି ସେ ରାଜ୍ୟ ପାଇବ, ଭଲ ମନ୍ଦ ହେଲେ ରାଜା ମୋତେ କାଢ଼ି ରାଜ୍ୟରୁ ତଡ଼ିଦେବେ । ମୁଁ ଏବେ କି ଉପାୟ କରିବି ?

In the southern regions there was a kingdom called Sindhu. Its ruler was a rajah named Birobahu. He had two queens. The older queen was called Premosila, the younger Konokomonjori. The younger queen was very beautiful and the rajah doted upon her, but the older queen he didn't care for at all. It happened that after a while the older queen gave birth to a son. Learning of this, the younger queen thought to herself, "She has borne a son who will rule someday. The first chance the rajah gets he will probably banish me from the kingdom. What am I going to do now?"

—MAHESVARA MISRA, *Tales of Abolakara*

Oriya is spoken in eastern India, principally in the state of Orissa, which faces the Bay of Bengal. It is closely related to Bengali, spoken to the north, and thus also belongs to the Indic branch of the Indo-European family. The distinctive Oriya script lacks the continuous horizontal top line of other Indian languages, most of its letters containing a large semicircle at the top. To one not familiar with the alphabet many of the letters appear at first glance to look alike. There are about 20 million speakers of Oriya. It is one of the official provincial languages recognized by the Indian constitution.

Assamese

অসমীয়া ভাষা অতি প্ৰাচীন আৰু ঐতিহ্যপূৰ্ণ। খৃষ্টীয় সপ্তম শতিকাতে বিখ্যাত চীনা পৰিব্ৰাজকাচাৰ্য্য হিউৱেন চাঙে ইয়াৰ বৈশিষ্ট্যৰ কথা প্ৰকাৰান্তৰে উল্লেখ কৰি গৈছে। হিউৱেন চাঙে লিখিছিল, "কামৰূপৰ ভাষা মধ্য ভাৰতৰ ভাষাৰ পৰা কিছু পৃথক।" অৰ্থাৎ সেই সুদূৰ অতীততে, হয়তো বা তাৰো বহু কালৰ পূৰ্ব্বেই আৰ্য্য সম্ভূত অসমীয়া ভাষাই স্থানীয় আৰ্য্যেতৰ বিভিন্ন ভাষাৰ প্ৰভাৱত পৰি স্বকীয়া ৰূপ গ্ৰহণ কৰিছিল।

Assamese is a very ancient language with a long tradition behind it. Hieun-Ts'ang, the great Chinese traveler of the 7th century A.D., made mention of its distinctiveness in an indirect way. He wrote, "The language of Kamarupa," *i.e.*, modern Assam, "differs a little from that of mid-India." This means that Assamese, which is derived from the Old Indo-Aryan language, acquired its distinctive shape and form in that distant past, maybe even long before that time, through the influence of the local non-Aryan languages surrounding it.

Assamese is spoken in easternmost India, in the state of Assam which borders Burma and China. Though it is spoken by only 9 million people (less than 2 percent of India's population), it is one of the constitutionally recognized languages of the country. Assamese is one of the Indic languages and is thus a member of the Indo-European family. Its alphabet is similar to that of Bengali, with slightly different characters for the letters *r* and *w*.

Bihari

अम्बरे वदन झपावह गोरि
राज सुनइछि चान्दक चोरि ।।
घरे घरे पहरी गेल अछ जोहि
अवही दूषण लागत तोहि ।।
सुन सुन सुन्दरि हित–उपदेश
सपनेहु जनु हो विपद-कलेश ।।
हास-सुधारस न कर उजोर
धनिके वनिके धन बोलब मोर ।।
अधर-समीप दसन कर जोति
सिंदुर-सीम वैसाउलि मोति ।।

O bright girl, please cover your face with a piece of cloth: they report the theft of the moon in the kingdom.

The watchman has carried out a house-to-house search and then he has gone away: now you will be accused of the offense.

Hear, O beautiful girl, this wholesome advice in order that you may not, even in dream, have any misfortune or trouble.

You should not let the nectar of your smile shine forth outside, or a wealthy trader will claim your face as his property.

On the skirts of your lips, the teeth are shining; they look like pearls set in vermilion.

—A Song of Vidyapati

Bihari is a somewhat imprecise designation for three related languages spoken principally in the state of Bihar, in northeastern India. The three languages are (1) Bhojpuri, with about 20 million speakers in western Bihar and eastern Uttar Pradesh; (2) Maithili, with about 15 million speakers in northern Bihar and another million in Nepal; (3) Magahi, with about 5 million speakers in central Bihar, including the capital city of Patna.

Because of this fragmentation, Bihari, despite its large number of speakers, is not one of the constitutional languages of India. Although a rich body of poetry exists from the 15th century onward, Bihari ceased to be cultivated as a written language in the 19th century. In this century a movement was begun to revive written Maithili and have it declared a separate language. (The above text is in Maithili.) While some success has been achieved in this direction, Hindi, rather than Bihari, is still used in Bihar for official correspondence and instruction in the schools.

Telugu

చెవులు గోరును మంచి జిలిబిలి పాటల,
తియ్యని మాటల తెరగు వినగ
చర్మంబు గోరును సరవి తోడుత శీత
మృదుల సంస్పర్శ సంపదలనెపుడు
కన్నులు గోరును కమనీయ వర్ణంబు
లైనట్టి రూపంబుల నువు తోడ
నాలుక గోరును, నయము తోడుత, తీపి,
యొగరు, కారమ్ము, చేదుప్పు, పులుసు,
ముక్కు గోరును సద్గంధములను జెలగి,
చెవులు చర్మంబు కన్నులు, జిహ్వ ముక్కు,
నిన్నియును గూడినటువంటి యిల్లు రోసి,
తన్ను గనుగొని సుఖయింప దగును వేమ.

The ears delight in gentle harmonious songs and sweet words well ordered; the skin in like manner is gratified by coolness and soft touches; the eyes desire forms adorned with lovely hues and delicately proportioned; the tongue naturally is pleased with tastes astringent, pungent, bitter, salt, and acid; and the nose takes pleasure in grateful scents. But let us abhor the corporeal mansion that renders us subject to the five feelings perceived by the ears, skin, eyes, tongue, and nose. See that thou art a being distinct from these earthly ties; and thus shalt thou be happy, O Vema!

—*The Verses of Vemana*

Telugu is spoken principally in the state of Andhra Pradesh, southeastern India. With about 45 million speakers, it is the most widely spoken of the four major Dravidian languages of southern India, each of which is recognized as an official provincial language by the Indian constitution. The Telugu alphabet most closely resembles that of Kanarese, both of them having developed out of the Grantha script, which appeared in India about the 5th century A.D.

Kanarese

ರಾಮ ಐತಾಳರು ನದಿಯನ್ನು ದಾಟಿ ಕಣ್ಮರೆಯಾಗುವ ತನಕ ಅವರ ತಂಗಿ ಸರಸೋತಮ್ಮ ನೋಡುತ್ತ ನಿಂತಿದ್ದಳು. ಅನಂತರ ಬೇಸರಬಂದು ಮನೆಯ ಕಡೆಗೆ ಹೊರಟಳು. ಆದರೆ ಪಾರೋತಿಯು, ಅವಳು ಕರೆದರೂ ಹೋಗಲಿಲ್ಲ. ಇನ್ನೂ ಅಲ್ಲಿಯೇ ನಿಂತಿದ್ದಾಳೆ. ಈಗ ಆಕೆಯನ್ನು ಗಂಡನ ಮರಳಿ ಬರುವ ಚಿಂತೆ ಕಾಡುತ್ತಲಿಲ್ಲ. ಬೇಸಾಯದ ಚಿಂತೆ ಕಾಡುತ್ತಿತ್ತು. 'ನೆರೆ ನೀರು ಇನ್ನು ನಾಲ್ಕು ದಿವಸ ಇದೇ ರೀತಿ ನಿಂತುಬಿಟ್ಟರೆ, ಮುಂದಿನ ವರ್ಷ ಉಣ್ಣುವುದೇನನ್ನು ?' ಎಂಬ ಚಿಂತೆ. ಹಾಗೆ ಕೇಳಹೋದರೆ ರಾಮ ಐತಾಳರ ಸಂಸಾರದಲ್ಲಿ — ಚಿಂತೆಯ ಭಾರವನ್ನು ಈ ಇಬ್ಬರು ಹೆಂಗಸರು ಹೊತ್ತಂತೆ ಯಜಮಾನರಾದ ಐತಾಳರೇ ಹೊರುವಂತಿಲ್ಲ. ಅವರಮ ಇದ್ದುದರಲ್ಲೇ ಲಘುಜೀವನ. ಪೌರೋಹಿತ್ಯದ ದೆಸೆಯಿಂದಾಗಿ ಅವರು ಸಾಗುವಳಿಯ ಕಡೆಗೆ ಸಮನಾಗಿ ಮನಸ್ಸು ಕೊಡುವುದೂ ಕಡಿಮೆ.

As Rama Aytala crossed the river and disappeared from view, his sister Sarasotamma stood there watching him. Then she felt tired and started out for home. But Paroti did not move, though she called to her. She still stood there. She was not troubled now by the thought of her husband's return. Only the thought of tilling the land bothered her. She thought, "If the floodwaters remain at their present level for many more days, what will we eat next year?" Such things mattered little to the master Rama Aytala, who could not bear the burden of thoughts and worries as these two women did. His life was easy, all things considered. Owing to his priestly duties, he gave little thought to matters of sowing and tilling.

—K. S. KARANTA, *Back to the Soil*

Kanarese, also known as Kannada, is spoken in southwestern India, principally in the state of Karnataka (formerly Mysore). A member of the Dravidian family of languages, it is spoken by about 22 million people. The Kanarese alphabet is similar to that used in Telugu, but the language itself is more closely related to Tamil and Malayalam.

Tamil

கொந்தவிழ் மலர்ச்சோலை நன்னீழல் வைகினுங்
குளிர்தீம் புனற் கையள்ளிக்
கொள்ளுகினுமங்ஙீ ரிடைத்திளைத்தாடினுங்
குளிர்சந்தவாடை மடவார்
வந்துலவுகின்றதென முன்றிலிடை யுலவவே
வசதிபெறுபோதும் வெள்ளை
வட்ட மதிப்பட்டப் பகற் போலநிலவுதர
மகிழ்போதும் வேலையமுதம்
விந்தைபெறவறுசுவையில் வந்ததெனவமுதுண்ணும்
வேளையிலுமாலைகந்தம்
வெள்ளிலைய டைக்காய் விரும்பிவேண் டியவண்ணம்
விளையாடி விழிது யிலினுஞ்
சந்ததமு நின்னருளை மறவாவரந்தந்து
தமியேனை ரக்ஷை புரிவாய்
சர்வபரிபூரண வகண்டதத்துவமான
சச்சிதானந்த சிவமே.

Whether in grateful shade I dwell of groves
Rich in clustered blooms, or cool sweet draughts
I quaft from limpid stream,
Or in its waters bathe and sport,
Or, fanned by fragrant breezes fresh.
That like maidens in the courtyard play,
I revel in the full moon's day-like splendor.
Or in dainties I feast where in ocean's ambrosia
Haply hath wondrous entered, or in garlands,
Perfumes, betel I joy, or rest in sleep,
Thy grace may I never forget! This boon
To me grant and from the world guard me,
O Sivam, all pervading, infinite, true,
Thou art the one Reality, Knowledge, Pure and Bliss!

—SAINT THAYUMANAVAR, *God and the World*

Tamil is one of the major languages of southern India. It is spoken principally in the state of Tamil Nadu (formerly Madras), located on the eastern coast and extending down to the southernmost tip of the Indian subcontinent. There are about 38 million Tamil speakers in India. In addition it is spoken by about 4 million people in northeastern Ceylon, about one million in Malaysia, and in smaller colonies in Singapore, Fiji, Mauritius, Trinidad, Guyana, Zanzibar, and parts of East Africa.

Tamil is the oldest and most richly developed of the Dravidian languages. The origin of the alphabet is uncertain, though it is believed to be about 1,500 years old. *Curry* and *mulligatawny* are two Tamil words that have entered the English language. The latter is a combination of the Tamil words for "pepper" and "water."

Malayalam

കളത്തിലെ കെട്ടുപിണഞ്ഞ നാഗങ്ങളെയും അവയിൽ കണ്ണുനട്ടിരിക്കുന്ന, ആ നിലവിളക്കിലെ നാളംപോലെ തിളങ്ങുന്ന, പെൺകിടാവിനെയും അവൻ മാറിമാറി നോക്കി. അവളുടെ കഴുത്തിൽ കുടുക്കിക്കെട്ടി കല്ലുപതിച്ച ആഭരണം വെട്ടിതിളങ്ങുന്നു. ദീപനാളങ്ങൾ മറച്ചിട്ടില്ലാത്ത മാറിൽ പുളഞ്ഞുമറിയുന്നു......... പതുക്കെപ്പതുക്കെ അവന്റെ കണ്ണിൽ നിന്നു പന്തലും മുററവും ആളുകളും ഒഴിഞ്ഞുപോയി. ഇപ്പോൾ കൊടുംകാട്ടിലാണ്. ഉയരത്തിൽ, മാനംമുട്ടിനില്ക്കുന്ന ഒരു വൃക്ഷത്തിന്റെ കവുളിയിൽ രാജകുമാരൻ ഇരിക്കുന്നു.

Appunni looked now at the interlocked snakes in the "square," now at the girl sitting amidst the lamps with her eyes fixed on the snakes, herself golden like the flame of the lamps. A jewel set with stones flashed and gleamed in the hollow of her neck. The flames turned and twisted like snakes on her bare breasts. Slowly, very slowly, the pandal and the people and the courtyard vanished from his sight. He was now in a thick forest. The prince was sitting on a tall tree whose top touched the heavens.

—M. T. VASUDEVAN NAIR, *Nalukettu*

Malayalam, with the stress on the third syllable, is spoken on the Malabar (western) coast of extreme southern India, chiefly in the state of Kerala. It is one of the Dravidian languages and is most closely related to Tamil. There are about 22 million speakers. The alphabet, which dates from the 8th or 9th century, also developed out of the script called Grantha. The English words *teak*, *copra*, and *atoll* all come from Malayalam.

Sinhalese

මල් රැසකින් බොහෝ මල් දම් ගොතන්නේ යම් සේ ද, එසේ ම, උපන් මිනිසා විසින් බොහෝ කුසල් කටයුතු ය.

සාමාන්‍ය මල් සුවඳක් හෝ සඳුන්, තුවරලා ඉද්ද වැනි මල්වල සුවඳක් හෝ උඩු සුළඟට නො යයි. එහෙත් සත්පුරුෂයන්ගේ (සිල්) සුවඳ උඩු සුළඟට ද යයි. සත්පුරුෂයා සියලු දිශාවල ම සිල් සුවඳ පතුරුවයි.

සඳුන්, තුවරලා, මහනෙල්, දෑසමන් යන සියලු මල් ජාතීන්ගේ සුවඳට වඩා සිල් සුවඳ උසස් ය.

As many kinds of garlands can be made from a heap of flowers, so many good works should be achieved by a mortal when once he is born.

The scent of flowers does not travel against the wind, nor that of sandalwood, of tagara, or jasmine. But the fragrance of good people travels even against the wind. A good man pervades every quarter.

Sandalwood, tagara, a lotus flower, jasmine—among these kinds of perfumes the perfume of virtue is unsurpassed.

—The *Dhammapada* (ancient Buddhist scriptures)

Sinhalese is the official language of Ceylon, now known as Sri Lanka. It is spoken by about 9 million people, living mainly in the southern and western two-thirds of the island. An Indo-European language descended from Sanskrit, Sinhalese was brought to Ceylon by settlers from northern India in the 5th century B.C. The alphabet, however, with its generally rounded letters, more closely resembles those of the Dravidian languages of southern India. The English words *tourmaline* and *beriberi* are of Sinhalese origin.

Nepali

एक दिन एउंटा कुकुर मासुको पसलबाट मासुको चोक्टो चोरेर बस्तीतिर भाग्यो। बाटामा ठूलो खोलो पर्थ्यो। त्यस खोलामाथि सांघु थियो। सांघुमा हिंड्दा त्यस कुकुरले तल खोलामा आफ्नो छाया देख्यो। यो ता अर्को कुकुर पो मुखमा मासु च्यापेर जांदो रहेछ भनी ठानेर त्यो मासु खोस्नलाइ झंट्यो। ङ्याङ गर्दा ता आफ्नै मुखको मासु पो पानीमा खस्यो। छायाका कुकुरको मुखको मासु नदेख्ता त्यसका मनमा आफूले च्यापेका मासुको समझ्ना भयो। तर पानीमा खसेको मासुको चोक्टो त्यस कुकुरले केही गरेर पनि पाएन।

One day a dog who had taken a piece of meat from a butcher shop set off for home. On the way he came to a large river. Over the river there was a bridge. While running across the bridge the dog looked down and saw his reflection in the river. Thinking that this was another dog with a piece of meat in its mouth, he set out to take it for himself. When he barked the meat fell from his mouth into the water. Not seeing the meat in the mouth of the dog reflected in the water, he remembered the meat which he himself had been holding. But no matter what he did, he could not find the piece of meat that had fallen into the water.

Nepali is the national language of Nepal. It is the mother tongue of about 6 million people there and is spoken fluently as a second language by about 2 million others. Nepali is also spoken in the Indian states of West Bengal (especially in the city of Darjeeling) and Assam, as well as in the Indian protectorates of Bhutan and Sikkim. All told, there are close to 10 million speakers of the language.

Nepali is one of the Indic languages and is thus related to Hindi and, more distantly, to the other Indo-European languages. The alphabet is the same as that used for Sanskrit and Hindi.

Tibetan

གསུང་དང་བླ་མ་རྣམས་ལ་ཕྱག་འཚལ་ལོ ༎
རྗེ་འགྲོ་བ་མགོན་པོའི་ཞབས་ལ་འདུད ༎
བླ་མ་མི་འགྱུར་ཆོས་ཀྱི་ངང་ལ་བཞུགས ༎
སྤྱན་རས་གཟིགས་ཀྱང་ཆོས་ཀྱི་ངང་ལ་བཞུར ༎
ཐུགས་རྗེ་ཆེན་པོ་ཆོས་ཀྱི་ངང་ལ་བཞུགས ༎
ཐང་སྟོང་རྒྱལ་པོ་ཆོས་ཀྱི་ངང་ལ་བཞུགས ༎
ལོ་ཆེན་གོང་མ་ཆོས་ཀྱི་ངང་ལ་བཞུགས ༎
རྒྱ་སྐྱེ་ཁྲིམས་པ་ཡིག་དྲུག་མ་ཎི་དྲོངས ༎
ཨོཾ་མ་ཎི་པདྨེ་ཧཱུྃ།

Let us salute the Teachers!
Bow to the feet of the Venerable Lord of Living Beings!
Abide in the spiritual essence of the Eternal Teacher!
Abide in the spiritual essence of Avalokiteçvara!
Abide in the spiritual essence of the All-Merciful One!
Abide in the spiritual essence of Thaṅ-stoṅ rgyal-po!
Abide in the spiritual essence of the sublime Paṇḍita!
You, country-folk, recite the six-lettered māṇi!
Oṁ māṇi padme hūṅ!
—The Ceremony of Breaking the Stone

Tibetan is spoken by about $1\frac{1}{4}$ million people in what was formerly Tibet, now the Tibet Autonomous Region of China. Another $1\frac{1}{2}$ million speakers live in the Chinese provinces of Szechwan, Tsinghai, and Kansu. Additionally about one million people in Nepal speak Tibetan as a second language.

Of the major languages of Asia, Tibetan has the most in common with Burmese. The two languages belong to the same branch of the Sino-Tibetan family. The Tibetan alphabet dates from the 7th century A.D. It is based on the Sanskrit, having been adapted by a Tibetan minister sent to study Sanskrit in Kashmir.

Uigur

كەچ مەزگىلى ئۈرۈمچى كوچىلىرىنى تاماشا قىلماقتىمەن.
كوچىنىڭ نېرىقى دوخمۇشىدىن بىر كىشى كۆزىنى مېنىڭدىن ئۈزمەي
قاراپ كېلىۋاتىدۇ. مەن ئۆزەمنىڭ تۇرقۇمدىن قورقۇپ چاپانلىرىمنى
قېلېشتۇرۇپ، قولاقچامنى تۈزەۋرەك كىيىپمۇ ئالدىم. قىزىرىپ
كەتتىم ئېھتىمالىم، پۈتۈن بەدەنلىرىم ئوت ئېلىپ يېنىۋاتقاندەك
بولدى. «نېمانچە قارايدىغاندۇ، بۇ ئادەم»

نامەلۇم كىشى ماڭا يېقىنلىشىپ كېلىۋاتىدۇ. تېخىچە
مېنىڭدىن كۆزىنى ئالغىنى يوق. ئۇنىڭ چىرايىدا يېقىن
كەلگەنسېرى قىزىرىپ كۈلۈمسىرەش ئالامىتى پەيدا بولدى. ماڭا
ئۇ ئەندى يېنىمدا. ئۇ ماڭا قول ئۇزۇتۇپ: «سىز مېنى ياخشى
تونالمايۋاتىسىز ھە؟» — دېدى

It is evening. I am walking along the streets of Urumchi. On the other side of the street, not taking his eyes off me, stands a man. Concerned about my appearance, I straighten my clothes and adjust my hat. Apparently I even blushed. Suddenly I felt hot. "I wonder why that man is watching me."

The stranger comes closer and closer without ever taking his eyes off me. The closer he comes, the broader the smile on his face. Finally he walks right up to me and, extending his hand, says, "It seems you do not recognize me, correct?"

Uigur is spoken principally in China and to a lesser extent in the Soviet Union. In China the Uigurs number some 4 million, most of whom live in a vast area of western China called the Sinkiang Uigur Autonomous Region (capital: Urumchi). In the Soviet Union Uigur speakers number only 150,000, living mainly in the Kazakh and Kirgiz republics, near the Chinese border.

Uigur is a Turkic language and thus of the Altaic family. The Uigurs are an ancient people whose history can be traced back to the early centuries of the Christian era. About the middle of the 8th century they established a large and powerful state in eastern Turkestan. When this was overrun a hundred years later, they established a new kingdom in western China that survived until the rise of the Mongol Empire.

The ancient Uigurs developed a script of their own, which was written vertically from left to right. Though not completely original (having been adapted from an earlier script called Sogdian), it had considerable influence upon writing in Asia even after the dissolution of the Uigur kingdom. In the 13th century the Mongols adopted the Uigur script for writing their own language, and in turn passed it on to the Manchus, who were to rule China for over 250 years.

Meanwhile the Uigurs had long since adopted Islam, and with it the Arabic script, but a new Roman-based alphabet introduced in the 1960s is gradually taking hold. In the Soviet Union Uigur has been written in the Cyrillic alphabet since 1947.

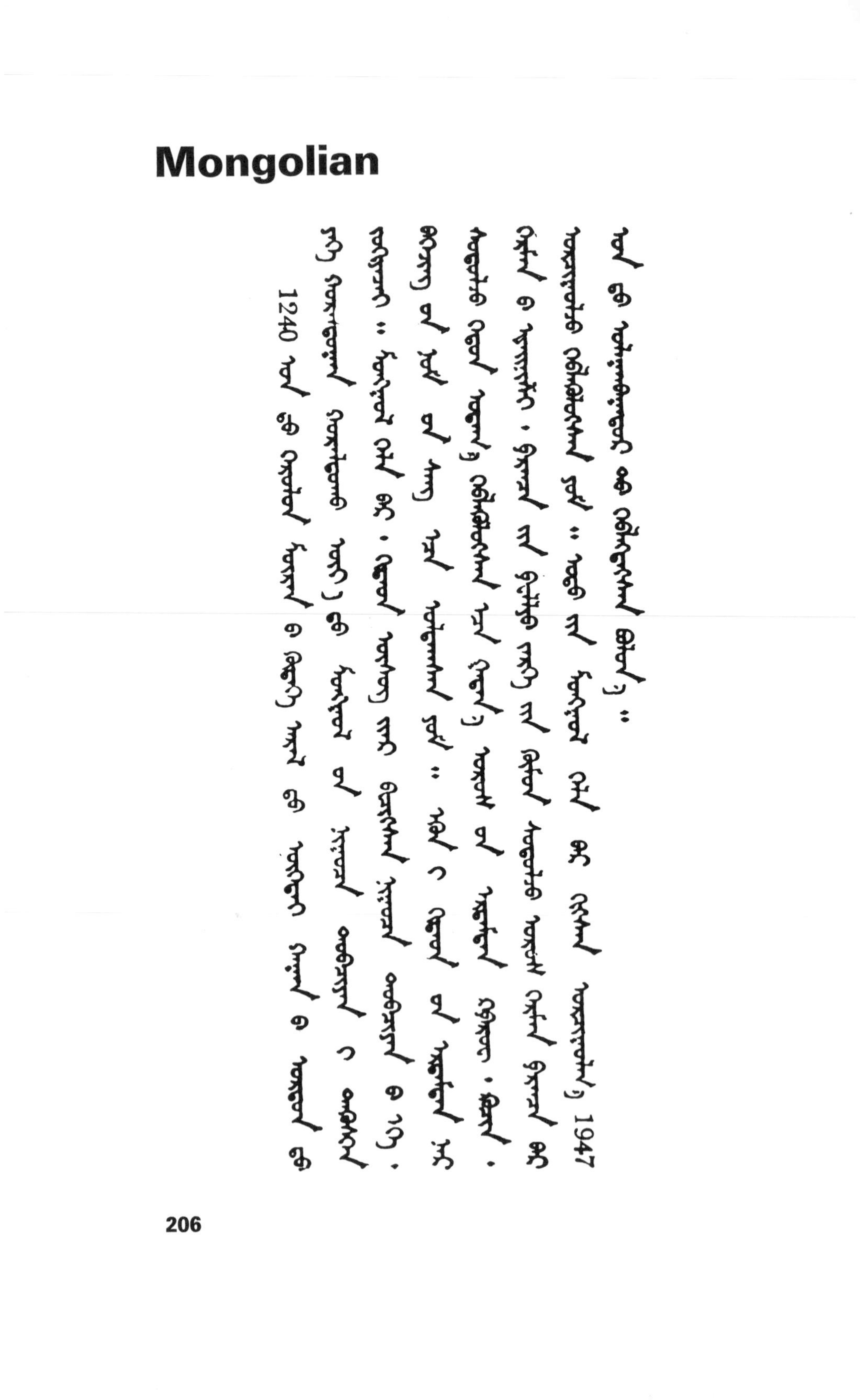

Mongolian

[illegible]

1240 онд Хэрлэн мөрний хөдөө аралд Огөөдэй хааны ордонд их хуралдаан хуралдах үед Монголын Нууц товчоог төгсгөн зохиожээ. Монгол хэлэн дээр хятад үсгээр бичсэн Нууц товчооны эх нь Бээжингийн номын сангаас олдсон юм. Үүнийг Хятадын эрдэмтэн нар судлаж хэдэн удаа хэвлүүлснээс гадна Оросын эрдэмтэн Кафаров, Кучин, Германы Хайниш, Францын Пеллио зэргийн хүн судлаж орос, герман, францаар орчуулж хэвлүүлсэн юм. Одоогийн монгол хэлээр хийсэн орчуулга 1947 онд Улаанбаатарт хэвлэгдсэн болно.

In 1240, when the great Khuraltai (Assembly) was held in the Palace of Ogodai Khan in the valley of the Kerulen River, the writing of the Secret History of Mongolia was completed. The original of the Secret History, printed in Mongolian using Chinese letters, was found in the Peking Library. It has been studied and published several times by Chinese scholars, while the Russian scholars Kafarov and Kuchin, Haenisch of Germany, and Pelliot of France have studied and published it in Russian, German, and French. In 1947 a translation in the modern Mongolian language was published in Ulan Bator.

Mongolian is spoken in both Mongolia and China. In the Mongolian People's Republic (the area traditionally known as Outer Mongolia) there are about $1\frac{1}{4}$ million speakers, while the Inner Mongolian Autonomous Region of China (traditionally known as Inner Mongolia) has about one million. With an additional 200,000 speakers in northwest China, and another 150,000 in Manchuria, the total number of speakers of Mongolian is slightly over $2\frac{1}{2}$ million.

Standard Mongolian is often referred to as Khalkha to distinguish it from a number of related languages and dialects. These include Buryat and Kalmyk, spoken in the Soviet Union. All of these belong to the Mongolian branch of the Altaic family of languages.

The original Mongolian alphabet was adapted from that of the Uigurs in the 13th century. It is written vertically, perhaps under Chinese influence, but unlike most vertical scripts it begins at the left. It was used in Outer Mongolia until 1941, and is still used among Mongolian speakers in China, though in a somewhat modified form.

In 1941 the Mongolian People's Republic replaced the old alphabet with a new one based on the Cyrillic. It was the first appearance of Cyrillic in Asia outside the Soviet Union. The alphabet is the same as the Russian, but contains two additional vowels, the ө and ү.

Chinese

既然必须和新的群众的时代相结合，就必须彻底解决个人和群众的关系问题。鲁迅的两句诗，“横眉冷对千夫指，俯首甘为孺子牛”，应该成为我们的座右铭。“千夫”在这里就是说敌人，对于无论什么凶恶的敌人我们决不屈服。“孺子”在这里就是说无产阶级和人民大众。一切共产党员，一切革命家，一切革命的文艺工作者，都应该学鲁迅的榜样，做无产阶级和人民大众的“牛”，鞠躬尽瘁，死而后已。知识分子要和群众结合，要为群众服务，需要一个互相认识的过程。这个过程可能而且一定会发生许多痛苦，许多磨擦，但是只要大家有决心，这些要求是能够达到的。

> Since integration into the new epoch of the masses is essential, it is necessary thoroughly to solve the problem of the relationship between the individual and the masses. This couplet from a poem by Lu Hsun should be our motto: "Fierce-browed, I coolly defy a thousand pointing fingers, head-bowed, like a willing ox I serve the children." The "thousand pointing fingers" are our enemies, and we will never yield to them, no matter how ferocious. The "children" here symbolize the proletariat and the masses. All Communists, all revolutionaries, all revolutionary literary and art workers should learn from the example of Lu Hsun and be "oxen" for the proletariat and the masses, bending their backs to the task until their dying day. Intellectuals who want to integrate themselves with the masses, who want to serve the masses, must go through a process in which they and the masses come to know each other well. This process may, and certainly will, involve much pain and friction, but if you have the determination, you will be able to fulfill these requirements.
>
> —MAO TSE-TUNG, Talk at the Yenan Forum on Literature and Art (1942)

Chinese is spoken by more people than any other language in the world. Since estimates of the current population of China are only approximate, figures for the number of speakers of Chinese must likewise be approximate. An educated guess would be about 750 million in the Chinese People's Republic, to which must be added another 15 million on Taiwan, 4 million in Hong Kong, 4 million in Thailand, 4 million in Malaysia, $1\frac{1}{2}$ million in Singapore, one million in Vietnam, and lesser numbers in other countries including the United States. Thus Chinese has more than twice the number of speakers of English, though of course it lacks the universality of English and is spoken by few people not of Chinese origin. Chinese has been an official language of the United Nations since the founding of the organization in 1945.

Though Chinese has many dialects, Mandarin, based on the pronunciation of Peking, is considered the standard and is spoken by about two-thirds of the population. The other major dialects are (1) Wu, spoken by about 50 million people in the Shanghai area and in Chekiang Province to the south; (2) Cantonese, spoken by about 45 million people in the extreme southern provinces of Kwangtung and Kwangsi; (3) Fukienese, or Min, spoken by about 45 million people, and generally subdivided into Northern Fukienese, or Foochow (15 million speakers), of northern Fukien, and Southern Fukienese, or Amoy (30 million speakers), of southern Fukien, Amoy Island, and Taiwan; (4) Hakka, with 20 million speakers in northeastern Kwangtung and southern Kiangsi provinces; (5) Hsiang, with 15 million speakers in Hunan Province. In addition the Fukienese dialects are widely spoken in Malaysia and Singapore, while Cantonese is also spoken in Hong Kong and on the Southeast Asia mainland. Nearly all Chinese in the United States speak Cantonese.

Chinese, like the other languages of the Sino-Tibetan family, is a tonal language, meaning that different tones, or intonations, distinguish words that otherwise are pronounced identically. The four Chinese tones are (1) high level; (2) high rising; (3) low rising; (4) high falling to low. It is not unusual for a syllable to be pronounced in each of the four tones, each yielding a word with a completely different meaning. For example, the word *ma* in tone one means "mother," while *ma*^{2} means "hemp," *ma*^{3} means "horse," and *ma*^{4} means "to curse." In fact each tone usually offers a large number of homonyms. *Yi* in tone one can mean, among other things, "one," "clothes," "doctor," and "to cure"; *yi*^{2} "aunt," "doubt," "suitable," and "to shift"; *yi*^{3} "already," "because of," and "by"; *yi*^{4} "easy," "strange," "benefit," and the number "100 million."

Chinese is written with thousands of distinctive characters called ideographs which have no relation to the sound of a word. In a large dictionary there are 40–50,000 characters, while the telegraphic code book contains nearly 10,000. A Chinese child learns about 2,000 characters by the time he is ten, but it takes two or three times as many to be able to read a newspaper or novel. One kind of Chinese typewriter has 5,400 characters. The number of strokes required to draw a Chinese character can be as high as 33.

The earliest Chinese characters were pictographs, such as a crescent for the moon, or a circle with a dot in the center to represent the sun. Gradually these gave way to nonpictorial ideographs which, in addition to standing for tangible objects, also represented abstract concepts. Today two characters—sometimes the same, sometimes different—often stand side by side to form a third. Thus two "tree" characters mean "forest," while "sun" + "moon" = "bright" and "woman" + "child" = "good." Sometimes the two characters are superimposed upon each other, their relative position giving a clue as to the meaning of the newly formed character. Thus when the character for "sun" is placed above the character for "tree" the new character means "high" or "bright," but when it is placed below, the new character means "hidden" or "dark." No matter how many single characters are combined into one, the resulting character always has the same square appearance and is the same size as any other character.

The majority of Chinese characters, however, consist of two elements —a signific, which indicates the meaning of a word, and a phonetic, which indicates the sound. The significs, or radicals, number 214 in Chinese, and indicate the class of objects to which the word belongs. For example, all words relating to wood, such as "tree" and "table," contain the "wood" radical. The phonetic consists of the character for a word whose meaning is totally unrelated to the word in question, but whose pronunciation happens to be the same. Thus the character for "ocean" consists of the signific "water" plus the phonetic "sheep," the word for "sheep" being pronounced the same as the word for "ocean." In some cases the phonetic stands alone, as in the case of the character for "dustpan" which also stands for the Chinese possessive pronoun, since the word for the pronoun is the same as the word for "dustpan."

Despite their staggering complexity, the Chinese characters do have the advantage of making written communication possible between people speaking mutually unintelligible dialects and languages. A given word may be quite different in Mandarin and Cantonese, but it would be written identically in the two dialects. Since the Chinese characters are also used in Japanese, each language, when written, is partially intelligible to a speaker of the other, despite the fact that the two spoken languages are totally dissimilar.

Numerous attempts have been made over the years to simplify the Chinese system of writing. In 1955 the Chinese People's Republic initiated a plan to simplify more than 1,700 characters, this number to be increased gradually so that over half of the most commonly used symbols would eventually be simplified. But the ultimate hope for easy readability of Chinese would appear to be an alphabetic script. In 1958 a new Chinese alphabet based on the Roman script was introduced, but thus far it appears to have made little headway.

English words of Chinese origin include *tea*, *typhoon*, *sampan*, *kaolin*, *kumquat*, *kowtow*, and *shanghai*.

Chuang

Daƅsam bəima le, ceзŋeiƅ couƅ sieŋз banƅfap haiƅ de, Ƃɵnƨ ƌeu, de heuƅ Daƅsam ma ranƨ guƅcəmƨ, couƅ gaŋз:“ Nueŋч ha! Mɯŋƨ nəuƨ mɯŋƨ youƽ laз saŋƽ, rəmч daŋƽ mɯŋƨ ciч gieŋƅ, mɯŋƨ səɯƽ rɵŋƨ laз saŋƽ bəi, gou əu rəmч dəuз daŋƽ, yəɯз mɯŋƨ gieŋƅ Ƃouз gieŋƅ?” Daƅsam Ƃouз roч Daƅŋeiƅ sieŋз haiƅ de, ciч rɵŋƨ laз saŋƽ bəi ninƨ. Daƅŋeiƅ əu rəmчgɵnз ma daŋƽ, Daƅsam couƅ dai lo.

After Dasam's return, her middle sister began to think of how she could do away with her. Once she invited Dasam to her house for a chat and said, "Sister! You used to say that if you sat in a big tub and were splashed with water, you would instantly become beautiful. Why don't you climb into the tub and let me splash water on you to see if you become beautiful?" Dasam did not suspect that Daney was planning to kill her and slid down to the bottom of the tub. Daney then took some boiling water and poured it all over her. Dasam died instantly.

The Chuang are the largest ethnic minority in China. Numbering about 8 million, they live chiefly in the Kwangsi Chuang Autonomous Region which borders Vietnam.

Of the major languages of Asia, Chuang is most closely related to Thai. The alphabet, developed in the 1950s, is based largely on the Roman. There are thirty-two letters in all—nineteen consonants, eight vowels, and five to indicate tones.

Miao

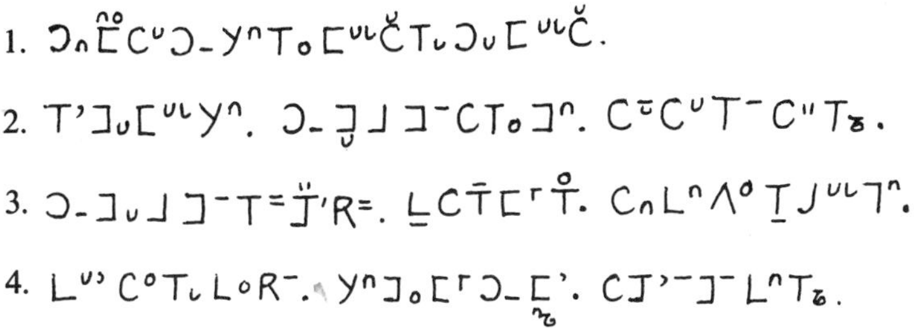

1. Hearken: Behold, the sower went forth to sow.
2. And it came to pass, as he sowed, some seed fell by the wayside, and the birds came and devoured it.
3. And other fell on the rocky ground, where it had not much earth; and straightaway it sprang up, because it had no deepness of earth.
4. And when the sun was risen, it was scorched; and because it had no root it withered away.

—From Luke viii

Miao is spoken by about 2½ million people in southern China, principally in the province of Kweichow, but also in Yunnan, Hunan, and Kwangtung. There are also some 200,000 speakers in Vietnam, 100,000 in Laos, and 50,000 in Thailand, though in these countries it is generally referred to as Meo. Miao and another language known as Yao constitute a separate branch of the Sino-Tibetan family.

Miao was first written in an ideographic script, but in 1904 a missionary, Samuel Pollard, developed the so-called Pollard script shown above. The simple, purely geometric symbols each stand for a syllable rather than a word. Although it enjoyed considerable success for many years, it is now giving way to a new Roman-based alphabet.

Yi

1. In ancient times there were differences between man and animal.
2. January likes the autumn rain.
3. February likes the leaves of the grasses.
4. March likes the frog.
5. April is the four-legged snake.
6. May is the house lizard.
7. June assumes the form of man.
8. July has mother's transformation.
9. August unites mother's spirit.
10. September is in mother's bosom.

—Passage describing the growth of a child during its mother's pregnancy

Yi, also known as Lolo, is spoken by about 3 million people in Yunnan Province, southern China. It is a member of the Tibeto-Burman subgroup of the Sino-Tibetan family of languages. The origin of the Yi script is unclear. The characters are mainly ideographic, possibly adaptations of the Chinese, but a number seem to be phonetic. In 1958 the Chinese government introduced a Roman-based alphabet for use in Yi.

Sibo

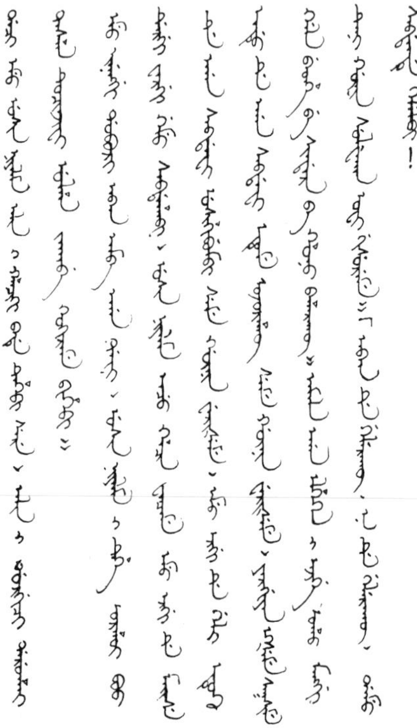

Once upon a time there was a farmer living in the vicinity of the mountains. In the mountains there always appeared tigers which caused harm to animals. One rainy night the farmer's house was leaking everywhere. The farmer was very angry. He did not know what to do. Later when the rain let up he wanted to take a rest. Then he said, "I'm not afraid of the sky and I'm not afraid of the earth, but I am afraid of the leaking!"

Sibo is spoken by a mere 20,000 people in northwestern China. An offshoot of the now extinct Manchu language, it is a member of the Tungusic branch of the Altaic family of languages. The vertical Sibo script is similar to the Manchu, which in turn was adapted from the Uigur script in the 13th century.

Nakhi

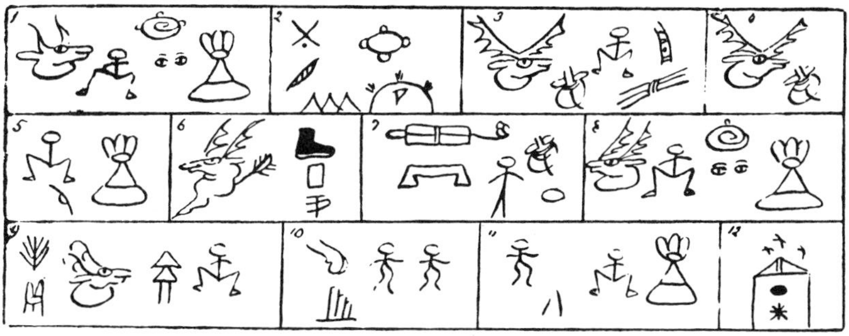

Box 1: The yak he dances there it is the custom
Box 2: on La-ts'ü-höddü gko
Box 3: the stag said he would like to dance there.
Box 4: For the stag
Box 5: to dance is not the custom,
Box 6: the elkskin shoes with the white front
Box 7: the sons of bitterness wear;
Box 8: the stag he dances there it is the custom.
Box 9: Where the pines are the young deer wanted to dance,
Box 10: the cloven-hoofed they sway in rhythm,
Box 11: they sway and dance as is the custom.
Box 12: All the people of the village.

—Excerpt from *Mun Ndzer Ä Lä Dzhu*, or Song of the Dead, Relating the Origin of Bitterness

Nakhi is spoken in Yunnan Province, southern China, by about 140,000 people. Called Moso by the Chinese, it is of the Tibeto-Burman family, and its script represents one of the few pictographic systems still in use in the 20th century.

Japanese

ああ、天の河と、島村も振り仰いだとたんに、天の河のなかへ體がふうと浮き上つてゆくやうだつた。天の河の明るさが島村を掬ひ上げさうに近かつた。旅の芭蕉が荒海の上に見たのは、このやうにあざやかな天の河の大きさであつたか。裸の天の河は夜の大地を素肌で巻かうとして、直ぐそこに降りて來てゐる。恐ろしい艶めかしさだ。島村は自分の小さい影が地上から逆に天の河へ寫つてゐさうに感じた。天の河にいつぱいの星が一つ一つ見えるばかりでなく、ところどころ光雲の銀砂子も一粒一粒見えるほど澄み渡り、しかも天の河の底なしの深さが視線を吸ひ込んで行つた。

The Milky Way. Shimamura too looked up, and he felt himself floating into the Milky Way. Its radiance was so near that it seemed to take him up into it. Was this the bright vastness the poet Basho saw when he wrote of the Milky Way arched over a stormy sea? The Milky Way came down just over there, to wrap the night earth in its naked embrace. There was a terrible voluptuousness about it. Shimamura fancied that his own small shadow was being cast up against it from the earth. Each individual star stood apart from the rest, and even the particles of silver dust in the luminous clouds could be picked out, so clear was the night. The limitless depth of the Milky Way pulled his gaze up into it.

—YASUNARI KAWABATA, *Snow Country*

Japanese, spoken by more than 100 million people in Japan, ranks among the top ten languages of the world.

No definite link has been established between Japanese and any other language, living or dead. Though it adopted the Chinese pictographic characters in the 3rd century A.D., Japanese is not, as is sometimes thought, genetically related to Chinese. Japanese does resemble Korean in grammatical structure, and though some scholars have suggested that they are related, this remains to be proven.

The Japanese ideographs, known as *kanji*, number in the thousands. An educated person can read 10,000 of them and the government has published a list of 1,850 that it considers basic. The *kanji* designate the chief meaningful words of the language—nouns, verbs, and adjectives. They are, however, supplemented by the *kana*, or syllabic characters, which are used chiefly to designate suffixes, particles, conjunctions, and other grammatical forms. There are two types of *kana*, each consisting of fifty characters: the *hiragana*, which is cursive in shape and in general use, and the *katakana*, which is angular in shape and is used mainly in imperial proclamations and in the transcription of foreign words. Each *kana* character stands for a single syllable rather than for a whole word. Theoretically any Japanese word can be written exclusively in the *kana* (children's primers are written entirely in *katakana*) but the large number of homonyms in the language makes this impractical. Modern Japanese, therefore, is written with a mixture of *kanji* and *kana* characters. As can be seen in the passage above, the *kana* are easily distinguishable from the *kanji* by their greater simplicity of design.

Japanese is generally written vertically beginning on the right, but many texts today are written horizontally to permit the inclusion of English words, Arabic numerals, and mathematical and chemical formulas. Though various movements over the years have advocated the adoption of the Roman script, native tradition and the great Japanese literary heritage militate against such a change.

English words of Japanese origin include *kimono*, *geisha*, *sukiyaki*, *hibachi*, *jiujitsu*, *karate*, *samurai*, *hara-kiri*, and *kamikaze*.

Yasunari Kawabata was the winner of the Nobel Prize for Literature in 1968.

Korean

진달래꽃

나 보기가 역겨워
가실 때에는
말없이 고히 보내 드리우리다。

영변(寧邊)에 약산(藥山)
진달래꽃
아름따다 가실 길에 뿌리우리다。

가시는 걸음걸음
놓인 그 꽃을
사뿐히즈려 밟고 가시옵소서。

나 보기가 역겨워
가실 때에는
죽어도 아니 눈물 흘리우리다

THE AZALEA

When you take your leave,
Tired of seeing me,
Gently and silently I'll bid you go.

From Mount Yag of Yongbyon
An armful of azaleas I shall pick,
And strew them in your path.

Go now, I pray, with short steps!
Let each footstep gently tread
The flowers which I have spread for you.

When you take your leave,
Tired of seeing me,
Though I should die, I shall not weep.

—KIM SO-WOL

Korean is spoken in both North and South Korea by about 50 million people. There are also about one million speakers in China, 500,000 in Japan, and 350,000 in the Soviet Union.

Korean's linguistic affiliation is uncertain, though in its grammatical structure it is most similar to Japanese. It is certainly not related to Chinese, although it has borrowed many Chinese words and has used the Chinese characters, together with the Korean alphabet, for many centuries. This latter practice was abolished in North Korea after World War II and is gradually being phased out in South Korea. In the fourth line of the poem above the proper nouns *Yongbyon* and *Yag San* appear with the Chinese characters following in parentheses.

The Korean alphabet, invented in the years 1443–46, is the only true alphabet native to the Far East. Each of the twenty-five letters represents a single consonant or vowel—not a syllable as in Japanese, or a concept as in Chinese. Korean writing differs from that of most other languages, however, in that the letters of each syllable are grouped together into clusters—as if the English word "seldom" were written
S D
E O or S E D O . The third word of the last line of the poem
L M   L   M
above, for example, consists of two clusters, each containing three letters arranged vertically. The first contains the letters *n*, *u*, and *n*, the second *m*, *u*, and *l*. *Nun* is the Korean word for "eye," *mul* the word for "water." Together they form the word *nunmul* which means "tear" or "tears."

Burmese

မဲဇာချောင် တောင်ခြေက လွမ်းပါရ
ပွဲခါညောင် ရေစင်သွန်းချိန်မို့
သဲသာသောင်မြေကျွန်းရယ်က ခွေပတ်လည်။

ရော်လို့သာ ရမ်းပါရ
တမ်းတကာ တဖိုဖိုနှင့်
ပြည်ရွှေဘို အောင်ဌာနဆီသို့
မြတ်ဘိုးတော် စေတီယတို့ကို
ဦးချစိတ်ရည်။

လေပြည်လာ တုန်ကာအေးတာမို့
နေခြည်ဖြာ ချုံလွှာနှင့်ထွေးပါရ
ဆွေးသပ ဖြေမတည်
ရေကြည်ကြည်ကျ သွင်သွင်မစဲ။

ဆီးနှင်းငယ်ထန်
မိုးလောက်ပင် ပုံသဏ္ဍာန်မို့
မှန်ပြာလုံ့ တောင်ယံထဲမှာ
မှိုင်းရီလို့မဲ။ ။

From Mèza Mountain's melancholy shade my heart turns homeward.
There Bo tree roots now run with water poured by festive hands.
Here gray sands lie about me, desolate.

Thoughts span the wastes that lie between.
Pulsing, throbbing, longing
Toward Shwébo, seat of victory where
Great Bo Daw sits enthroned among the myriad shrines.
Deep in obeisance I incline.

Sun rays fold me round about when cold winds
Whining, mourning, thrusting,
Search and chill. No shield I find
When sad, disconsolate remembrances come crowding.
Here pure, clear waters sound unceasingly.

Dews fall and fill the skies as thick as rain
Gathering, darkening, glooming,
The far off mountain summits breasting,
The whole of heaven's vault to mists of blue is changing.

—AWAY-YAUK-MIN ("The Exiled Noble"), *Mèza-gyaung*

Burmese is spoken by about three-fourths of the population of Burma, or between 20 and 25 million people. It is one of the Tibeto-Burman languages, which constitute a branch of the Sino-Tibetan family. The distinctive Burmese alphabet consists almost entirely of circles or portions of circles used in various combinations. It evolved at a time when writing was generally done on palm leaves, the letters traced by means of a stylus. Thus straight lines were impossible because they would cause the leaf to split. There are forty-two letters in all—thirty-two consonants and ten vowels.

Thai

นาคีมีพิษเพี้ยง สุริโย
เลื้อยบ่ทำเดโช แช่มช้า
พิษน้อยหยิ่งโยโส แมลงป่อง
ชูแต่หางเองค้า อวดอ้างฤทธี

ผลมะเดื่อเมื่อสุกไซร้ มีพรรณ
ภายนอกดูแดงฉาน ชาดบ้าย
ภายในแมลงวัน หนอนบ่อน
เหล่าเช่นชนชาติร้าย นอกนั้นดูงาม

Great indeed is the power of the dragon as the sun,
Yet humbly and slowly it meanders its way shy,
Minuscule indeed is the power of the tiny scorpion,
Yet it swaggers its tail and boasts to the sky.

Ripened figs are pretty and pleasing to the eyes,
Their colors seduce both the sight and palate,
Alas, the cores rot with maggots inside,
For evils are but false fronts and gilded waste.

—Old Thai Verses

Thai is spoken by over 85 percent of the population of Thailand, or about 35 million people. It is a member of the Sino-Tibetan family of languages, which means that it is distantly related to Chinese. It is closer, however, to Lao, spoken in Laos, and to the Shan language of northern Burma. Like Chinese, Thai is a tonal language, meaning that different tones, or intonations, distinguish words that would otherwise be homonyms.

The origin of the Thai alphabet is obscure, but it is believed to have had its origin in southern India. It consists of forty-four consonants and thirty-two vowels, the latter consisting not of an individual letter, but of a mark written above, below, before, or after the consonant with which it is pronounced. Of the five tones, four are indicated by signs over the consonants, the absence of a sign indicating that the fifth tone is to be used. Words are not separated from each other and the letters generally flow uninterruptedly until the idea changes.

Malay

Maka ada-lah kira-kira sa-puloh minit lama-nya, maka mělětup-lah ubat bědil itu saperti bunyi pětir; maka těrbongkar-lah batu kota itu sa-běsar-běsar rumah, dan ada yang sa-běsar gajah, bětěrbangan ka-dalam laut; maka ada batu yang těrbang sampai ka-saběrang dan měngěnaï rumah-rumah. Maka těrkějut-lah orang sěmua-nya sěbab měněngar bunyi-nya itu, sěrta děngan běsar-běsar hairan, sěbab sa-umor hidup měreka itu bělum pěrnah měněngar bunyi yang děmikian, dan sěbab mělihatkan bagaimana běsar kuasa ubat bědil itu, sampai boleh ia měngang-katkan batu sa-běsar-běsar saperti rumah.

In about ten minutes' time the gunpowder exploded, with a noise like a clap of thunder. The masonry of the fort went up, in great masses the size of houses. Some pieces, as big as elephants, were hurled into the sea, others flew across the river and struck some houses on the other side. Everybody was thunderstruck by the noise, and amazed, because in all their lives they had never heard anything like it, and because they saw how great was the power of gunpowder, that it could lift rocks as big as houses.

—ABDULLAH BIN ABDULKADIR,
Hikayat Abdullah (autobiography)

Malay is spoken principally in Malaysia and, to a lesser extent, in neighboring Thailand and Singapore. Before 1945 its speakers extended through much of the Indonesian archipelago, but with the establishment of the Republic of Indonesia the Malay of that country was designated Indonesian. In Malaysia it is the mother tongue of about 6 million people, or about half the total population. Speakers in Thailand number one million, in Singapore 250,000.

Malay is a member of the Malayo-Polynesian family of languages. Beginning in the 14th century, with the conversion of many Malays to Islam, a variation of the Arabic script known as Jawi was used for writing. In the 19th century the British constructed a Roman-based alphabet that is in general use today. It differs slightly from the one used in Indonesia, which was developed by the Dutch, but the resulting variations in spelling are in fact the only difference between the two languages. A few examples of these differences may be found in the article on Indonesian.

Grammatical concepts in Malay differ radically from those in Western languages. Prefixes and suffixes as we use them are virtually absent, their functions being assumed by additional words. The plural of a noun is most commonly indicated by simply saying it twice, as in *rumah-rumah* in the above passage, which means "houses." After numbers, however, the noun reverts to the singular and an additional word is added, similar to the English construction "seven head of cattle." Malay has many of these "numerical coefficients"—one for people (*orang*—man), one for animals (*ekor*—tail), and others for flowers, jewels, threads, and even fishing nets. "Two cats" in Malay is *dua ekor kuching* ("two-tail-cat"), while "two children" is *budak dua orang* ("child-two-man").

Malay contains many words of Sanskrit and Arabic origin. English words of Malay origin include *orangutan, gingham*, *sarong*, *bamboo*, *rattan*, *kapok*, *paddy*, and *amok*.

Lao

ໂອ້ດວງຈຳປາ ເວລາຊົມນ້ອງ ນຶກເຫັນພັນຊ່ອງ
ນອງເຫັນຫົວໃຈ ເຮົານຶກຂຶ້ນໄດ້ ໃນກິ່ນເຈົ້າຫອມ
ເຫັນສວນດອກໄມ້ ບິດາປູກໄວ້ ຕັ້ງແຕ່ບານມາ
ເວລາງ່ອນເຫງົາ ເຈົ້າຊ່ວຍບັນເທົາ ເຮົາຫາຍໂສກາ
ເຈົ້າດວງຈຳປາ ຄູ່ຄຽງເຮົາມາ ແຕ່ຍາມນ້ອຍເອີຍ

ກິ່ນເຈົ້າສຳຄັນ ຕິດພັນຫົວໃຈ ເປັນຫນ້າຮັກໃຄ່
ແພງໄວ້ເຊີຍຊົມ ຍາມເຫງົາເຮົາດົມ ໂອ້ຈຳປາຫອມ
ເມື່ອດົມກິ່ນເຈົ້າ ປານພົບຊູ້ເກົ່າ ທີ່ພາກຈາກໄປ
ເຈົ້າເປັນດອກໄມ້ ທີ່ງາມວິໄລ ຕັ້ງແຕ່ໃດມາ
ເຈົ້າດວງຈຳປ່າ ມາລາຂວັນຮັກ ຂອງຮຽມນີ້ເອີຍ.

Oh Champa! When I sense your fragrance, a thousand memories stir in my heart.
Your sweet scent reminds me of the garden of my father.
And I recall all my dreams, all my melancholy, and all my childhood joys.
Champa, you are for me the flower of my childhood.

Your perfume awakens in me delightful memories.
When I inhale your fragrance I seem to recall in my heart
My beloved whom I have lost.
Champa, the most beautiful flower of Laos, you are for me the flower of my love.

—*Champa, Flower of Laos*

Lao is the official language of the Kingdom of Laos. Like Thai, to which it is closely related, it is a member of the Tai subgroup of the Sino-Tibetan family of languages. Lao is spoken by about $2\frac{1}{2}$ million people. Its script was adopted from that of the Mons, the earliest civilized people of Burma. It contains forty-five consonants, but only about half of these signs represent pure consonantal sounds, the others being merely tonal indications.

Khmer

ចំណោទកំសាន្ត

បងប្អូន ៣នាក់ ចង់ចែកគ្នា នូវដបចំនួន ២៤, ក្នុងចំណោមដបទាំងអស់នេះ មានដបធំចំនួន ១២– ដបតូចពាក់កណ្ដាលចំនួន១២ដែរ ។ ក្នុងចំណោមដបធំទាំង១២ មាន៧ដាក់ស្រាពេញ មាន៥គ្មានស្រាទេ ។ ក្នុងចំណោមដបតូច១២មាន៧ដាក់ស្រាពេញ មាន៥គ្មានស្រាដែរ ។ តើត្រូវចែករបៀបណា ដើម្បីឲ្យម្នាក់ៗ បានចំនួនដបទាំងធំទាំងតូចស្មើគ្នា ហើយចំនួនស្រាក៏ឲ្យបានស្មើគ្នាដែរ ដោយឥតចាក់ស្រាចេញពីដបមកចែកទេ ?

A CAMBODIAN RIDDLE

Three brothers wish to divide twenty-four bottles amongst themselves. Of the twenty-four bottles, twelve are large and twelve are small. Of the twelve large bottles, seven are filled with alcohol and five are empty. Of the twelve small bottles, seven are filled with alcohol and five are empty. The question is: How should the three brothers divide up the bottles in such a way that each obtains the same number of large and small bottles?

Khmer is the national language of Cambodia. It is spoken by over 6 million people there, or about 85 percent of the population. There are also some 750,000 speakers in Vietnam and Thailand.

Khmer is the most important member of the Mon-Khmer family of languages. The Khmers were once a powerful people who dominated much of Southeast Asia from the 9th through the 12th century. Their alphabet, like most of those of the area, had its ultimate origin in southern India.

Vietnamese

Đầy vườn cỏ mọc lau thưa,
Song trăng quạnh-quẽ, vách mưa rã-rời.
Trước sau nào thấy bóng người,
Hoa đào năm ngoái còn cười gió đông.
Xập-xè én liệng lầu không,
Cỏ lan mặt đất, rêu phong dấu giầy.
Cuối tường gai góc mọc đầy,
Đi về nẩy những lối này năm xưa.

The grass had grown all over the garden. Here and there reeds raised their slender stalks.
At the window from which she used to contemplate the room there was no one. The outer walls, beaten by the rain, had lost their paint.
Neither behind nor before was there trace of a living soul.
Yet a flowering peach branch, sole witness of the past, still smiled at the eastern breeze.
In the empty buildings the swallows fluttered.
The grass had grown up everywhere, the footprints were covered with moss.
The corners of the walls were overgrown with brambles and thorns.
This was the road which he traversed in days gone by.

—*Kim-Van-Kieu*

Vietnamese is spoken in both North and South Vietnam by about 35 million people. Its linguistic affiliation is uncertain, and though it is sometimes thought to be distantly related to Chinese, this remains to be proven. Like Chinese, Vietnamese is a tonal language and it has borrowed nearly half of its vocabulary from the Chinese.

The Vietnamese alphabet was devised in the 17th century by Catholic missionaries. It contains a complex system of diacritical marks, some distinguishing certain vowel sounds, others indicating tone. As can be seen in the few lines above, a letter may often contain two diacritical marks.

Kim-Van-Kieu is the Vietnamese national poem. Written by Nguyen Du (1765–1820), it contains a total of 3,254 lines, of which only eight are cited above.

Indonesian

Setiap kita bertemu, gadis ketjil berkaleng ketjil
Senjummu terlalu kekal untuk kenal duka
Tengadah padaku, pada bulan merah djambu
Tapi kotaku djadi hilang, tanpa djiwa

Ingin aku ikut, gadis ketjil berkaleng ketjil
Pulang kebawah djembatan jang melulur sosok
Hidup dari kehidupan angan-angan jang gemerlapan
Gembira dari kemajaan riang

Duniamu jang lebih tinggi dari menara katedral
Melintas-lintas diatas air kotor, tapi jang begitu kauhafal
Djiwa begitu murni, terlalu murni
Untuk bisa membagi dukaku

Kalau kau mati, gadis ketjil berkaleng ketjil
Bulan diatas itu, tak ada jang punja
Dan kotaku, ah kotaku
Hidupnja tak lagi punja tanda.

Every time we meet, little girl with your begging bowl,
Your smile is too eternal to know sorrow,
You look up at me, at the light red moon,
But my city has disappeared, soulless.

I want to go with you, little girl with your begging bowl
To your home, under the bridge, which expunges every shape,
To live from the life of radiant fantasies,
To be gay in the illusion of happiness.

Your world that is higher than the cathedral spire
Flashes past on the dirty water, but you know it by heart,
Your soul is so pure—far too pure
To share my sorrow.

If you die, little girl with the begging bowl,
Then the moon up there will no longer have an owner,
And my city, ah, my city
Will live on without a beacon.

—TOTO SUDARTO BACHTIAR, *The Beggar Girl*

Indonesian is the national language of the Republic of Indonesia. When independence was declared in 1945, *bahasa Indonesia* ("Indonesian language") was decreed as the country's official language. Although it is the mother tongue of only about 12 million people out of a population of 125 million, it is estimated that as much as three-fourths of the population now understand it.

Indonesian is virtually the same language as Malay, the latter spoken in Malaysia. The principal difference is in the spelling, the Indonesian system having been developed by the Dutch, the Malay by the British. Thus the Indonesian *j* is *y* in Malay (*e.g.*, *kaju*—wood, Malay: *kayu*); Indonesian *dj* is *j* in Malay (*gadjah*—elephant, Malay: *gajah*); Indonesian *tj* is *ch* in Malay (*kutjing*—cat, Malay: *kuching*); and Indonesian *sj* is *sh* in Malay (*sjarat*—condition, Malay: *sharat*). The Indonesian plural, like the Malay, is formed by merely repeating the word, as in *angan-angan* in the poem above, which means "fantasies."

Javanese

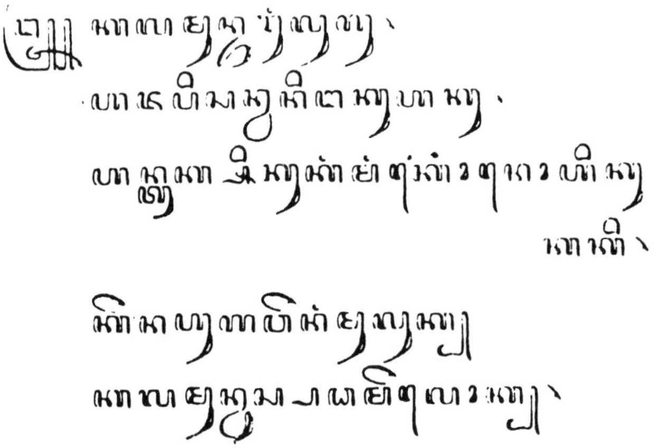

Kulamun durung lugu
Aja pisan dadi ngaku-aku
Antuk siku kang mangkono iku kaki
Kena uga wenang muluk
Kalamun wus pada melok

If you do not understand all these teachings perfectly, do not presume to boast of possessing the knowledge they contain. He who does shall incur wrath, my friend. For only he who has first mastered them completely has the right to consider them his own.

Javanese is spoken in the central and eastern parts of Java, the most populous island of the Republic of Indonesia. A member of the Malayo-Polynesian family, it has about 45 million speakers. The traditional Javanese script is of ancient origin, having been brought to Java from southern India more than a thousand years ago. The passage above appears first in the Javanese, then in the Roman script to which it is gradually yielding ground.

Sundanese

Dumadakan aja angin ribut katjida di laut, nepi ka ombak-ombak ngarungkup kana parahuo. Tidinja murid-murid njalampeurkeun, seug Andjeunna digugahkeun, bari undjukan: Aduh Gusti, mugi tulungan, abdi tiwas! Dawuhana Na ka maranèhna: Naha maranèh sarieum, èh nu leutik kapertjajaan? Geus kitu tuluj gugah, sarta njeuseul ka èta angin djeung kana laut, djep djèmpe-rèhè pisan Ari èta djelema pada hèraneun, sarta ngaromong kieu: Na ieu tèh djelema naon, nepi ka angin djeung laut gè narurut ka Andjeunna!

Behold, a great storm arose on the sea, so that the boat was being swamped by the waves, but he was asleep. They went and woke him, saying: "Save us, we are perishing!" He said to them: "Why are you afraid, you faithless ones?" Then he went and rebuked the sea, and there was a great calm. The men marveled, saying: "What sort of man is this, that even the wind and the sea obey him?"

Sundanese is one of the major languages of Indonesia, spoken in western Java by about 13 million people. It is a member of the Indonesian branch of the Malayo-Polynesian family of languages. Sundanese is written in both the Javanese script and the Roman alphabet shown above.

Madurese

E dimma bhḁi bḁḍḁ bengko se elebbhoenana dhibiqna, ngotjaq dhilloe bḁrijḁ: paḍḁ salamet sabhḁlḁ bengko areja. Lamon e dissa bḁḍḁ anaq salamet, tanto katebhḁnan salamma dhibiqna, nangeng lamon taḍḁg, salamma dhibiqna abḁlijḁ pole ka dhibiqna. Monḍhoek e bengko djḁroewa, ngakan bḁn ngenom sabhḁrḁng apa se esoghoewaghi biq oreng djḁroewa, karana oreng se alako patot olle opa, addjhḁq le-ngalle pamondhoeghḁn.

When you enter a house, say first: "Peace be on this house." And if a peaceful person is present there, your peace shall rest upon him; but if not, it shall return to you. Remain in the same house, eating and drinking whatever is given to you, do not go from house to house.

Madurese is spoken on the small island of Madura, lying adjacent to Java, as well as that part of eastern Java which faces Madura. Like Sundanese, it was traditionally written in the Javanese script but recently the Roman alphabet has come into use. Madurese is another of the Malayo-Polynesian languages. There are about 8 million speakers.

Buginese

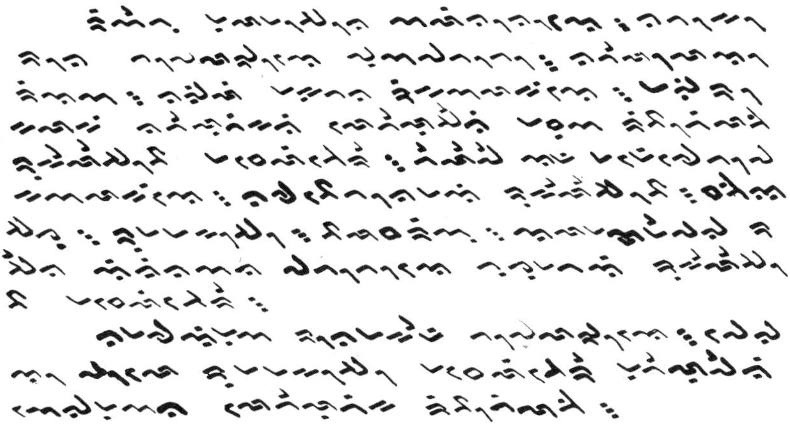

When the sun is shining the Creator, holder of Man's destiny, asks the escort, "Why, oh people, have Rukkelengpoba and his family for three days and three nights left the top of the sky?" Before the escort can answer, Rukkelengpoba, Sangiang padju, Rumamakkompo, Balassariú, immediately appear. The Creator is not pleased when he sees Rukkelengpoba and his family. In an angry voice the Creator asks, "Where hast thou been, oh Rumamakkompo and thy family? For three nights already thou hast been absent from the top of the sky."

—*Galigo* (Buginese mythology)

Buginese is spoken on the island of Celebes, Indonesia. There are about 2½ million speakers, living mainly on the southwestern peninsula. The Buginese alphabet is believed to have had its origin in Java. Like the other languages of Indonesia, Buginese is of the Malayo-Polynesian family.

Batak

When they got back to their village Adji Panurat stole away to the jungle; he is afraid to see his younger brother. Adji Pamasa told his balbal [spirit that can beat up people or other things] to head him off. "When you meet him drive him home. If he doesn't want to, hit him over the head but don't kill him, so be it," said Adji Pamasa. The balbal went to head (Adji Panurat) off. He met Adji Panurat. He led him (toward the house). He refused. Therefore he hit him over the head. Adji Panurat saw stars in front of him. Therefore he consented to go home.

Batak is spoken on Sumatra, the westernmost of the major islands of Indonesia. There are about $1\frac{1}{2}$ million speakers, living mainly in the north-central part of the island, but also scattered along the eastern coast. The distinctive Batak alphabet consists of sixteen basic characters, each of which may be modified by the use of certain marks. It is rapidly disappearing in favor of the Roman alphabet, and relatively few people remain today who are able to read it. Batak belongs to the Malayo-Polynesian family of languages.

Pidgin English

Long Muglim klostu long Mount Hagen planti man i belhat tru. As bilong trabel em i man Kei na Ruri na Maga Nugints—tripela i bin trikim moa olsem 1000 man. Ol i tok ol man hia i mas tromoim $10 inap long $100 bilong baim sampela retpela kes. Samting olsem 300 retpela kes ol i bin haitim insait long wanpela haus. Ol i makim de bilong opim sampela kes na soim ol man ol kes hia i mas pulap long mani. Ol i opim sampela bek na 5-pela bokis hia na ol ston tasol na sampela nil i kapsait i kam daun. Ol man i lukim, ol sampela i lap na narapela gen i belhat.

At Muglim near Mt. Hagen there are many very angry people. The reason for this is that three men—Kei, Ruri, and Maga Nugints—tricked more than 1,000 people. They told the people they had to buy red wooden suitcases, which cost from $10 to $100 apiece. They then hid approximately 300 such boxes inside a house. They set a date when they would publicly open the boxes and show the people that they were now full of money. They did open five sacks and five of the boxes but only some stones and nails fell to the ground. Some of those who saw this laughed and others got very angry.

Pidgin English exists in a number of varieties, but the most important is Melanesian Pidgin of eastern New Guinea and other nearby islands. It is spoken and understood, with varying degrees of proficiency, by an estimated 300–400,000 people and the number is increasing rapidly. As the indispensable lingua franca of the area, it has been given official status in the country now known as Papua New Guinea.

A pidgin language is generally based on one of the major world languages, such as English, Spanish, or Portuguese. Arising out of commercial activities, it contains a sharply reduced grammar and vocabulary, making it much easier to learn than the parent tongue.

Melanesian Pidgin, which appears in the text above, has a vocabulary of about 1,500 words. Many others are curious compounds, such as *haus kuk* ("house cook"), meaning "kitchen"; *haus sik* ("house sick"), meaning "hospital"; and *haus pepa* ("house paper"), meaning "office." The common word *bilong* (from "belong"), which simply means "of," appears in *glas bilong lukluk* ("glass belong look-look"), meaning "mirror"; *smok bilong graun* ("smoke belong ground"), meaning "dust"; *lait bilong klaut* ("light belong cloud"), meaning "lightning"; and *man bilong longwe ples* ("man belong long-way place"), meaning "foreigner." The ubiquitous suffix *-pela* (from "fellow") appears in the plural of personal pronouns (*e.g.*, *mi*—I, *mipela*—we), in numerals up to 12 (*wanpela*—one, *tupela*—two), in one-syllable adjectives (*bikpela*—big, *gutpela*—good), and in some other common words (*dispela*—this, *sampela*—some).

Tagalog

Hagurin ng tanaw ang ating palibot:
taniman, gawaan, lansangan, bantayog,
lupa, dagat, langit ay pawang sinakop,
at kamay ng tao ang nagpapakilos.

Ang mga kamay ko'y binihasang sadya
sa kakaharaping gawai't dalita;
pangit ang daliring humabi ng sutla,
tumuklas ng ginto'y kamay ng paggawa.

Habang ang kamay mo o aking Pagibig,
kambal na bulaklak—mabango, malinis;
kung may sakit ako o nasa panganib,
dantay ng kamay mo ay isa nang langit.

Nguni't tingnan yaong kamay ng Orasan,
may itinuturo't waring nagsasaysay:
"Tao, kayong lahat ay may katapusan
na itatadhana nitong aking kamay!"

Observe carefully our world:
fields, factories, streets, statues,
earth, sea, sky have been dominated
by the hands of men, which can move mountains.

I too trained my hands for expert work,
to prepare for the hard days ahead;
how ugly my words woven in silk,
compared to the hands of the worker mining gold.

My hands, oh dearest love, were
like flowers, clean and fragrant;
and when I am ill or in danger,
the touch of your hand is healing balm.

And all the while the hands of the clock,
point to the prophetic mouth:
"Man, all of you will meet the end
decreed by this—time's hand."

—AMADO V. HERNANDEZ, *The Hand*

Tagalog, with the stress on the second syllable, is the national language of the Philippines. In 1962 it was made the country's official language and given the new name of Pilipino. Tagalog is the mother tongue of about 10 million people, most of whom live in southern Luzon in an area that includes Manila. Its study has been strongly encouraged by the government and it is estimated that over 75 percent of the population at least understands the language.

Tagalog is a member of the Malayo-Polynesian family of languages. The three centuries of Spanish rule in the Philippines left a strong imprint on the vocabulary. *Mesa* (table), *tenedor* (fork), *papel* (paper), and *asero* (steel) are only a few of hundreds of Spanish words in Tagalog.

Visayan

May usa ka magtiayon dugay nang katuigan nga nangagi nga may usa ka anak nga lalaki nga ilang ginganlan si Juan. Sa nagatubo si Juan, nalipay usab ang iyang mga ginikanan uban ang pagtuo nga aduna na silay ikatabang sa panimalay. Labi na ang amahan nalipay gayud pag-ayo tungod kay duna na man siyay ikatabang sa pagpangahoy nga maoy iyang pangita alang sa panginabuhi sa matag adlaw.

Many years ago there was a couple who had a son whom they named John. As John grew up, his parents were happy, believing that now they would have help in the household. The father especially was very happy because now he would have help in gathering firewood which was the means by which he earned his living from day to day.

Visayan, with the stress on the second syllable, is a collective term for three closely related yet distinctly different languages spoken mainly on the middle islands of the Philippine archipelago. The three languages are (1) Cebuano, spoken by about 8 million people on Cebu, Bohol, eastern Negros, western Leyte, and northern Mindanao; (2) Hiligaynon, spoken by 3 million people on Panay and western Negros; (3) Samaran, spoken by $1\frac{1}{2}$ million people on Samar and eastern Leyte. The above passage is in Cebuano. Like Tagalog, the Visayan languages are of the Malayo-Polynesian family.

LANGUAGES OF OCEANIA

Maori

Ki a au nei e rua tahi ngaa waahine o teenei ao, araa ko te wahine tangata nei, na, ko te wahine oneone. E rua eenei mea, e rite tahi ana, te wahine, te whenua. Ma te wahine ka tupu ai te hanga nei, te tangata, ma te whenua ka whai oranga ai. Ki te tangohia too whenua e te iwi kee, ka ngau te poouri ki roto i a koe; naa, ki te tangohia too wahine e te tangata kee, ka tupu hoki ko taua poouri anoo. Ko ngaa puutake nunui eenaa o te whawhai. Koia i kiia ai, "He wahine, he whenua i ngaro ai te tangata."

To me there are two kinds of female in this world, human women, and land. These things are two, yet they are equal, women, and land. Women bring forth children, and the land sustains them. If your land is taken by strangers, you are consumed with anger, if your wife is taken by a stranger you feel that same anger. These are the two great causes of strife. Hence it is said, "By women and land were men destroyed."

The Maori are the native inhabitants of New Zealand. Historically they are a Polynesian people whose original home was Tahiti. Their migration halfway across the Pacific Ocean is believed to have occurred in successive waves, the last and greatest taking place in the middle of the 14th century. Today the Maori number about 200,000, almost all of whom live on North Island. Only about half of them still speak the Maori language, which is slowly giving way to English.

Chamorro

Manhanao mameska ham gi painge yän si Kimio yän si Juan. Manmangone' ham mas de dos sientos libras na guihän. Pues, anai manmunhayan ham mameska gi oran a las dos, nu mandeskansa ham. Despues nai manana guenao gi oran a las siete, humanao ham yän si Kimio para in bende i guihän gi äs Bernado. Despues nai munhayan ma fahan i sisienta libras, humanao ham para Sinajana yä lumiliko' ham manbende sina buente kuarenta libras na guihän.

Kimio, Juan (and I), we went fishing last night. We caught more than two hundred pounds of fish. Then, when we finished fishing at two o'clock, we rested. Then in the morning at six o'clock, Kimio and I went to sell the fish at Bernardo's. Then we finished, they bought sixty pounds, we went to Sinajana and went around selling maybe forty pounds of fish.

Chamorro is spoken on the island of Guam in the western Pacific Ocean. Latest figures show approximately 40,000 speakers of the language out of a total population of 87,000. Chamorro is one of the Micronesian languages, which form a part of the Malayo-Polynesian family. Numerous Spanish words in the vocabulary reflect the three centuries of Spanish rule in Guam.

Marshallese

M̍ahjeł yej tijtiryik yew r&yhar-tahtah yilew Tiraj Teyr&yt&wr&y. Majr&w yej yijew j&yban kiyen yew han M̍ahjeł yim yeleg harm&j jan kajj&wj&w hay&l&g kew yilikin rej j&q&y yi'y&y. Yepjay, yilew hay&l&g yin Kiwajleyen yej jikin yew k&yin kariwew han kiyen yilew hay&l&g yin M̍ahjeł. Harm&j r&yin yewen Yepjay rej jerbal yilew Kiwajleyen, jikin kekkeylaq miyjeł han rittarin̍ahyey yin Hamedkah. Pikinniy yim Yan&ywey-tak rej yijekew Hamedkah yehar teyej baham̍ yi'y&y.

The Marshalls District is the easternmost of the Trust Territory of the Pacific Islands. Majuro is the capital, and many people from the outer islands live there. Ebeye on Kwajalein Atoll is the subcapital of the Marshalls. The people on Ebeye work at Kwajalein, the missile testing range of the American military. Bikini and Eniwetok are the atolls where America tested bombs.

Marshallese is spoken in the Marshall Islands, which lie north of the equator and just to the west of the International Date Line. It is one of the Micronesian languages, which form a branch of the Malayo-Polynesian family. The alphabet includes an ampersand (&), which represents a vowel sound somewhere between *e* and *i*, as well as seven special consonants: *m̍*, *n̍*, *ł*, *g̎*, *n̎*, *l̎*, and *r̎*. There are about 20,000 speakers.

Fijian

Na gauna e dau qolivi kina na kanace e na mataka lailai sara, ni sā bera ni cadra na mata ni siga. E na gauna oqō era moce tū kina. Ni ra sā moce tū, era qeleni sara vakalewelevu, ia na gauna sā katakata mai kina na mata ni siga era sā dui veilakoyaki. E na gauna sā via yakavi kina na vanua era sota tale ki na vanua era via lakova, me ra laki moce kina.

The time to catch mullet is in the very early morning before the sun appears. At that time the fish are asleep. While they are asleep they lie close together in large numbers, but when the sun becomes hot they disperse. When the evening draws in, they assemble again in the spot they visit, to go to sleep there.

Fijian is the indigenous language of newly independent Fiji in the central Pacific Ocean. It is spoken by about 200,000 people, or about 40 percent of the population. Fijian is one of the Melanesian languages, which form a subgroup of the Malayo-Polynesian family. The alphabet lacks the letters *h*, *x*, and *z*, while the letters *f*, *j*, and *p* appear only in foreign words. The letter *b* is pronounced *mb*, *d* is pronounced *nd*, *g* is *ng* as in "sing," and *q* is pronounced *ng* as in "finger." A line over a vowel lengthens its sound.

Samoan

E i ai le fale o le tagata Samoa i totonu o le nu'u, ae peita'i o ana fa'ato'aga e masani ona i ai i le maila po'o le sili atu i uta. Na te tōtō i ana fa'ato'aga ana mea'ai, taro, fa'i, ma 'ulu; na te tōtō fo'i niu mo popo, ma koko. O nei mea na te fa'atau atu i le fai'oloa i totonu o le nu'u po'o i Apia. Mai tupe ua maua na te fa'atau ai pisupo ma apa i'a, ma 'ie mo ona lavalava atoa ma lavalava o lona aiga.

A Samoan has his house in the village, but his plantations are often a mile or more inland. In his plantation he grows his foodstuffs, taro, bananas, and breadfruit; he also grows coconuts for copra, and cocoa. These things he sells to the merchants in the village or in Apia. With the money received he buys tinned meat and tinned fish, and materials for clothes for himself and his family.

Samoan is spoken by about 125,000 people in Western Samoa (an independent island state) and by 25,000 in American Samoa (a U.S. territory) in the South Pacific Ocean. It is a member of the Polynesian branch of the Malayo-Polynesian family of languages. The Samoan alphabet contains only fourteen letters—the five vowels plus the consonants *f*, *g*, *l*, *m*, *n*, *p*, *s*, *t*, and *v*. The letters *h*, *k*, and *r* appear only in words of foreign origin, while *b*, *c*, *d*, *j*, *q*, *w*, *x*, *y*, and *z* are missing entirely. The sign ' represents a break or hesitation between two vowels (*e.g.*, *la'au*—tree, *fa'i*—banana).

Many Samoan words are simple compounds. *Fale* (building) + *oloa* (goods) = *faleoloa* (store), while *vai* (water) + *tafe* (to flow) = *vaitafe* (river). English has contributed innumerable new words such as *taimi* (time), *apu* (apple), *aisa* (ice), *loia* (lawyer), *kolisi* (college), and *niusipepa* (newspaper).

Tahitian

Teie te ravea no to te feia Tahiti taioraa i te mau "mahana" i tahito ra, mai te tahi aahiata te taioraa e tae noa'tu i te tahi. Te taio ra hoi ratou i te mau pô o tei ohie hoi i te faataa no te mea ua huru ê te marama i te tahi arui i to te tahi, e to'na vairaa i nia i te ra'i, e mea ê atoa ïa. Te mau mahana râ, ua huru â te huru, aore hoi te râ e huru ê, e aore hoi to'na vairaa ê i nia i te ra'i tera mahana e tera mahana, (e mea ê rii roa'e, eiaha i te rahi). No reira, te haapao ra te maohi i te pô ei faataaraa taime; ua topa hoi ratou i te i'oa i nia i te pô hoe ra. E 28 (piti ahuru ma vau) "auri" ta te ava'e hoe i taua anotau ra, e te mairihia ra te i'oa o taua maororaa taime ra: e marama.

This is how the ancient Tahitians counted the "days" from one daybreak to the next. They counted the nights instead, which were easy to distinguish from each other, the moon never being the same shape or in the same place two nights in a row. The days were all alike, with the sun always the same shape and in the same place (approximately). That is why the natives arranged their life by the nights to which they had given names. The month had 28 "nights," the period being called a "moon."

Tahitian is the indigenous language of Tahiti, one of the Society Islands located in the South Pacific Ocean. It is a Polynesian language with about 50,000 speakers. The alphabet contains only thirteen letters—the five vowels plus the consonants *f*, *h*, *m*, *n*, *p*, *r*, *t*, and *v*. The English word *tattoo* is of Tahitian origin.

Tongan

Ko te taupoou ko Hina, pea na feongoaki mo te manaia ko Sinilau, pea faifai tena feongoaki kua ka la kei manofo ia Hina kua tokanga kia Sinilau. Pea hau leva i te aho e taha o too mai tona kiefau o vala, pea too mai leva mo tona kafakula o fau; pea alu atu leva mo te vaa-akau o hopo ki tai, o kaukau; o tau leva ki te fenua o Sinilau.

There was a virgin named Hina, and she and the handsome man Sinilau heard reports of one another, and as time went on and they continually heard one another's praises, Hina could rest no longer, because of her thoughts of Sinilau. So one day she clothed herself with her fine mat, and took her necklace and put it on, and she went with a pole and leaped into the sea, and swam, and came to the land of Sinilau.

Tongan is spoken in the Tonga Islands, a kingdom in the South Pacific Ocean just west of the International Date Line. Another of the Polynesian languages, it has about 75,000 speakers. The English word *taboo* is of Tongan origin.

LANGUAGES OF THE WESTERN HEMISPHERE

Hawaiian

AKA AME KA MANO

O Aka he menehune uuku momona.
I kekahi la ua luu o Aka,
Ua nahu ka mano i kona manamana wawae nui.
Alaila ua huhu loa ka mano,
No ka mea ua pololi loa oia.

Ua huhu pu no ka menehune,
No ka mea he hoaloha o Aka no lakou.
Nolaila hana lakou i hinai koali,
A ua hoopiha ia me ka maunu.

Me keia ua paa ia lakou ka mano.
Ua huki ia iluna o ke one e make.
Ua hoike mai na iwi keokeo
"Mai hoopa i ka menehune."

AKA AND THE SHARK

Aka was a fat little men-e-hu-ne.
One day when Aka was diving,
A shark bit off his big toe.
Then the shark was very angry,
Because he was very hungry.

The menehunes were also very angry,
Because they were Aka's friends.
So they made a basket of bindweed
And filled it with bait.

In this they captured the shark,
Pulled him up onto the sand to die.
His bleached bones warned other sharks,
"Do not touch a menehune."

Hawaiian, the indigenous language of the Hawaiian Islands, is steadily losing ground to the all-pervasive influence of English. It is estimated that at present only 7,500 people—about one percent of the Islands' population—are still fluent in Hawaiian. On one island, Niihau, a few hundred speakers are kept out of contact with the outside world, and it is probably only here that pure Hawaiian is spoken. Elsewhere the language has been strongly influenced by English. Conversely, local English speech contains many Hawaiian words.

Hawaiian is a Polynesian language, brought from the Society Islands, 2,500 miles to the south, between the 2nd and the 8th centuries. It is considered one of the most musical in the world, containing only the five vowels and seven consonants—*h, k, l, m, n, p*, and *w*. The paucity of consonants, plus the fact that every Hawaiian syllable and word ends in a vowel, produces curious renditions of certain English expressions, such as the Hawaiian equivalent of "Merry Christmas," *Mele Kelikimaka*. Perhaps the best known Hawaiian word is *aloha*, meaning "love" or "affection," but also used both for "hello" and "good-bye." *Ukulele* is also a Hawaiian word, as are *hula, lei, luau*, and *poi*.

Eskimo

niviarsiarqat mardluk mêránguanik amârdlutik narssákut ingerdláput. ingerdlaniardlutik iterssarssuarmut nákarput. sunauvfa tássanĩtoq inupilorujugssuaq. táussumarssûp amâgángue nerivai, niviarsiarqatdlo oqarfigalugit aqagumut neriumâramigit.

kisiáne niviarsiarqat inorujugssuaq arajutsisârdlugo qimãput angerdlardlutigdlo. oqalugtuarmatalo ilaisa inupilorujugssuaq sorssugkiartorpât.

angutit ilât iterssarssuarmut arqarpoq agdlunâmik nagsardlune. táussumínga inorujugssuaq terdlinganit singerneragut qilerpâ. ilaisalo qulânît amôrpât toqutdlardlugulo.

Two girls carrying small babies in back-pouches were walking over a plain. On their way they tumbled into a large cave. In it there was a really huge ogre. This bad fellow ate their small babies and told the girls that he would surely eat them the next day.

But the girls fled without the ogre noticing it and went home. And when they told their story their relatives set out to fight the ogre.

One of them went down into the big cave carrying a rope with him. He stole up on the ogre and tied the rope around its instep. And from above his fellows pulled the ogre up and killed it.

Eskimo is spoken over a vast area extending from Greenland across Canada and Alaska, and into Siberia. Speakers in Greenland number 40–45,000, in Alaska 25,000, and in Canada 15,000. In the Soviet Union about 1,000 Eskimos live in northeasternmost Siberia, in the area nearest the Bering Strait.

Considering this vast territory, it is remarkable that there are only two major dialects of Eskimo, and that one of them, known as Inupik, is spoken almost uniformly across Greenland, Canada, and northern Alaska. But at an imaginary line running east-west across central Alaska there is an abrupt change: Eskimos living south of this line speak a dialect, known as Yupik, that is completely unintelligible to

Inupik speakers. The line reaches Norton Sound on the west coast between the towns of Unalakleet, where Inupik is spoken, and St. Michael, which is Yupik-speaking. Yupik, or variations thereof, is also spoken in Siberia.

The only language known to be related to Eskimo is the Aleut language of the Aleutian Islands. The two are not mutually intelligible, but there are sufficient similarities to indicate that they were a single language several thousand years ago. Together they form the Eskimo-Aleut family.

The Eskimos call themselves *inuit*, or "people." The word Eskimo comes from the language of the Cree Indians—their immediate neighbors to the south in the area of Hudson Bay—and means "eaters of raw flesh." *Igloo* and *kayak* are two Eskimo words that have entered the English language. In Eskimo they simply mean "house" and "boat" respectively.

The writing of Eskimo dates back as far as 1721 when the Roman alphabet was introduced into Greenland. In 1937 the Soviet government developed a Cyrillic-based alphabet for the use of Russia's 1,000 Eskimos.

Aleut

Ag̔ánan, ag̔ánan, tánan a̔kúya, a̔kúya,
Wákun qayáxtalkinín ag̔anágan
Cuqígan tamadág̔in, tamadág̔in
Ayágag̔ílik taĭyág̔ug̔ílik;
Ag̔ánan, ag̔ánan, tánan a̔kúya, a̔kúya,
Wákun ayagángin, wákun taĭyág̔ungin
Ásik kukíming álulik a̔ladaqalidáqing
Tág̔a axtagalíkumán,
Tutaqangúluk tutálik wángun sag̔álik ulálik ulalíting.

These countries are created, created.
There are hills on them.
There are little hills on each of them, each of them.
There are women, there are men.
These countries are created, created.
On them are women, on them are men.
With me they laughed and joked.
And so when we separated [they did the same]
I have not heard [such things] as if in a sleep
I heard or felt pleasure.

Aleut is spoken by about 1,000 people in the Aleutian Islands and by some one hundred more on the Commander Islands, which belong to the Soviet Union. It is related to Eskimo but only distantly, the two languages being in no way mutually intelligible. The first alphabet for the Aleut language was developed by a Russian missionary about 1825 and was based on the Cyrillic alphabet. Although the islands passed with Alaska to the United States in 1867, the Roman alphabet was not introduced until the 20th century.

Tlingit

Athapaskan tóo-nux̲ uyúh kawsi.àh hah Lingít k̲oostèeyee. Lingít tlàgoo tóo-x' uyúh yéi kudoonéek, yúh hah shugóon súkw, àn g̲uluk̲óo yéig̲ah, àg̲ah uwéh dak̲-x' hus woolilàh. Yáh yeedút dlèit k̲ách Arctic Circle yéi yuságoo yei-x' uwéh hus woolilàh. Dlèit k̲áh k̲oonujéeyee, hús uwéh yéi's kawjixít, hah shugóon súkw nakée, t'éex' kàh-nux̲, yáh-nux̲ yun hus oowu.át. Yúh sh-kulnèek k̲o.àh tléil uwooyàh. Doo toondutánee k̲oodziteeyee k̲áh tléil yúh áh k̲oosu.at'ee yéi-dei doo yútx'ee tèen goog̲u.àt, k̲uh yun dug̲awútx'ee tèen, ch'uh yúh t'éex' kàh-nux̲ yun hus g̲wa.àdit. Tléil tsoo hus uh wooskóh t'éex' áh yéi tèeyee. K̲oosu.át'ee yéh uyóo yóo nakée; tléil dah súh áh koo.éix̲; tsoo ut woo.àdee útx'ee sánee tsóo tléil áh yéi ootíh. Tléil tsoo áh yéi k̲ootée. Tákw-x' tlukw k̲ookooshgítch. Wooch g̲oowunádei k̲ah utx̲àyee tsóo tléil áh yéi ootíh. Tléil uh t'éi-t uh yux̲doowuhanee út k̲oostíh. Yát'ah tléil yéi x̲'awdután uyúh, tléil àdei út koowoog̲agoowoo yéh. Adei k̲o.àh shukdéi k̲oogoox̲lus'ées. Yéi ut kuwoo.àk̲w àdei uh n'g̲u.àdee, yut'ix'ee út-x̲ k̲ah jèe-x' goox̲sutée.

The Tlingit tribe is one of the Athapascan tribes. It is told in some of the Tlingit legends that during Noah's flood the Athapascan tribe, as the waters subsided, landed in the area of the Arctic Circle. The theory of many writers is that the Athapascans came across the Bering Ice Bridge. This doesn't stand to reason. Why should a family or group of people—men, women, children, and older people—go up North? Just to cross an Ice Bridge that they did not know existed? It was a cold, desolate, uninhabited place, dark during part of the year, without much variety of food and with no protection. This is not to say that a group of people could not land at such a place by accident. But to go there willfully, at great discomfort to the whole group, is not reasonable.

The Tlingit Indians live in the Alaskan Panhandle—in and around the cities of Juneau, Sitka, and Ketchikan, as well as on a number of islands in the Alexander Archipelago. Their language shows a number of similarities with those of the Athapascan family, but its exact linguistic classification remains uncertain. There are about 1,000 speakers.

Cree

ᐚᐤ ᑲᓴᑭᐦᐁᑕᐣ ᓂᑐᑌᒼ
ᐊᐯᓯᐢ ᐁᑳᐧ ᒥᓇ ᑭ ᐃᐧ ᒪᓯᓇᐊᒪᑎᐣ
ᓇᒥᐢᑳᐧ ᑯᑕᐠ ᑭ ᒪᓯᓇᐯᑳᐣ ᓂ ᐊᐧᐸᑎᐣ ᐊᐢᐯᐣ ᑲᑭ
ᒪᓯᓇᐊᒪᑕᐣ ᑕᓀᓯᑐᑭ ᐁᓯ ᐊᔭᔭᐣ ᒪᑖᐧᓀᒋ
ᐣ ᒥᔪᐊᔭᐣ ᒥᑐᓀ ᓂ ᓄᑎᐯᑎᐣ ᑭᔭᐎᐤ ᐅᒋ
ᐁᑳᐧᓀ ᒪᑲ ᐁᐢᑳᐧᔭᒋ- ᑭᑕ ᑕᑯᐸᔨᐠ ᐯᒥᔭᑲᐣ ᐊᓄ-
ᑲᑭᓯᑲᐠ ᐸᑎᒪ ᐁᑳᐧ ᑭ ᐊᑳᐧᑎᑭ ᐁᐊᐧᑯ ᐅᒋ ᑭᓴ-
ᐊᓄ- ᑲᑭᑭᓯᐸᔨᐠ ᑲ ᒪᓯᓇᐁᑭᔭᐣ ᓯᒪᐠ ᑭᑕ
ᓯᐻᑎᓴᐊᒪᐣ. ᓂ ᒥᔪᐊᔭᐣ ᓂᐢᑕ ᒥᑳᐧ-

How! ka sakihāytan nitootem

apāysis āykwu minu ki wi musinuumatin numeskwa kootuk kimusinuāykun niwaputen uspāyn ka ki musinuumatan tanāysitookwe āysi uyayun mutwanāytshi ki miyooayun. mitoonāy ni noote pāyten kiyuwuoo ootshi āykwanāy maku āyskwayatsh kitu tukoopuyik pemiyakun unootsh ka kisikak patima āykwa ke ukwatikih āywukoo ootshi kisatsh unootsh ka kekisepuyik ka musinuāykeyan semak kitu sipwāytisuuman. ni miyooayan nistu mekwatsh.

Greetings, my very dear friend,

I am writing to you again, a little. I have not seen another letter from you since I wrote to you. I am wondering how you are. I wonder if you are in good health. I would really like to hear from you folks. Today's mail-plane will be the last to arrive before the freeze-up; therefore I am writing this letter this morning so that I may send it off immediately. I myself am well at this time.

Cree is one of the major Indian languages of Canada. It is spoken by about 30,000 people in the provinces of Ontario, Manitoba, and Saskatchewan. Cree to this day is written in a system of syllabic symbols introduced by a Protestant missionary in the year 1840. The language belongs to the Algonkian family.

Navajo

Naakidi neeznádiin dóó ba'ąą hastą́diin dóó ba'ąą náhást'éí nááhaiídąą' Naabeehó Yootó dóó kinteel bita' Dinétah hoolyéegi kéédahat'į́į ńt'éé', dóó índa shádi'ááh dóó e'e'aahjigo dadeezná jiní. Ła' t'éiyá Tséyi'jigo adahaazná jiní; náánáła' t'éiyá Mą'ii Deeshgiizh dóó Soodził bine'jį' adahaazná jiní, dóó náánáła' éí Tóntsaajį' adahaazná jiní. Táadi neeznádiin dóó ba'ánígo nááhaiídą́ą' Naabeehó dibé dóó łį́į' bee dahazlį́į' dóó díí naaldlooshii shódayoost'e'go nikidadiibaa' jiní. Naakaii ádaaníigo t'éiyá 165 nááhaiídą́ą' Naabeehó 3500 yilt'éego kéédahat'į́į ńt'éé' —díishjį́įgóó 100,000 yilt'é jiní.

Until about 268 years ago the Navajo lived in an area between Santa Fe and Aztec called *Dinetah,* and after that time they began to move southward and westward. Some moved toward the Canyon de Chelly; others migrated toward Jemez and to Mount Taylor, and still others to Tunicha. More than 300 years ago the Navajo acquired sheep and horses and began to raid the settlements. According to Spanish accounts 165 years ago the Navajo population was about 3,500—today there are about 100,000.

The Navajo are the largest Indian tribe in the United States. They number about 100,000, the majority living on the vast reservations in New Mexico, Arizona, and Utah. They are an offshoot of the Apache, who are believed to have migrated from Canada to the American Southwest about a thousand years ago. The Navajo language, like the Apache, is of the Athapascan family. The Navajo call themselves Diné—"The People."

Cherokee

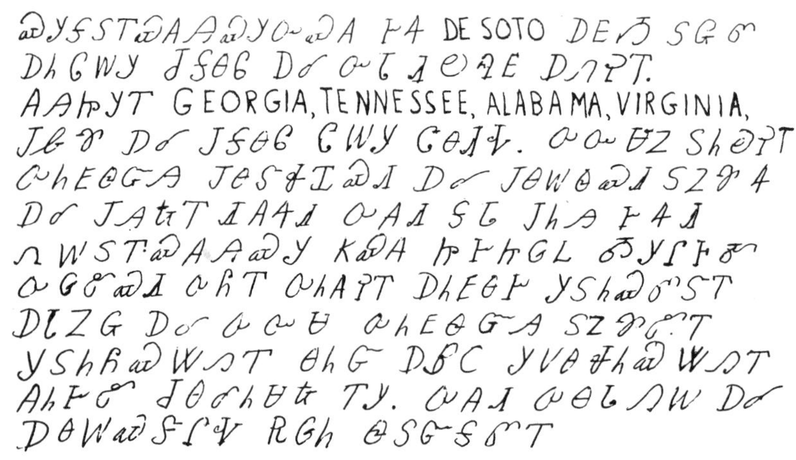

The Cherokees when first discovered by De Soto in 1540 were living in the southeastern part of the United States, known today as Georgia, Tennessee, Alabama, Virginia, North and South Carolina. They had their own tribal government, schools, churches, and were prosperous landowners. Their forced removal in the 1830s to what is now Oklahoma is a dark episode in the history of this country. They endured great hardships during the Civil War, with its destructions, suffering, and tragedy, and finally the dissolution of their tribal government with the coming of Oklahoma Statehood. Yet they rose above these hardships and struggles, and today they contribute greatly to the wealth and stability of this nation and the world.

Cherokee is spoken by upwards of 10,000 people, the great majority living near the town of Tahlequah in northeastern Oklahoma. About 1,000 speakers live in western North Carolina, on a reservation near the town of Cherokee. The Cherokee language is of the Iroquoian family, most closely related to Seneca, Mohawk, and Oneida.

Cherokee writing, pictured above, is the creation of Sequoyah, one of the great names in the history of the American Indian. Convinced that the key to the white man's power lay in his possession of a written language, he set about bringing this secret to his own people. In 1821, after twelve years of work, he produced a syllabary of eighty-six characters, representing every sound in the Cherokee language. The system was quickly mastered by thousands of Cherokees and within three years a newspaper began to be published, and a constitution for the Cherokee Nation was drawn up in the Cherokee language.

Sequoyah borrowed many of his characters from English, but since he actually neither spoke nor read English, they represent completely different sounds in the two languages. The letter *D*, for example, is pronounced *a*, while *h* is pronounced *ni*, *W* is pronounced *la*, and *Z* is pronounced *no*. But the Sequoyah syllabary has remained in use to the present day, with no modifications considered necessary in 150 years. That an unlettered hunter and craftsman could complete a task now undertaken only by highly trained linguists must surely rank as one of the most impressive intellectual feats achieved by a single man.

Sioux

Ehanni, kangi kin zintkala ata ska heca. Nahan tatanka ob lila kolawicaye lo. Lakota kin tatanka wicakuwapi na wicaktepi iyutapi cannas, kangi kin u kte na tatanka kin iwahowicaye s'a. Heon Lakota kin lila acanzekapi. Hankeya, Lakota kin kangi kin oyuspapi. Iyopeyapi kta on, can hanska wan oinkpa el kaskapi na kuta peta tanka wan ilegyapi. Sota lila sapa ca wankatakiya iya icunhuh, kangi kin ata sapa hingle. Hankeya, peta kin wikan kin kihugnage naha kangi kin kinyan kigle,—tka itahena ata sapa heca.

A long time ago, the crow was a bird that was completely white. He was also a very good friend of the buffalo. When the Indians would try to catch and kill the buffalo, the crow would come and warn them. For this reason, the Indians were very angry at the crow. Finally, the Indians caught the crow. In order to punish the crow, they tied him to the top of a tall pole and built a big fire under him. As the black smoke rose, the crow became completely black. Finally, the fire burned the rope in two and the crow flew away,—but he has been black ever since.

—*How the Crow Became Black*

Sioux, also known as Dakota, is spoken principally in South Dakota, and to a lesser degree in North Dakota, Montana, and Nebraska. It is the largest division of the Siouan family, which includes Winnebago, Crow, and a number of other languages. There are about 20,000 speakers of Sioux. The name Dakota is a Sioux word meaning "friends" or "allies."

Ojibwa

eppi· ko me·no·kkemikin kecci-mo·škeˀan iw si·pi·we˜ e·nta·ya·n.
mi· tašš kwa ema· ekote ˀowa·t ekiw keno·še·k keye· kwa ekiw ešikume·-
kok. nentatto·n tašš kwa iw pi·wa·pekko·ns menka·we·penakwa·
wi·-pwa·-ša·pekkošuwa·t ekiw keno·še·k keye· ešikume·kok. pi·cin
tašš ekwa nentawa-ena·p ema· si·pi·we·nˀink e·ya·mekakk iw nentasso·-
na·kan. nuwa·penta·n kwa kuma·ppi·cc iw mema·sekka·k iw pi·-
wa·pekko·ns. mi· a·ši ki·-tekoššink aw ki·ko˜. mi· tašš eša·ya·n
keye· kwa mi· nena·ˀetta·ppenama·n iw nentanitt. mi· tašš pecipuwak
aw ki·ko˜. na·nenkotenonk ni·š nente·-pecipuwa·k ci-pwa·-kekkina-
-kencipeˀiwe·wa·t.

In springtime the creek near my house runs very deep. Then the pike and dogfish swim upstream there. Then I put wire netting there to keep the pike and dogfish from swimming through. At frequent intervals I go and look there in the creek where my trap is placed. In time I see the wire moving. That is when the fish have arrived. Then I go and tie fast my fish spear. Then I spear those fish. Sometimes I manage to spear two of them before they all get away.

Ojibwa, perhaps better known as Chippewa, is an Indian language spoken both in the United States and Canada. In the United States there are about 30,000 speakers, located in Michigan, Wisconsin, Minnesota, and North Dakota, while in Canada there are about 20,000, in Ontario, Manitoba, and Saskatchewan. Ojibwa belongs to the Algonkian family of languages.

Blackfoot

A-chim-oo-yis-gon.
e-spoo-ta kin-non-a na-do-wa-bis
ke-ta-nik-goo-ye
oo-da-keen-non. ke-sto-wa a-ne-chiss
ke-che-sta-ne a-nom cha-koom-ma
e-spoo-che-ka ne-too-ye a-ne-chiss
kip-pe-soo-kin-on na-pa-yen
ee-seen-mo-kin-on ke-che-na-pon-sa-ko
da-ke-boo-che-kim-ma ma-da-pee-wa.
moo-ka-mo-che-pew-kin-on ka-mo-che-pew-kin-on
ma-ka-pe-ye nee-na-kee-sta-ta-poo. Kin-na-ye.

Lord's Prayer.
Our Father who art in heaven,
hallowed
be thy name. Thy kingdom come.
Thy will be done on earth,
as it is in heaven.
Give us this day our daily bread.
And forgive our debts,
as we forgive our debtors.
And lead us not into temptation,
but deliver us from evil. Amen.

The Blackfeet Indians live in Montana and the Canadian province of Alberta. In Montana they number about 6,000, most of them living on the reservation near the town of Browning, just east of Glacier National Park. In Canada they number about 2,500. The Blackfoot language is of the Algonkian family.

Crow

Ush-ke-she-de-sooua bob-ba-sah uh-caw-sha-asede Usha-esah-ughdia be-lay-luc Ugh-ba-dud-dia coush aho-hake. Ish-gawoun besha-ahsoua-luc, dagh-gosh-bosho-luc, bah-couh-we-sha cou-cwah ah-cou-duke. Usha-esah-ughdia esa-ba-lay-duc, acouh-bah-goo-sa e-gee-lay-duc. Oogah chia-luc, hish-sha-luc, she-lay-luc, e esa bah-lah-gic. Oogah-luc, alah-coo-sio-luc, ewah-ah-cou-dua-luc, cou-cwah ushuma-la-chia ala-whoua-lawah cone bah-quoc.

On the first day of the sun dance as the sun breaks over the horizon, the sponsor enters the lodge and begins his fast which is in appreciation of past favors by the Great Spirit. Inside the lodge are a buffalo head and eagle feathers which are symbols of all the animals and birds that live on the great plains and in the Rocky Mountains. The sponsor is barefooted and is uncovered above the waist. His face is painted with white, red, or yellow clay. The color of the paint, the application, and the symbols are handed down from generation to generation by each clan.

Crow is a Siouan language, once spoken over a large area of Montana and Wyoming, between the Yellowstone and Platte rivers. Today almost all the Crow Indians, numbering about 3,500, live on the Crow Indian Reservation, near the town of Hardin, Montana.

Seneca

wayatihãẽ' ne nyakwai' khuh ne tyihukwaes. ne' nyakwai' thutẽcunih tyawe'ũh teyucũtaikũke'ũ thutẽcunih. taneke'ũ tyihukwaes neke'ũ ẽyuhẽsek. teyu'kœhtũk, teyu'kœhtũk, teyu' kœhtũk. tyihukwaes wãẽ': ẽyuhẽsek, ẽyuhẽsek, ẽyuhẽsek. tanenekyũ' tyihukwaes waatkwenii'. tanekyũ' kayũnih ne' unẽh wa'uhẽt wa'u'kœ khuh. tanenẽhke'ũ waunũ'khwẽ' ne nyakwai'. taneke'ũ uthuchiyuu' ne tyihukwaes haswe'nũkeh. tanenẽ'kyũ' kayũnih sẽniyũ tetya'tetanũ haswe'nũkeh ne' tyihukwaes.

The Bear and the Chipmunk quarreled. The Bear wanted it to be night all the time, it is said. The Chipmunk, it is said, wanted it to be day and night. (The Bear said) "Dark all the time, dark all the time, dark all the time" (faster and faster). The Chipmunk said, "Day and night, day and night, day and night" (faster and faster). Then, it is said, the Chipmunk won. That is why it now dawns and grows dark. Then, it is said, the Bear got angry. He scratched the Chipmunk on his back. That is why the Chipmunk has three stripes down his back.

The Seneca Indians lived for centuries in the western third of New York State, being one of the Five Nations that formed the League of the Iroquois. Today about 4,400 Senecas live on two reservations in western New York—the Cattaraugus Reservation near the town of Irving, and the Allegany Reservation near Salamanca.

The Seneca language belongs to the Iroquoian family. The alphabet consists of only twelve letters of the English alphabet (*a*, *c*, *e*, *h*, *i*, *k*, *n*, *s*, *t*, *u*, *w*, *y*) plus the additional vowel *œ*.

Mohawk

Niyawehkowa katy nonwa onenh skennenji thisayatirhehon. Onenh nonwa oghseronnih denighroghkwayen. Hasekenh thiwakwekonh deyunennyatenyon nene konnerhonyon, "Ie henskerighwaghtonte." Kenyutnyonkwaratonnyon, neony kenyotdakarahon, neony kenkontifaghsoton. Nedens aesayatyenenghdon, konyennedaghkwen, neony kenkaghnekonyon nedens aesayatyenenghdon, konyennethaghkwen, neony kenwaseraketotanese kentewaghsatayenha kanonghsakdatye. Niyateweghniserakeh yonkwakaronny; onidatkon yaghdekakonghsonde oghsonteraghkowa nedens aesayatyenenghdon, konyennethaghkwen.

Great thanks now, therefore, that you have safely arrived. Now, then, let us smoke the pipe together. Because all around are hostile agencies which are each thinking, "I will frustrate their purpose." Here thorny ways, and here falling trees, and here wild beasts lying in ambush. Either by these you might have perished, my offspring, or, here by floods you might have been destroyed, my offspring, or by the uplifted hatchet in the dark outside the house. Every day these are wasting us; or deadly invisible disease might have destroyed you, my offspring.

—*The Iroquois Book of Rites*

The Mohawk Indians lived originally in the Mohawk Valley of New York State, between the modern cities of Schenectady and Utica. The easternmost of the Five Nations that formed the League of the Iroquois, they sided with the British during the Revolutionary War and were forced after the Revolution to flee to Canada. Today the largest concentration of Mohawks (about 2,000) is on the St. Regis Indian Reservation in St. Regis, New York, facing the St. Lawrence River and bordering Canada. A few thousand more live in various parts of Ontario and some are to be found in Quebec. The Mohawk language is of the Iroquoian family.

Choctaw

ATIKEL I.

Aiʋlhpiesa Makosh Ʋlhpisa

Nana isht imaiʋlhpiesa moma i̱shahli micha, Kʋfamint yoka keyu hosh ilʋppa ka tokma atobacha aiʋlhpisa chi̱ mako yakohmashke.

SEK. 1. Hattak yuka keyu hokʋtto yakohmit itibachʋfat hieli kʋt, nan isht imaiʋlhpiesa atokmʋt itilawashke; yohmi ka̱ hattak nana hohkia, keyukmʋt kanohmi hohkia okla moma nana isht aim aiʋlhpiesa, micha isht aimaiʋlhtoba he aima ka̱ kanohmi bano hosh isht ik imaiʋlhpieso kashke. Amba mo̱ma kʋt na̱na isht imachukma chi̱ ho tuksʋli hokmakashke-

SEK. 2. Oklah moma hatokmʋt, na̱na kʋt aiʋlpiesa hinla kʋt afoyoka ho̱ mʋhli hatokma ko̱, na̱na kʋt ʋlhpisa na Okla moma kʋt isht imachukma̱ chi̱ ka̱ a̱pisa he ʋt imaiʋlhpiesa cha Kafanmint yuka keyu ikbashke, yohmi tok osh i̱shahlit isht a maha̱ya hinla kʋt otani hokma̱, nittak na̱na hohkia na̱na ho̱ apihinsa tok ʋt kobafi, keyukmʋt mosholichi cha i̱la̱ chit ikbi bʋnna hokmʋt imaiʋlhpiesashke.

ARTICLE I

Declaration of Rights

That the general, great and essential principles of liberty and free government may be recognized and established, we declare:

Sec. 1. That all free men, when they form a social compact, are equal in rights, and that no man or set of men are entitled to exclusive, separate public emolument or privileges from the community, but in consideration of public services.

Sec. 2. That all political power is inherent in the people, and all free governments are founded on their authority and established for their benefit, and therefore they have at all times an inalienable and indefeasible right to alter, reform, or abolish their form of government in such manner as they may think proper or expedient.

—Constitution of the Choctaw Nation

The Choctaw Indians lived originally in southern Mississippi, but in the 1830s were forced to cede their lands to the United States Government and move to what is now Oklahoma. There, together with the Chickasaws, Seminoles, Creeks, and Cherokees, they formed the so-called Five Civilized Tribes, each with its own territory, government, and code of laws. This independent status continued until 1907, when Oklahoma was admitted to the Union as a state.

Speakers of Choctaw today number about 7,000. About three-fourths live in southeastern Oklahoma, the rest on a reservation in central Mississippi. The Choctaw language is most closely related to Chickasaw, the two belonging to the Muskogean family. The name Oklahoma means "red people" in Choctaw.

Chickasaw

Chikasha, Chahta, Mushkoki Micha Chukhoma mǫt Mushkoki aiǫchololi achi cha tok.

Yakni aiasha yummut Oshapani i̱ Okhata ǫ hekia cha Hushi Akocha Bok Misha Sipokni onna mut Fulummi pila ǫ aiya ot Bok Fulummi abuiydchit ulhchuba Bok tuklo itti̱tukla aiya ot Hushi Akocha Okhata Ishto ot talhi tok.

Chikasha hatuk owutta ulheha mut mona impona kut immaiya tok, nunna aiyaka tawa̱. Ikimmilho cha immaiyachit ik tikabo ot unoa mah momut aiyukpachit isht anumpoli cha tok.

Chepota i̱ki keyuk mut ishki ot illi hokma i̱ kanomi fehna kut himmonali i̱ chuka achufa ikbi cha i̱ hullo kut immi che yummushchi cha tok.

The Chickasaws are of the Muskogean family, whose principal nations were the Chickasaw, Choctaw, Creek, and Chockhoomas. The country occupied by them extended from the Gulf of Mexico up the east side of the Mississippi River, then up the Ohio to the dividing ridge between the Tennessee and Cumberland rivers and on eastward to the Atlantic Ocean.

As trackers and hunters the Chickasaws had no superiors. They were celebrated for their personal bravery and indomitable spirit and had almost endless endurance. There were no Chickasaw orphans. If the mother or father died, or the father was slain in battle, the child was immediately placed with a near relative able to care for him and was thereby adopted into the new family and no differences were shown in the children.

The Chickasaw Indians lived originally in Mississippi, just north of the Choctaws, to whom they are linguistically related. About 1830 they were moved to what is now Oklahoma, where today they number about 5,000. Most of them live near the town of Ardmore, in the southernmost part of the state. About 2,500 people are still able to speak the language. Chickasaw belongs to the Muskogean family.

Fox

Nenī'w äʽkī'wānī^{d}tc ä'ʽcīʽcā^{d}tc^{iʽ}, äʽpeʽcegeʽsiweʽciʽᴀg^{kiʽ}. Äʽᴀʽcki'meguʽu'wīwi^{d}tc äʽnawänenī'ʽäʽi^{d}tc^{iʽ}. Ī'nᴀ nā'ʽk iʽkwäw äʽwäwe'neʽsi^{d}tc^{iʽ}. Tcäwīʽcwi'megu äʽwäwene'ʽsiwā^{d}tc^{iʽ}. Äʽtᴀgwāgī'ʽinig äʽuwīwe'tīwā^{d}tc^{iʽ}. Nōmᴀgä'w uwīwe'tīwā^{d}tc īni^{d}tcā'ʽip äʽmawikīwānī^{d}tc^{iʽ}. Kᴀbōtwe'megu äʽpōnikeʽkä'netᴀgi wä'^{d}tcīgwän^{niʽ}. Keyäʽᴀpᴀgä'ʽipi kīʽceʽsōn aiyāpōtānᴀgīgwänegu'teʽe wä^{d}tcipwāwi'megukeʽkä'netᴀgi wä'^{d}tcīgwän^{niʽ}. Äʽkīʽcāgu^{d}tci'täʽä^{d}tc äʽkī'wānī^{d}tc^{iʽ}. Äʽwᴀ'niʽe^{d}tc^{iʽ}.

A man was lost when hunting, when hunting deer. He had just been married and he was a fine-looking man. And the woman was beautiful. Both were beautiful. It was in the fall when they married. When they had been married a short time, then it is said he went out and was lost. Soon he ceased to know whence he had come. It is a fact, so it is said, that the reason why he did not know whence he had come was because his eyes had been turned upside down by the moon. He felt terrible when he was lost. He was missed.

—The One Whom the Moons Blessed

The Fox Indians, who number only about 500, live on a reservation in eastern Iowa, near the village of Tama. About two centuries ago they merged with the neighboring Sac, or Sauk, tribe who spoke the same language, and thus the language is sometimes referred to as Fox and Sac. The Sac Indians now live in central Oklahoma and number about 1,000. The Fox language is of the Algonkian family.

Creek

Ma-ómof fû'suă ok'holátid 'lákid á'latis; ihádshî tcháp-gīd, ímpafnita lámhi imántalidshid. Níta umálgan alágit ístin pasátît pápît á'latis. Hókti ahákin háhit, hía fûsuă á'latin ihuiläidsháχadis. Hía fúsua ma nákî inhahóyadi í'hsit isayipatítut, hofónen i'lisaláχatīs. Ódshipin ómad ná-kitäs hítchkuidshi wäitis kómakatis. Hofóni hákin tchíssi tchátit hī'tchkatis; mómen ma fúsuat i lkitó-aitis kómaχatis. Ma tchíssin itimpunayágit istumidshakátit í'lgi imilid-ha-gi-táyad itimpunäyákatis. Ma fúsuă ítcha=kuadáksin ín'li apákīn ō'dshid ómatis. Mómen ma tchī'ssit ítsa=kuadáksi îfákan kalágit intádshatis, istómit issi-imanäítchiko-tidáyin háyatis; mómen man ilidsháχatis. Ma fúsuă fúsuă ómal immíkkun käidsháχatis. Lámhi-u míkko 'lákid ō'mis kóma-gid ómis; mómiga hú'lidäs apíyis, adám hí'lka hákadäs fúllis mómof lámhihádshi ko'htsaktsahídshid isfúllid ómis. Tchátad hó'lit ómin, hátgātît hí'lka ahopákat ómis. Ihú'lit táfa hátkin isnihäídshit idshú'kuan hatídshit awolä'dshit lámhi ókit hákin ómat, istófan ilí'htchikos.

At that time there was a bird of large size, blue in color, with a long tail, and swifter than an eagle, which came every day and killed and ate their people. They made an image in the shape of a woman, and placed it in the way of this bird. The bird carried it off, and kept it a long time, and then brought it back. They left it alone, hoping it would bring something forth. After a long time a red rat came forth from it, and they believe the bird was the father of the rat. They took counsel with the rat how to destroy its father. Now the bird had a bow and arrows; and the rat gnawed the bowstring, so that the bird could not defend itself, and the people killed it. They called this bird the King of Birds. They think the eagle is also a great King; and they carry its feathers when they go to War or make Peace: the red mean War; the white, Peace. If an enemy approaches with white feathers and a white mouth, and cries like an eagle, they dare not kill him.

—The Migration Legend of the Kasi'hta Tribe

The Creek Indians lived originally in Georgia and Alabama. Frequent clashes with advancing white settlers eventually led to the Creek War of 1813–14, in which the Creeks were decisively defeated and forced to cede more than half their land to the United States. In the 1830s they were forced to move to Oklahoma, where today they number about 15,000. Most of them live near the town of Okmulgee, which lies due south of Tulsa. Probably not more than half still speak the Creek language. Creek is closely related to Seminole, both of them belonging to the Muskogean family.

Osage

E′-dsi xtsi a′, a bi^{n} da, ţsi ga,
U′-ba-mo^{n}-xe i-tse-the a-ka′, a bi^{n} da, ţsi ga,
E′-dsi xtsi a̧′, a bi^{n} da, ţsi ga,
Da′-ķ'o i-the ga-xe a-ka′, a bi^{n} da, ţsi ga,
O′-da-bthu i-the ga-xe a-ka′, a bi^{n} da, ţsi ga,
Mo^{n}′-xe a-tha ķ'a-be do^{n} a′, a bi^{n} da, ţsi ga,
Da′-zhu-dse i-no^{n}-the a-ka′, a bi^{n} da, ţsi ga,
He′-dsi xtsi a′, a bi^{n} da, ţsi ga,
Zhi^{n}′-ga ķi-no^{n} gi-the ţse a-tha e-ķi-a bi a′, a bi^{n} da, ţsi ga,
He′-dsi xtsi a′, a bi^{n} da, ţsi ga,
Ţsi′-zhu Ų-dse-the Ƥe-tho^{n}-ba′, a bi^{n} da, ţsi ga,
U′-ça-ķa thi^{n}-ge i-he-the a-ka′, a̧ bi^{n} da, ţsi ga.

Verily, at that time and place,
They placed beneath the pile of stones and in the spaces between them the dry branches.
Verily, at that time and place,
They set fire to the dead branches placed within and about the pile of stones,
And the flames leaped into the air with vibrating motions,
Making the walls of the heavens
To redden with a crimson glow.
Verily, at that time and place,
They said to one another: Let the reflection of this fire on yonder skies be for the painting of the bodies of the little ones.
Verily, at that time and place,
The bodies of the people of the Tsi-zhu Fireplaces
Became stricken with the red of the fire, leaving no spot untouched.

—Painting Ritual of the Osage War Ceremony

The Osage Indians lived originally in Missouri, but in 1872 were settled on the Osage reservation in northeastern Oklahoma. The reservation has the same boundaries as Osage County, with tribal headquarters in the town of Pawhuska. The Osage language is of the Siouan family. Only a few hundred speakers remain today.

Delaware

yukwi′n·ek·e^{c} k^{cw}tcu′k^{c}hɔk·e^{c}hel·a$^{a′}$k·e lowe$^{e′}$n ga′ci·k^{c}tu′he^{e} nun·-hu′k·we yut·a′ lamha′k·i·ye^{e}. ɔk^{c} pe′tci k^{c}tale$^{e′}$tan pu′ŋg^{w} ɔk kwe^{e}-c^{c}ha′t·e^{e}k ɔk aha′m·e^{e}ni·^{1} pe′tci k^{c}tal·e$^{e′}$tan ke$^{e′}$ko ma′l·aci· ka$^{a′}$nosli·-na′k·wat^{e} suk^{c}pe$^{e′}$k·at^{c} nen·i·ke$^{e′}$ko ge^{e}t^{c}pe′^{c}hel·a^{a}t^{c} la^{a}mha′ki·ye·ne′n·i ə′nda^{c} ama′ŋgi tu$^{u′}$χk^{c}hak·i·e′^{c}hel·ak^{c} yu′endalausi·′eŋg^{c} ga^{c}he$^{e′}$sə·n·a oto^{c}he$^{e′}$p·iŋ.

yuk·we pe′tci ako′^{u} wa^{c}k·ɔt·u′^{u}wi ke$^{e′}$ko e^{e}li·mgɔ′t·uk^{c} ne^{c} suk^{c}pe$^{e′}$k·a ke$^{e′}$ko ge^{c}t·ala$^{a′}$mwiŋg$^{c′}$. ne^{c} ə′nda^{c} ki·$^{1′}$skak·e′^{c}hel·a^{a}k ha′k·i· ɔk ən·en·$^{1′c}$ ənda′n·e^{ec}gɔ′t·ək^{c} pu′ŋg^{c} ɔk kwe^{e}c^{c}ha′t·e^{e}k^{c} lo′we^{e}n nale′tən·en ule^{e}χ-e$^{e′}$yan ma^{c}ta′n·t^{c}o.

Now at the time when the earth quaked, so it is said, a great cracking, rumbling noise arose here from down in the ground below. And there came rising dust and smoke, while here and there came rising something sticky, looking like tar, a black fluid. That substance overflowed down into the earth. That was when the great gaps opened in the ground, here where we dwell upon our mother's body.

So even it was not known what purpose was intended for the black fluid substance blown forth from below. There the earth lay gaping open and when the dust and smoke were seen, it was said to be the breath of the Evil Spirit.

—The Delaware Indian Big House Ceremony

In early colonial times the Delaware Indians inhabited the Delaware Valley, in the states of New Jersey, New York, Pennsylvania, and Delaware. Beginning about 1720 they were gradually driven westward, first by the hostile Iroquois, later by the white man. Today they number less than 1,000, most of whom live in Oklahoma, near the town of Anadarko, the rest in southern Ontario, near the city of Brantford. The Delawares call themselves Lenape—"The People." Their language is of the Algonkian family.

Papago

Sh am hebai ha'i o'odhamag g kakaichu. Kutsh e a'ahe matsh wo u'io g ha'ichu e-hugi. Atsh am e nahto wehsijj, k am hihih gam huh mash am s-mu'ij, k gam huh dada k am u'u hegai. Tsh g wisag am hahawa wabsh jiwia, ash hegam si ha gewichshulig kakaichu. Kutsh ga huh amjeD s-kuhkim wo i him k am wo si e wamigid k ia huh he'ekia wo ha gewichshul, hab e juhka'i. T wabshaba hemako al kakaichu gam huh si e ehsto sha'i wecho. Atsh heg al i wih. Tsh im hab wa ep wehs ha hugio hegam kakaichu. Kutsh heg am ta'iwuni k meh am uhpam. K ash im huh meD e-kih wui, ch ash hab kaijhim: "Wahm att ha'ichu am chum ko'itohio. T g ohbi am jiwia. Wehs t-hugio! Wehs t-hugio!"

It is said that somewhere there lived some quail. The time came to go for their food. They all got ready, and went to the place where it was abundant, and arrived there and were taking it. Then the hawk came, striking down those quail. He would swoop down from above and raise himself and strike down a number of them in this manner. But one little quail completely hid himself under the brush. He was the only one that was left. The hawk destroyed all the rest of the quail. And he [the quail] rushed out and ran back. And he was running to his home saying: "We just went to try to get something to eat. The enemy came. Destroyed us all! Destroyed us all!"

Papago, pronounced POP-a-go, is spoken by about 8,000 people in southern Arizona and about 1,000 more in the province of Sonora in northern Mexico. It is closely related to Pima, with about 5,000 additional speakers in southern Arizona—in fact the two are really dialects of the same language. They are sometimes referred to collectively as O'odham, the Papago and Pima word for "people." Papago belongs to the Uto-Aztecan family of languages.

Nahuatl

Manoce ca ye cuel nelti muchiua
in quimattiuitze ueuetque, ilamatque in quipixtiuitze:
in ualpachiuiz topan mani,
in ualtemozque tzitzitzimi
in quipoloquiui tlalli, in quiquaquiui maceualli,
inic cemayan tlayouaz tlalticpac: in acan yez tlalticpac:
in quimattiuitze, in quipixtiuitze,
in cultin, in citi in inpial yetiuitze,
in muchiuatiuh, in neltitiuh.

Perhaps now is coming true, now is coming to pass,
what the men and women of old knew, what they handed down:
that the heavens over us shall sunder,
that the demons of the air shall descend
and come to destroy the earth and devour the people,
that darkness shall prevail, that nothing be left on earth.
Our grandmothers and grandfathers knew it,
they handed it down, it was their tradition
that it would come to pass, that it would come to be.

—A Prayer to Tlaloc

Nahuatl, with the stress on the first syllable, was the language of the great empire of the Aztecs. At one time spoken over all of present-day Mexico, it is still the most important Indian language in the country. Its 800,000 speakers live mainly in the states of Puebla, Veracruz, Hidalgo, and Guerrero, to the north, east, and south of Mexico City. Nahuatl belongs to the Uto-Aztecan family, which also includes a number of languages of the western United States. English words of Nahuatl origin include *tomato*, *chocolate*, *avocado*, *coyote*, and *ocelot*.

At the time of the Spanish conquest Aztec writing was entirely pictographic. The Spanish introduced the Roman script and soon recorded a large body of Aztec prose and poetry. The full text of the prayer to Tlaloc, the god of rain, runs about 200 lines.

Maya (Quiché)

C'ä c'ä tz'ininok, c'ä c'ä chamamok, cätz'inonic, c'ä käsilanic, c'ä cälolinic, c'ä tolon-na puch upacaj.

Wae' c'äte' nabe tzij, nabe uch'an: Majabi' jun winak, jun chicop, tz'iquin, cär, tap, che', abaj, jul, siwan, c'im, c'iche'laj; xa u tuquel caj c'olic. Mawi k'alaj uwächulew, xa u tuquel remanic palo, upacaj ronojel. Majabi' nac'ila' cämolobic, cäcotzobic, jun-ta cäsilobic cämalcaban-taj, cäcotzcaban-taj pa caj, x-ma gkowi nac'ila' c'olic yacalic.

Xa remanic ja', xa lianic palo, xa u tuquel remanic; x-ma c'o-wi nac'ila' lo c'olic. Xa cächamanic, cätz'ininic chi k'ekum chi akab.

This is the account of how all was still, the waters lay calm, there was no wind, and the expanse of the sky was empty.

This is the first account, the first narrative. There was neither man nor animal, birds, fish, crabs, trees, stones, caves, ravines, grasses, nor forests; there was only the sky. The surface of the earth had not appeared, there was only the calm sea and the great expanse of the sky. There was nothing brought together, nothing which could make a noise, nor anything which might move, or tremble, or fly, nor was anything standing.

There was only the calm water, the placid sea, alone and tranquil; nothing whatever existed. Only the expanse of water, and tranquillity in the darkness, in the night.

—*Popul Vuh*

Maya, the language of the great Maya civilization that flourished more than a thousand years ago, is still spoken in various forms by several million people in present-day Mexico, Guatemala, and British Honduras. Since earliest times the Maya language has contained numerous dialects, which today are sufficiently different to be regarded as separate languages. There are about eight such languages in Mexico and more than a dozen in Guatemala.

Maya proper, sometimes called Yucatec, is spoken by about 450,000 people on the Yucatán Peninsula of Mexico as well as in northern British Honduras. In the adjacent Mexican states of Chiapas and Tabasco, there are, from south to north, Tzotzil (100,000 speakers), Tzeltal (100,000), Chol (50,000), and Chontal (20,000). Farther up the coast, in Veracruz, and inland in San Luis Potosí, Huastec is spoken by about 65,000 people. In Guatemala, which has about $2\frac{1}{2}$ million Maya Indians, the big four languages are Quiché (750,000 speakers), Cakchiquel (400,000), Mam (350,000), and Kekchi (300,000). Kekchi is also spoken in southwestern British Honduras.

The *Popul Vuh*, the sacred book of the Mayas, is a stirring account of Maya history and traditions, beginning with the creation of the world. The most outstanding example of native American literature that has survived the passing of centuries, it was first reduced to writing (in the Roman alphabet) in the middle of the 16th century.

Alone among the Indians of America, the Mayas possessed a fully developed system of writing. The Maya hieroglyphs, a sample of which appears at the right, have posed a formidable challenge to scholars and linguists ever since the 16th century. They appear to be a combination of ideographs, phonetic signs, and also rebus writing, in which an ideograph is used to represent another word which happens to have the same pronunciation. (For example, in English the sign for "eye" could be used to represent the pronoun "I.") The first signs to be deciphered were those dealing with the calendar and astronomy, but progress in unraveling the rest of the system has been extremely slow and difficult. Even electronic computers have been applied to the problem in recent years, and new discoveries offer fresh hope that the mystery will eventually be solved.

MAYA HIEROGLYPHS

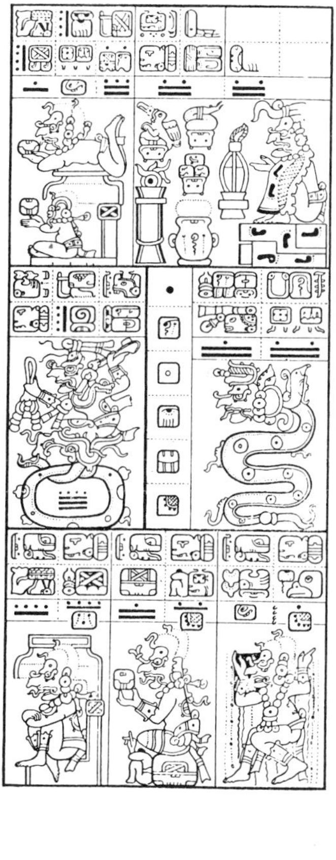

Papiamento

Despues cu e navegante spañó Alonso de Ojeda a bandona Curaçao cu destino pa Santo Domingo, el a discubri dia 15 di Agosto 1499 un cabo, cu el a yama San Román i dia 24 di mes luna el a hayé den un puerto i un lago grandísimo, cu el a duna nomber di San Bartolomeo, cuyo nomber despues tabata cambiá pa Maracaibo, na honor di un cacique riquísimo, biba cerca di e lago. Mui probable cu den e travesía Ojeda lo a toca Aruba, i casi sigur lo por yamé descubridor di e isla.

Tanto durante e tempo despues di descubrimento bao di dominio spañó, i despues di 1634 bao di poder holandes, nunca Aruba tabatin un propia historia. E gran distancia for di Curaçao, e corriente fuerte entre costa venezolana i e isla, e remontamento sin fin contra un biento fortísimo, i den un tempo cu lamar rondó di e islanan tabata cruzá cu frecuencia pa piratanan, a haci un comunicacion ligé i regular cu Curaçao mashá dificil pa veleronan.

After the Spanish navigator Alonso de Ojeda left Curaçao bound for Santo Domingo, he discovered on August 15, 1499 a cape which he called San Román. On the 24th of the same month he found himself in a port and huge lake, to which he gave the name of San Bartolomeo. This name was later changed to Maracaibo, in honor of a rich Indian chief living near the lake. It is most probable that en route Ojeda touched Aruba: it is fairly certain that he is the island's discoverer.

A period of Spanish rule followed the discovery of the island, and after 1634 it came under the dominion of the Dutch. But Aruba never had much of a "history." Its distance from Curaçao, the strong current between the Venezuelan coast and the island, its constant exposure to the relentless trade winds, the seas roundabout infested with pirates—all made rapid and regular communication very difficult for sailing vessels.

Papiamento is the native, though unofficial, language of the southern islands of the Netherlands Antilles—Curaçao, Aruba, and Bonaire. A creole language with Spanish as its base, it contains numerous words from Dutch, English, Portuguese, French, and many other languages. There are about 200,000 speakers.

Guarani

Ayajhe'óta pende apytepe
narötivéigui che vy' a y
ajhypyimita co pyjarepe
che resaype Paraguahy.

Che momoräva cu umi burrera
ipymandí jha jhesá jhovy
che py'apypente añopü jhera
jha che ajhogata co tesay.

Purajhei pope co che amocäva
yeroky jharupi che resay,
jha ñasaindyro romonguetava
che novia raicha, Paraguahy.

Let me relate to you
The sorrow that oppresses me,
And sprinkle the night with my tears
For my beloved Asunción.

I recall the women selling produce
With bare feet and blue eyes,
My bosom is burdened with anguish
And is choked with my crying.

Only the music can relieve
With its sweet notes my sadness,
And under a full moon will I declare
The love that I feel for you, Asunción.

—MANUEL ORTIZ GUERRERO, *Asunción*

Guarani, with the stress on the final syllable, is the native language of Paraguay. While Spanish is the official language of the country, and spoken by the majority of the population, it is estimated that as many as $1\frac{3}{4}$ million people, or 70 percent of the population, speak Guarani as well. No other Indian language is so widely used by all classes of society in a given country. There are also some speakers of Guarani in southern Brazil and Bolivia. The name Paraguay is a Guarani word meaning "place of great water."

Quechua

Pitu Salla, millay cutin	Pitu Salla, many times,
Chayllatatacc, chayllatatacc	Only this, only this,
Cunahuanqui ñoccaracctacc	You say to me.
Rimarisacc chaymi sutin	Now I will speak
Anchatan checnipacuni	The very truth.
Cay canchata cay huasita	This court, this house,
Caypi caspa cay ccasita	The useless life,
Ppunchau tuta ñacacuni	Days and nights I hate.
Cay payacunacc uyanta	The faces of the old women.
Ancha aputa ccahuascani	Above all I detest.
Payllatatacc ricuscani	That is all I can see
Chay ccuchu tiascaymanta	From the corner where I sit.
Manan cusi caypi canchu	In this place there is no joy,
Hueqquen uyancupi caicca	Only tears to weep.
Munaiñimpi canman chaicca	Your wish would be
Manan pipas tianmanchu	That none should live here.
Ccahuani puriccunata	They all walk, as I see,
Asicuspan ccuchicuncu	Between laughing and crying,
Maquincupi apacuncu	Their fate in their hands,
Llipipas samincunata	Full of anxiety.
Ñoccallachu huisccacusac	I am shut up here,
Mana Mamay casccan raycu	Because I have no mother.
Ccapac ttalla canay raycu	Having no good nurse to tend me,
Cunanmanta qquesacusacc	I have been to seek for one.

—*Ollantay*

Quechua, pronounced (and sometimes spelled) Kechua, is the most widely spoken Indian language of South America. Its 7 million speakers are located mainly in Peru (5 million), Bolivia ($1\frac{1}{2}$ million), and Ecuador (500,000).

Quechua was the language of the great Inca Empire, which at its zenith in the late 15th century extended from Ecuador in the north to central Chile in the south. The Spanish conquest of the 16th century did not diminish the importance of Quechua, for the new conquerors continued its use throughout the area, and in fact extended it to other areas not part of the original empire. In succeeding centuries many Indian languages of the area have died out, the natives adopting Quechua in some cases, Spanish in others. There are more speakers of Quechua at present than at the time of the Spanish conquest and the number is still increasing.

For all their great technological skills, the Incas never developed an alphabet. What written records there were, were kept by means of a quipu (the Quechua word for "knot"), an arrangement of cords of various colors which were knotted in different ways. All literature prior to the Spanish conquest was handed down by oral tradition. The Spanish introduced the Roman alphabet but to this day the spelling has not been standardized. Quechua grammar, however, has been found to be extremely regular and consistent. English words of Quechua origin include *llama*, *puma*, *vicuña*, *condor*, *quinine*, *coca*, and *guano*.

Ollantay, a drama of life at the Inca court, is perhaps the best-known work of Quechua literature. It was composed by an unknown author about 1470.

Aymara

Aimaranacaja ayllunacana utjapjataina. Jacha ayllunacaja ackam sutinipjatainau: Urus, Parias, Umasuyos, Pacajis, Sicasicas, Karankas, Yuncas, Laricajas. Aca ayllunacaja janira catocktasa Perú marcanacata jakenacan lurapjatapata ni jupanacap oracke yapuchiripjataynau, ucatsti ckori, colcke, cunaimanaca kollunacata apsuña yatipjataina.

Ukamaraqui, jacha ayllunaca utjataina, ackama sutichata: Charcas, Chichas, Kochapampas, Atacamas, Yuras, Killacas, cunaimananaca. Tacpacha aca ayllunacaja yatipjatainau tacke casta parlasiñanaca; jichuruna armthata, incanacan juchapata, quitinacateja kechua parlaña yatichapjataina.

Aimaranacaja janiua mayasapa marcan jacapjatainati sapa aylloja maya jiscka marcanua, jiliri mallkuta apnackata. Jacha jiscka apnackeri jackenau utjataina jilacata sata.

Aca jackenacaja challua catuña huali yatipjana, ucatsti huyhua ahuatiña yatipjataina manckañataqui.

The Aymaras lived in tribes or families. The large tribes were as follows: Urus, Parias, Umasuyos, Pacajis, Sicasicas, Karankas, Yuncas, Laricajas. Before they learned the customs of the Peruvians, these people worked the soil and mined gold, silver, and other minerals from the bowels of the earth.

Other large tribes were called: Charcas, Chichas, Kochapampas, Atacamas, Yuras, Killacas, and more. All these tribes and families once spoke distinct dialects, which were forgotten when the Incas taught them to speak Quechua.

Each of the Aymara tribes was subject to the orders of a great chief called Mallku, to whom other authorities of lower rank, such as the Jilacatas, deferred.

These people were good fishermen and hunters, and also raised llamas and sheep for food.

Aymara, with the stress on the final syllable, is the second of the major Indian languages of western South America. There are about $1\frac{1}{2}$ million speakers, of whom about two-thirds live in Bolivia, the rest in Peru. Aymara and Quechua constitute a single subfamily of the Andean Equatorial family of languages.

LANGUAGES OF AFRICA

Hausa

Ku̱rēgē Dą Būshiyā :—Wata rānā anā̱ ruwā : būshiyā taną̄ yāwo̧, ta zō bą̄kin rāmi̱ŋ ku̱regē : ta yi sallamą, ta cē̱ ‘ Kai, i̱nā ji̱n sanyī̭ : kō dą wuri̭n dą za̭m fa̭kę ? ’ Ku̱rēgē ya amsa̭ ‘ A̱lhamdu̧ li̱llāhi̱ ! Tō̧, gą̄ ɗaŋ wurī, shi̱gō ! ’ Suką zauną tą̄re : ji̱m kąɗaŋ ku̱rēgē ya cę̄ ‘ Kē būshiyā̭ ! Zaman nąn nāmu̱, dą kē̱, bā̭ shi dą dāɗī, ji̱kiŋki̱ yā ciką tsi̱nī. Sǎi ki̱ sākę wurī ! ’ Būshiyā ta cę̄ ‘A̭shę̄ ? Nī ku̱wā, dāɗī nikę̄ jī̱ : wa̭ndą wurin nąm bai̱ gąmē shi̱ ba, bą̄ sǎi yą sākę wani ba̭ ? ’

The Ground Squirrel and the Hedgehog:—One day it was raining: the hedgehog greeted the squirrel saying, “How do you like the cold? Is there anywhere I can shelter?” The squirrel replied, “I'm well, thank God. Here's a little place, enter!” They then lived together, but after a while the squirrel said, “Hedgehog! This stay of yours with me is unpleasant, your body is all prickles. Change your abode!” The hedgehog said, “Is that so? As for me, I enjoy it: the one whom this place doesn't suit, shouldn't he change it for another?”

Hausa is spoken by close to 20 million people in northern Nigeria, another 2 million in Niger, and by several million more in a number of other countries. With about 25 million speakers in all, it is far and away the most important language of West Africa.

Hausa belongs to the Chadic branch of the Afro-Asiatic (Hamito-Semitic) family of languages. Before the colonial period it was written in a variety of the Arabic script known as Ajami, but this has largely given way to a modified Roman script introduced by the British. The language contains many words borrowed from the Arabic.

Fulani

Jemma go'o alkali heɓti nder deftere komoi mari hore pẹtẹl be wakkude junde kanko woni patạdo. Alkali, marḍo hore pẹtẹl be wakkude junde, ẉi'i nder yọnki mako, 'Mi wawata ɓesdugo mangu hore am, amma mi ustan wakkude am'. O ḍaɓɓiti mekesje amma o heɓtai ḍe. Wala ferẹ sei o nangi reta wakkude nder jungo mako, o waḍi reta ferẹ ha pitirla, o wuli nde. Sa'i nde ḍemgal yite yotti jungo mako o yofti nde, wakkude fuh wuldama. Ni'i alkali lati semtuḍo gạm o gongḍini bindaḍum nder deftere.

One evening a judge found in a book that everyone who had a little head and a long beard was a fool. Now the judge had a little head and a long beard, so he said to himself, "I cannot increase the size of my head, but I will shorten my beard." He hunted for the scissors, but could not find them. Without further ado he took half of his beard in his hand and put the other half into the candle and burnt it. When the flame reached his hand he let go, and all the beard was burned. Thus the judge felt ashamed, for he had proved the truth of what was written in the book.

Fulani, also known as Fula or Fulbe, is spoken over a broad belt of western Africa. By far the largest concentration is in northern Nigeria, where approximately 6 million Fulani (out of a total of 10 million) live. But they are also to be found in sizable numbers in Guinea, Guinea-Bissau, Senegal, Gambia, Mauritania, Mali, Upper Volta, Niger, and Cameroon.

The light-skinned Fulani are apparently a people of great antiquity. Their ultimate origin is a source of much speculation, some even suggesting that they are one of the tribes referred to by biblical and classical writers. Their language is generally placed in the West Atlantic branch of the Niger-Congo family, but its richness and sophistication seem to set it apart from the other languages of the region.

Malinke

Dounou gna dan kouma Allah fé, a ye san kolo dan, ka dougou kolo dan, ka kocodjie baou dan, ka badji lou dan, ka kolou dan, ka yirilou dan, ka sogolou dan, ka mogo lou dan. A ba fen toumani ka djiro kè, a ko sogo bè makal ki bolobiri i niè la. Sogobè ya bolo fla biri i niè la. N'ka ba yè kègouyakè: a ma son ka niè da tougoun ka gna: a y'a bolokoni nou so bo niokon na; o ya to a y'a yè Allah ba-kan ka fèn diougou lou kè djiro: Sadiougoulou minignam, ninikin-nankan, bamba, mali. Kabini ô kèra, ba tè son ban Kadjiguing djiro. Hali ni san-ya gossi, a bè koulé bahou a ba lon mi yè djiro.

When God had finished creating the sky and the earth, he put trees, animals, and human beings on the earth. Then, when he wanted to cover the surface with water (oceans, streams, and rivers), he told all the animals to close their eyes. Every animal closed its eyes except for the goat. The goat, instead of covering its eyes with its hands, as everyone else was doing, spread its fingers in order to look through them. Thus it observed God putting nasty fish into the waters, dangerous snakes, alligators, hippopotamuses, and monsters. Since that day the goat has lost confidence in the water, and does not dare, under any circumstances, to go into the water, because it knows what there is in it.

Malinke is another important language of West Africa, spoken by about 2 million people in Senegal, Gambia, Guinea-Bissau, Guinea, Mali, and Ivory Coast. It belongs to the Mande branch of the Niger-Congo family of languages. Malinke is closely related to Bambara, of Mali, and Dyula, of Mali, Ivory Coast, and Upper Volta, the three often combined under the single term Mandingo.

Wolof

Bêne n'gone bêne khali guissena thi bêne têré ni kouame bop bou touti ak sikime bou goûde a moulou bop. Khali binak n'déké bop bou touti la am ak sikime bou goude mou dadini danâ dâgue sama sikime n'dâkhe menouma yokhe sama bop. Mouhoûte âye ciseaux wa n'dé guissouka. Moudâdi diape guène-valou sikimame thi lokhôme guène-valou bithié desse mou lakhe kâ thi sondèle boûye take. Bi safara aksê thi lokhome mou téguikâ sikime yop lâkhe khâli-bi roûsse n'dake-té limou guissone thi têrêbi douvône deûgue.

One evening a judge found in a book that everyone who had a little head and a long beard was a fool. Now the judge had a little head and a long beard, so he said to himself, "I cannot increase the size of my head, but I will shorten my beard." He hunted for the scissors, but could not find them. Without further ado he took half of his beard in his hand and put the other half into the candle and burnt it. When the flame reached his hand he let go, and all the beard was burned. Thus the judge felt ashamed, for he had proved the truth of what was written in the book.

Wolof is the principal language of Senegal, in westernmost Africa. There it is spoken by about $1\frac{1}{2}$ million people, while another 50,000 speakers are to be found in neighboring Gambia. Wolof belongs to the West Atlantic branch of the Niger-Congo family of languages.

Yoruba

Ajọ ìgbimọ ti awọn àgbàgbà ni imâ yan ọba lârin awọn ẹniti nwọn ní ìtan pàtàki kan ninu ẹ̀jẹ. Ilana kan ti o ṣe ajeiì amâ ṣâju ìyan ti ọba. Awọn olori amâ dan agbara ti ìrọju rẹ̀ ati iṣẹ́ akoso ara rẹ̀ wò. Li ọjọ́ ti a yàn fun dide e li ade, awọn olori amâ lọ si âfin ọba, nwọn a mu u dani pẹlu agbara, nwọn a si nà á pẹlu pàṣán. Bi ọba ba faradà aje nâ lai sún ara kì, nigbanâ nwọn yio de e li ade; bi bệkọ, nwọn yio yàn ọba miràn.

The king is chosen by a council of elders from among those who have a certain blood descent. A curious ceremony precedes a king's election. His powers of endurance and self-restraint are tested by the chiefs, who, on the day appointed for the coronation, go to the king's palace, get hold of him forcibly, and flog him with a whip. If the ordeal is suffered without flinching, then the king is crowned; if not, another king is chosen.

—A King's Election in Yoruba Land

Yoruba, with the stress on the first syllable, is one of the major languages of Nigeria. It is spoken in the southwestern part of the country, in the region whose principal city is Ibadan. There are about 12 million speakers.

Yoruba is one of the Kwa languages, which form a subgroup of the Niger-Congo family. The alphabet includes the letters ẹ, pronounced as in "bet" (*e.g.*, *ẹ̀jẹ*—blood); ọ, pronounced as in "ought" (*ọba*—king); and ṣ, pronounced *sh* (*erekuṣu*—island). All three appear in the word *ọṣẹ*, which means "soap." The grave and acute accents do not indicate stress, but rather the rise and fall of the voice.

Ibo

Orue otu mgbe, nne mbe we da n'oria; madu nile ma na ọ gagh aputa n'oria ahu. Mgbe mbe huru na ya enwegh ego ÿi we kwa nne ya otu okwesiri, ọ kwado ÿe. Tupu ọ pua, ọ gwara umu anumanu nile si ha na ya n'apu ÿe; ma onye ọbula akpọla ya karia ma ihe emebegh mbu omere.

O tegh aka mbe puru ÿe, nne ya nwua. Umu anumanu n'ile we zukọ itu alo otu agesi we lie, kwakwa nne mbe. Dika ome n'ala umu anumanu si di; ọdigh ihe obula ha nwere ike ime karia ma mbe ọ nọ n'ebe ahu. Otu onye n'ime ha we lota ihe mbe kwuru tutu ọ pua ÿe. Ihe a ghara umu anumanu n'ile ghari.

Once upon a time the tortoise's mother fell ill; everyone knew she would not survive. The tortoise, wishing to escape an expensive funeral befitting a woman of his mother's rank, decided to embark on a trip. Before leaving, he instructed all the animals in his village never to send for him unless an event hitherto unheard of happened.

Shortly afterward the tortoise's mother died. As was the custom in the land of the animals, the villagers gathered to consider the burial of the deceased. No funeral rites could be performed for her unless her son was present. One of the villagers recalled the instructions given by the tortoise. This posed a puzzle to them all.

Ibo, also known as Igbo, is one of the major languages of Nigeria. It is spoken chiefly in East-Central state with its capital at Enugu. Ibo belongs to the Kwa subgroup of the Niger-Congo family of languages. There are about 8 million speakers.

Mende

Mu va maminingɔ humɛniilɔ kɔɔlongɔ mu Lɔlɔ Lavai Wai, Kenɛi Miltin Magai, haalɛi ma. Dɔkita Magai haailɔ Eipril yenjii 28 volei ma ngi ye pɛlɛ bu miando ngiyei hu Friitauŋ. Ngi hegbɛngɔ yɛla gɛ ngalu lɛɛnga va. Gɔmɛntii i yɛ hugbatɛ wieilɔ ngi yoyo va Ingland a baloi hu wee, ngi hale va na. Kɛɛ, pɛiŋ ti ya a kpɔyɔ a yehugbatɛi ji yefolei na ma, Ngewɔ guilɔ i ngi loli li va ngi gama. I haailɔ leke yɛlɛiŋ i li kuwu hu Ngewɔ gama a hawɛi yepui gbelemɛi a kpindii folei na ma.

Saa (Sir) Miltin voi guni a (68) numu sawa gbɔyɔngɔ mahu wayakpa lɔ. Ti guilɔ naa ti Kena Wai ji gbɔu Ndɔlɔ-gomɛ-houwɛlɛ Wai gbelanga miando Friitauŋ.

We heard the sad news of the death of our Prime Minister, Mr. Milton Margai. Dr. Margai died on the 28th of April at his home on the hill in Freetown. He had been ill for some months. The government had made arrangements to send him to England by air for treatment. But before they had completed these arrangements on that day, God was able to call him to go to Him. He died peacefully and went home to God at 10 P.M. that day.

Sir Milton was 68. They were able to bury this great man near Parliament Building in Freetown.

Mende is the most important native language of Sierra Leone, on the west coast of Africa. It is spoken by about one million people, mainly in the southern half of the country. Mende is a member of the Mande branch of the Niger-Congo family of languages.

Kpelle

Nuahn dah ga nahn
Defa wellė de teka,
Kenoh dee a gba gbeyh
Dah nwehyn kashu.

Defa wolloh shungh nella
Ka shaangh quai gah
Dah welle shungh kela
A kur baddae gah de kleema.

Some stand and look while others do
Then come and say what ought to be,
To them the world is never right
For all is wrong that they can see.

They never see the good in things
That you and I would like to see
They seem to think whatever they say
Is just the thing that ought to be.

—BAI T. MOORE, *Some People*

Kpelle is the most important language of Liberia, on the west coast of Africa. It is spoken by about 500,000 people, or one-third of the total population. Kpelle belongs to the Mande branch of the Niger-Congo family of languages.

Twi

Nantwí bí redidí wɔ̀ sáre bí sò.
Saá sȧre ẏi bɛ̀ŋ atɛkyɛ́ bí â mpɔ̀torɔ áhyė ṁu mä hő.
Mpɔ̀torɔ nó hűu̇ ṅo̤ ṅo, wɔŋ́ mù bínom teɛ́ɛ̇m sè: „Akoá ýi ső mà nè hő baá nò.“
Saá â wɔ́kãė pɛ́, mpɔ̀torɔ nó mù biakő sè: „Mé dė, mĕtu̇mi ṁahòmáŋ áyė sɛ̂ nantwí ýi.“
Ɔ́kãà saá pɛ́, nà ofíì asé homáŋ̀ nè hő nà ɔhomáŋė ȧra kosíì sɛ̂ ɔ́paeė.

A cow was grazing in a field of grass.
This field was near a pond which was full of frogs.
When the frogs saw him some of them exclaimed, "This fellow is extremely big."
Just as they said this, one of the frogs remarked, "I can blow myself up as big as this cow."
No sooner had he said it, than he began to blow himself up, and he went on blowing until he burst.

Twi is the most important language of Ghana. Together with closely related Fanti it is spoken by about 4 million people in the forest area west of the Volta River. Twi belongs to the Kwa subgroup of the Niger-Congo family.

Ewe

'Mise alobalo loo!' 'Alobalo neva!' 'Gbe ɖeka hɔ̃ va fo flavinyɔnu dzetugbea ɖe yi ɖada ɖe koa ɖe dzi le tɔ dome. Fia di amewo be, woaxɔ ye vi la le hɔ̃ si vɛ na ye. Enumake fiafitɔ, adela kple nuhela wova. Fiafitɔ be, yeate ŋu afi nyɔnuvi la le hɔ̃ fe fego me. Adela be, ne hɔ̃ la kpɔ yẹwo be, yeagaxɔ nyɔnuvi la, yeafo tui, wòaku enumake. Nuhela be, ne hɔ̃ ge dze ʋua me wòfe la, yeagahee keŋkeŋ.'

'Wodze mɔ dzi ko la, eye fiafitɔ ɖafi nyɔnuvi la. Esi wova ɖo tɔ titina la, hɔ̃ la va be, yeafo nyɔnuvi la. Tete adela fo tui wòku hege dze ʋua me, wòfli tsayatsaya. Nuhela he ʋua enumake, eye wova afe dedie. Ame etɔ̃ siawo dometɔ ka wɔ wu, ne fia la nakafu?'

"Hear a parable!" "May the parable come!" "One day an eagle swooped down upon the beautiful daughter of a chief and carried her to an island in the river. The chief looked for people to fetch his daughter away from the eagle. A thief, a hunter, and a mender came at once. The thief said he could steal the girl from the talons of the eagle. The hunter said that should the eagle see them and try to recapture the girl, he would shoot him, so that he would die at once. The mender said that should the eagle (having been shot) fall into the boat and break it, he would patch it up.

"As soon as they had started off, the thief stole the girl. As they reached the middle of the river, the eagle came to take the child. Then the hunter shot him, so that he fell into the boat, which was shattered into a thousand pieces. The mender immediately patched the boat, so that they reached home safely. Which of these three people did the most, thereby gaining the praise of the chief?"

Ewe, pronounced *ay-way* or *ay-vay*, is spoken on the southern coast of West Africa between the Volta River in Ghana and the Mono River in Togo. There are about one million speakers in Ghana and about 750,000 in Togo. Ewe belongs to the Kwa subgroup of the Niger-Congo family. The English word *voodoo* is of Ewe origin.

Mossi

Sõñg f mẽñga ti Wennam sõñg fo. Ti bakargo n bâs a mẽñga, dar a yemre, ti taõñg ñyok a la ra ka niñg pãñg n pam a mẽñg ye, a da kosda Wennam a sõñgre, la Wennam sẽ da logĕd a segẽ yela la woto: "Niñg pãñga bilfu t m sõñg fo." Ti a yaol n man dabar bilfu ti winri kaoge. Ren yeta neba sẽ zindb zalĕm la b yetẽ dar fã: "Wennam waoga; a nã kõ ma m sẽ date!" Wennam kõ kõ ba bumbu, b sã deñge n sõñg b mense, ye.

Help yourself and Wennam will help you. One day a hen fell into a trap but made no effort to extricate herself. She begged Wennam for help but Wennam, who was passing by, said, "First make an effort yourself and then I will come to your aid." The hen then made a slight motion and the rope snapped. This is addressed to all those who sit idly and repeat endlessly, "Wennam is great; he will grant my any wish." Wennam will not give them anything unless they begin by helping themselves.

Mossi, also known as Moré, is the principal language of Upper Volta, in West Africa. It belongs to the Gur, or Voltaic, branch of the Niger-Congo family of languages. There are about 3 million speakers.

Fang

E n'aboa na Ku ba Fifi vœlar angom; bœnga to ki dzal avori. Ni mbu mœtsi o nga so, Ku vœ zo Fifi na: "A monœdzãn, ma komœna o kœm mœlœr a tsi." Edo Fifi œnga zo Ku na: "A mi, ma kon va abi, nlo wa sim mœna bim, bim, bim! mœkoe lœr dzo afoe." Edo Ku œnga kœe tam afan eti. A so anga so ngoṙ a sœ, an' anga kwè Fifi z'abom mbè. A n'anga silœ ṉœna: A mi, yœ nkokon w'abobom mbè? Edo anga kœ adzira yœ ṉœ, yœ domœ ṉœ. Nnœangom Ku ba Fifi e nga wu valœ.

Once upon a time the hen and the cockroach, who were good friends, lived in the same village. During the season when all the inhabitants of the village were engaged in working in the fields, the hen invited her friend with these words: "Friend, come with me into the forest to help me clear my field." The lazy cockroach excused himself saying: "Friend, I really cannot accompany you today, I have been having violent headaches; I will go another time." The hen proceeded to the forest alone. Upon her return that evening she was astonished to find the cockroach playing the tom-tom. Becoming angry, she ran after him and began to peck him. That is why since that time hens cannot look at cockroaches without pecking them.

Fang is the major language of three countries on the west coast of Africa. It is spoken in southern Cameroon by about one million people, in mainland Equatorial Guinea by about 200,000, and in northern Gabon by about 175,000. A Bantu language, it is closely related to Bulu, another language of Cameroon.

Swahili

Mtego wanaotega, ninaswe nianguke,
Sifa yangu kuvuruga, jina liaibike,
Mungu mwema mfuga, nilinde lisitendeke,
Na wawekao kiaga, kudhuru watakasike.

Kwa wingi natangaziwa, maovu nisiyotenda,
Na habari nasikia, kila ninapokwenda,
Lakini Allah mwelewa, atalifanya kuwanda,
Jina wanalochukia, badala ya kukonda.

Badala ya kukonda, jina litanenepa,
Ugenini litakwenda, lisipopendeza hapa,
Kutafuta kibanda, ambako halitatupwa,
Huko wataolipenda, fadhili litawalipa.

A trap they set, for me to get caught,
My reputation they blemish, to spoil my name.
Oh, Lord the Keeper, save me from the plight,
And those who promise me harm, remove their aim.

Many slanderous charges are published against me,
And these I hear, wherever I go.
But God who understands, my name will clear,
The name they hate, He will surely emancipate.

Rather than wither, my name will thrive,
Abroad it will succeed, if here they will not heed.
Shelter it will find, where it will not be remiss,
Where those who care, it will reward and recompense.

—SHAABAN ROBERT, *The Name*

Swahili, more correctly called Kiswahili, is the most important language of East Africa. It is the official language of both Tanzania and Kenya, and is also spoken in Uganda, Rwanda, Burundi, and Zaïre. (In Zaïre a separate dialect is spoken, known as Kingwana.) Swahili is the mother tongue of perhaps only a million people, but at least 10 million more speak it fluently as a second language, and many millions more at least understand it to some degree.

Swahili is one of the Bantu languages, which form a branch of the Niger-Congo family. Its vocabulary is basically Bantu but with many words borrowed from Arabic. The name Swahili is derived from an Arabic word meaning "coastal," having developed among Arabic-speaking settlers of the African coast beginning about the 7th century. During the 19th century it was carried inland by Arab tradesmen, and was later adopted by the Germans as the language of administration in Tanganyika. In modern Tanzania it is the national language, and in 1970 it was proclaimed the official language of Kenya.

The Swahili alphabet lacks the letters *c*, *q*, and *x*, but contains a number of its own. The letter *dh* is pronounced like the *th* of "this" (*e.g.*, *dhoruba*—hurricane), *gh* like the German *ch* (*ghali*—expensive), and *ng'* like the *ng* in "thing" but not as in "finger" (*ng'ombe*—cow). Whereas English grammatical inflections occur at the end of the word, in Swahili everything is done at the beginning. *Kitabu* is the Swahili word for "book" but the word for "books" is *vitabu.* This word falls into the so-called Ki Vi class, one of eight in the Swahili language. Others are the M Mi class (*e.g.*, *mkono*—hand, *mikono*—hands; *mji*—town, *miji*—towns), and the M Wa class, used mainly for people (*mtu*—man, *watu*—men; *mjinga*—fool, *wajinga*—fools). Furthermore these prefixes are carried over to verbs of which the noun is the subject, as well as to numerals and modifying adjectives. Thus "one big book" in Swahili is *kitabu kikubwa kimoja* ("book-big-one"), but "two big books" is *vitabu vikubwa viwili.*

Amharic

፩ ዲት ፡ ቂንተል ፡ ከአንድ ፡ ሀገር ፡ ሌላ ፡ አውሬ ፡ ሳታይ ፡ ትኖራ
ለች ፡ ለባልንጀራዋ ፡ እንዲህ ፡ አለቻት ፤ እኔን ፡ የሚያህለኝ ፡ ትልቅ ፡
አውሬ ፡ የለም ፡ በድምጽም ፡ የሚተከለኝ ፡ የለም ። አዎን ፡ እውነት ፡
ነው ፡ አለቻት ፤ ፪ ቱም ፡ አላዩምና ፡ ሌላ ፡ ነገር ። ቀንም ፡ አንበሳ ፡
ሲጮህ ፡ ሰምታ ፡ እኔም ፡ እንደርሱ ፡ እጮሀለሁ ፡ አለቻት ። ባልንጀ
ራዋ ፡ ግን ፡ እንዲህ ፡ አለቻት ፥ እኔ ፡ ፪ ታችሁንም ፡ እሰማለሁ ፡
ጩሂ ፡ አለቻት ። ያችም ፡ ቂንተል ፡ ሰሚኝ ፥ ብላ ፡ ሆዷን ፡ ነፍታ ፡
ጮኸች ፡ ባልንጀራዋም ፡ እንዲህ ፡ አለች ፤ ያንበሳው ፡ ድምጽ ፡ ትልቅ ፡
ነው ፡ ያንችስ ፡ ድምፅ ፡ አይሰማም ፡ አለቻት ። ፪ተኛ ፡ ተናደደችና ፡
ሰሚኝ ፡ ስጮህ ፡ አለች ። ከዚህ ፡ በኋላ ፡ ቂንተል ፡ እንደ ፡ አንበሳ ፡
እጮሀለሁ ፡ ብላ ፡ ከ፪ት ፡ ተሰንጥቃ ፡ ሞተች ። እንደዚህም ፡ ሁሉ ፡
ከባለጸጋ ፡ ጋራ ፡ የሚጣላን ፡ ደሀ ፡ ደሀችን ፡ ያገኜ ፡ መከራ ፡ ያገኝዋል ።

A hare lived in a country where there was no other kind of animal. "There is no animal as big as I and none whose voice can equal mine," he said to one of his friends. "That is true," replied the other, for they had never seen another. One day, hearing a lion roar, the first hare said, "I shall cry like him." "Good. I'll stay to hear you. Cry!" said his friend. "Listen," said the hare, and, swelling his chest, he cried. His friend said to him, "The lion's voice is strong; yours, on the other hand, cannot be heard." The hare became very angry and said a second time, "Watch and listen how I cry." And under the illusion of roaring like a lion, he split in two and died. The same fate awaits the poor man who vies with the rich.

—Amharic fable

Amharic is the national language of Ethiopia. It is spoken in the vicinity of the capital, Addis Ababa, and the area just to the north. Its speakers number 9 million, about one-third of Ethiopia's population.

Amharic is one of the Semitic languages. Together with a number of the lesser languages of Ethiopia it constitutes the Ethiopic branch of this family. All the Ethiopic languages are descended from Geez, the ancient literary and ecclesiastic language of Ethiopia.

It is generally believed that the Semitic languages were introduced into Ethiopia from the Arabian Peninsula sometime in the first millennium B.C. The Ethiopic alphabet used in Amharic is also believed to have had its ultimate origin in Arabia. Originally written from right to left, it eventually switched, probably under Greek influence, from left to right. Two dots are placed after each word to separate it from the next.

Somali

Sidii koorweyn halaad oo
Kor iyo Hawd sare ka timid
Kulayl badan baan qabaa

Shimbiro geed wada koraa
Midi ba cayn bay u cidaa
Carro ba waa camaladdeed
Illayn Lays ma cod yaqaan

Hal baa hilin igaga jaban
Hilbaha yaan ka ceshadaa
Habeenkii ka ma lulmoodoo
Dharaartii ka ma hadh galo

Sankaa qori igaga jabay
Sintaa midig baan ka jabay
Il baa sachar igaga dhacay
Haddana waan soconayaa

Like a she-camel with a large bell
Come from the plateau and upper Haud,
My heat is great.

Birds perched together on the same tree
Call each their own cries,
Every country has its own ways,
Indeed people do not understand each others' talk.

One of my she-camels falls on the road
And I protect its meat,
At night I cannot sleep,
And in the daytime I can find no shade.

I have broken my nose on a stick,
I have broken my right hip,
I have something in my eye,
And yet I go on.

—*Fortitude* (anonymous)

Somali is the national language of Somalia, in easternmost Africa. It is spoken by the great majority of the population (about 3 million people), as well as another 1½ million in Ethiopia, and about 300,000 in Kenya. Somali is one of the Cushitic languages, which form a branch of the Afro-Asiatic (Hamito-Semitic) family. In 1973 it was made the official language of Somalia.

Kikuyu

Gikuyu ni gitikitie Ngai
mumbi wa Iguru na Thi,
na muheani wa indo ciothe.

Ngai ndarimuthia kana githethwa,
Ndari ithe kana nyina,
Ndataragwo na arutaga wira ari wiki.

Aikaraga Matu-ini
no ni ari mucii ungi bururi-ini wa Gikuyu
uria Ahurukaga riria okite gucera Thi;
mucii ucio uri Kirima-ini gia Kirinyaga.

Arathimaga Kana akaruma mundu
kana Kirindi, na
Aheanaga na agatunyana
kuringana na ciiko cia ciana Ciake.

Gikuyu ni kigocaga Ngai hingo ciothe
tondu wa uria anagitanahira muno,
ni gukihe bururi mwega
utagaga nyama, irio kana Mai.

The Gikuyu believe in God
the creator of heaven and earth,
the giver of all things.

God has no beginning nor end,
He has no father nor mother,
He takes no advice and works singlehandedly.

He lives in heaven
but has another home in Gikuyuland,
where He rests when He visits earth;
this home is on Mount Kenya.

He blesses and curses individual
and society, and
He gives and withholds His gifts
according to the actions of His children.

The Gikuyu praise their God always
because of His genuine generosity,
in giving them fertile country
which lacks no meat, food, or water.

—MAINA KAGOMBE, *The Gikuyu Concept of God*

The Kikuyu are the largest tribal group in Kenya, numbering about 2 million people. They inhabit the fertile land around the slopes of Mount Kenya to the north of Nairobi. The Kikuyu language is of the Bantu family.

Luba

Muntu wakatompele mbao. Wafika katompa mbao, ino watana mulubao lumo lupye ntambo. Ino muntu wadi kāsake kumutapa; ntambo kānena'mba: Ngabule, kokantapa. Shi ubangabula nankyo nāmi nkakupa mpalo. Ino muntu wamwabula; ino kwadi'mba: Ke nkudi. Muntu amba: Nanshi e mo wadyumukila. Kwivwana padi mpuku mu lubao'mba: Iya bidi pano, ntambo; le kukīye? Nanshi umōngwelanga palubao.

Penepo ntambo'mbo: Mfwene; waponene mōnka mu lubao. Mpuku waita muntu amba: Iya umutape. Pēnepo muntu wafwena kāmutape, wamwipaya. Penepo ntambo pa kufwa kwadi muntu amba: Le nkupa ka, abe mpuku? Aye mpuku amba: Nsaka twisambe nōbe bulunda, unsele kōbe kunjibo, untule pa kapala. Nāndi wamusela wamutula pa kitala kāikele'tu nyeke.

A man went to examine his pit-traps. He came and looked at the traps, and found in one pit a lion. As the man was about to spear him the lion said, "Lift me out, do not spear me. If you lift me out, I will give you a reward." So the man lifted him out, but he said, "Now I will eat you." But hark, a rat in the pit said, "Come here, lion; why don't you come?" Now he was tricking him about the pit.

So the lion thought, "I will go near." So he fell once again into the pit. The rat called the man and said, "Come and spear him." So then the man came near and speared him, killing him. Then when the lion was dead, the man said, "What shall I give you, O Rat?" The rat replied saying, "I would like you to carry me home to your house, and put me on the tall food-rack." And as for the man, he carried him away and put him on the rack, and he lived there always.

Luba, also known as Chiluba, is one of the major languages of Zaïre (formerly Congo-Kinshasa). It is spoken by about 3 million people, mainly in the southeastern part of the country. The language belongs to the Bantu family.

Lingala

Tokosepelaka míngi na botángi o kásá malúli ma báníngá baíké, bakosɛ́ngɛ te báléndisa bolakisi kóta ya Pútú o kelási ya baíndo. Yangó malámu míngi sɔ̂lɔ́. Kási bandeko ba bísó bâná bakobósanaka te malúli ma pámba pámba makomɔ́nisa moto lokóla mwána mokɛ́. Mwána sɔ́kɔ́ azalí na límpa sikáwa, ekomɔ́nɔ yě sukáli, akobwáka límpa pé akolela sukáli. Loléngé lɔ́kɔ́ sɔ́kɔ́ bakolakisa bísó lingála, kiswahíli, kikɔ́ngɔ́, tsiluba, b.n.b., toébí naíno malámu tɛ́, tokoíbwáka pé tokolela français, flamand, anglais. Wâná níni? Tokomɛmya kóta ya bísó tɛ́; tokoíbébisa bobébisi. Na yangó mindɛ́lɛ́ bakolomɔ́na bǒ bána bakɛ̂ ba bilúlélá pé bakosɛkɛ bísó.

We are pleased to read in the newspapers that many of our friends are pressing for the teaching of European languages in the schools for Blacks. This is an excellent idea. But our friends often forget that impractical ideas often make a man look like a small child. If the child who has, for example, a piece of bread, should see a piece of sugar, he will toss away the bread and take the sugar. It is the same with Lingala, Swahili, Kongo, Luba, etc., which we have not yet thoroughly mastered, but which we are discarding in favor of French, Flemish, and English. What then? We will no longer respect our own languages and can only debase them. Thus the whites look upon us as small children filled with vain desires and they make fun of us.

Lingala is spoken in northern and northwestern Zaïre (the former Congo-Kinshasa) and the northern part of the Congo-Brazzaville. There are about 1½ million speakers in the former and about 300,000 in the latter. Lingala is another of the Bantu languages.

Kongo

Kilumbu kimosi M'vangi wa vova kua bibulu. "Tuka ntama yitudi banza nani vakati kua beno yigufueti kala n'tinu, bubu nsoledi vo mbua sikakala n'tinu. Bonso luzeyi, mbua yi n'kundi wa unene wa muntu. Siyakubika n'kinzi, situa dia buna si tuayadisa mbua."

Kansi na nsiesi kazola yalua kua mbua ko. Mpimpa yina kaleka ko wabanza ye wa sosa nzila mu vunzakisa luzolo lua M'vangi. Kilumbu ki landa bibulu bia vuanda ga mesa, na nsiesi wa vuandila lukufi ye mbua. Buna wa geta kiyisi ga n'totu, muna ntangu yina mbua watimuka ye landa kiyisi. Bibulu biakulu biayituka mu mavanga ma mbua. Buna na nsiesi watelama ye vova, "Bue yani mbua kafueti yadila beto yani muntu gakena mavanga ka mazimbuka ko e?" Mbua kani yadisua kayala ko mu kilumbu kina, nate ye bubu M'vangi ukini sosa nani fueni gana kifulu kana kikala mbua.

Once upon a time the Creator said to the animals, "For a long time I've been thinking about who shall rule among you, and at last I've decided that it should be the dog. He is, after all, man's best friend. I invite each of you to a feast at which the dog will be crowned king."

But the hare could not stand the idea of being ruled by a dog. He lay awake all night thinking how to thwart the Creator's plan. The following day at the feast he sat next to the dog. Suddenly he threw down a bone, whereupon the dog leaped from the table to grab it. All the animals were shocked. Then the hare stood up and said, "How can the dog pretend to govern us if he is ignorant of the basic elements of good manners?" The crowning of the dog was, of course, canceled, and it is said that the Creator is still seeking a king for the animals.

Kongo, more correctly called Kikongo, is spoken near the mouth of the Congo River—in western Zaïre (formerly Congo-Kinshasa), in the southern part of the People's Republic of the Congo (capital: Brazzaville), as well as in northern Angola. Its speakers number nearly 3 million—about 2 million in Zaïre, 300,000 in Congo-Brazzaville, and 500,000 in Angola. Kongo is another of the Bantu languages.

Ganda

Lumu ensolo zawakana okudduka nti anasooka okutuka kuntebe gyezali zitadewo yanaba omufuzi. Ngabulijjo wampologoma yeyasokayo, naye, teyamanya nti munne nawolovu yali yekwese mumukiragwe. Kale bweyali agenda okutula kuntebbe nawulira nga nawolovu amugamba nti, sebo tontuulako. Nawolovu ngayetwalira bufuzi. "Amagezi gakira amanyi."

The animals had no leader and decided to choose one. A race was held, and a chair was placed a long distance away. The first animal to reach the chair and sit on it would be the leader. As usual, the lion was the fastest, but he did not know that the chameleon was sitting behind his tail. As he sat on the chair, he heard a cry. He jumped up and was surprised to find the chameleon, who claimed he was first and therefore the leader. "Wisdom is better than strength."

Ganda, also known as Luganda, is the most important language of Uganda, in East Africa. Its speakers, the Baganda, live principally in the former kingdom of Buganda, which is located in the southern region and includes the capital city of Kampala. They number about 2 million, or 20 percent of the country's population. Ganda is another of the Bantu languages.

Ruanda

Impundu z'urwunge zavugiye mu muli Maternite y'i Kigali, zivugilizwa umubyeyi wabyaye umwana uteye imbabazi. Uwo mwana yavutse afite ibiro bine na grama magana ane. Yaba ali umwe mu bana banini cyane bavukiye muli iyo nzu y'ababyeyi y'i Kigali, niba rero atali we ubaye uwa mbere.

At the Kigali Maternity Hospital a mother was highly congratulated for having given birth to a child breaking the record in weight for this maternity hospital. The child weighed at birth 4 kilos, 400 grams. It is the first baby born in the Kigali Maternity Hospital to weigh that much.

Ruanda, more properly known as Kinyarwanda, is an important language of east-central Africa. It is spoken by virtually everyone in the republic of Rwanda (about 4 million people), and by perhaps a million more in neighboring Zaïre. Ruanda is one of the Bantu languages.

Rundi

Kuva aho Uburundi bwikukiriye ibintu bitari bike vyarateye imbere mu gihugu. Kuva aho Republika ituvyagiriyemwo na ho, amajambere yarongerekanye muri vyinshi, cane cane mu butunzi bwa Leta. Mugabo ikinzindukanye aha lero, n'ukugira turabe aho ukurera abanyagihugu kugereye. Musanzwe muzi lero ko indero y'umuntu ihagaze kuri vyose: ari ku bwenge, ku magara, canke ku mutima. Rimwe narigeze kwandika muri Ndongozi, ko ubu hariko haraba ikirere amahanga hagati y'abize n'abatize. Na none birumvikana kuko bamwe baguma bikarihiriza ubwenge, abandi na bo bakaguma mu buhumyi bâmanye.

Since Burundi became independent, many things have improved within the country. And since the advent of the Republic, progress has been made in many fields, especially in the state's economy. But the reason I am writing today is to try to see how education has progressed. You already know that human progress depends on many things: on education, on health, on spiritual values. I once wrote in Ndongozi [a magazine] how the gap between the educated people and the illiterate is growing wider and wider. This is understandable, since the former continue to learn while the latter remain in their illiteracy.

Rundi, or Kirundi, is the national language of Burundi, in east-central Africa. It is spoken by the entire population of the country, or some 4 million people. A Bantu language, Rundi is closely related to Ruanda of neighboring Rwanda—in fact, the two are little more than dialects of the same language.

Nyanja

Kalekale Kunali munthu wina dzina lace Awonenji. Anzace Sanalikumuwelengela Koma iye Sanadzipatule. Tsiku lina pamene anawalondolela Ku ulenje, anthu odzikuzawo Sanawonjeko ndi maukonde awo. Pomwe analikubwelela Ku mudzi anakumana ndi njoru. Iwo anacha maukonde yawo. Njoru zitawonjedwa, zinazula mphompho zaukondewo ndi Kupitililabe. Awonenji anatemapo imodzi ndi buma mmaso ndipo imagma pansi ndi Kufa cifukwa inalikuphupha ndi infa. Awonenji amapha njoru ndi buma.

Once upon a time there lived a man whom his community generally regarded as an idiot. In spite of this he did not isolate himself. On a certain day he followed his companions on a hunting trip during which they did not kill any game. While returning home they met elephants which they trapped with nets that the elephants had tramped over. The idiot picked up a stone and struck one elephant in the eye. The elephant fell dead because it had already been very seriously wounded by a hunter. . . . An idiot killed an elephant with a small stone.

Nyanja, more correctly known as Chinyanja, is a major language of both Malawi and Zambia. In the former, where it is known as Chewa, it is spoken by more than half the population, or over $2\frac{1}{2}$ million people, while in Zambia it is spoken by another 750,000. Nyanja is another of the Bantu languages.

Bemba

Calandwa ukutila indimi ishilandwa mu calo ca Africa shaba pakati kampendwa imyanda mutanda ne myanda cine konse konse. Cintu cayafya ukwishiba bwino impendwa ya ndimi ishilandwa ngatwati tweshe ukupatulula ululimi lumo lumo, mpaka fye ilyo lintu kukaba ifilangililo ifingi kabili ifyalondololwa bwino bwino. Kwena, impendwa ishilangilwe pamulu, shilelanga apabuta tutu ukutila indimi mu calo ca Africa shaba ishingi kabili ishalekana lekana, nokucila ku kuboko kwa kulyo ukwa ciswebebe ca Sahara.

The number of languages spoken on the African continent is estimated to be between six and eight hundred. Until more information is available, and until a more precise criterion as to what constitutes a separate language is agreed upon, no exact number can be given. The figures quoted, however, clearly indicate the great linguistic diversity of Africa, particularly that portion which lies south of the Sahara.

Bemba is the most widely spoken language of Zambia. Its $1\frac{1}{2}$ million speakers live mainly in the northeastern part of the country. Bemba is one of the Bantu languages, most closely related to Luba, spoken in neighboring Zaïre.

Shona

Zuʋa rese ŋgoma yakaswera icicema,
Ʋanhu ʋakatamba kutamba kusina rufaro.
Mambo akaswedza zuʋa ari mumba,
Haana kumboɓuɗa kana kweŋguʋa shoma cete.
Asi ʋahosi, mukadzi mukuru wamambo,
Ndiʋo ʋakaɓuɗa ʋakapembera nesimba,
Simba rinoshamisa iɀo risakabva mukudya.
Curu mukuru wakaswera agere paɗare,
Aciridza ŋgoma kuɗaidzira ʋanhu ʋese
Kuti, 'Uŋganai imi mose ʋaManyika,
Zuʋa riya razoȿika, zuʋa rokugumisira,
Nokuti Nyatene akafanira kutinzwa nhasi,
Kana acizotinzwa kana narini muiyi nhamo.'

Ʋarume ʋazhinji ʋakaŋge ʋakapfeka
Macira nematehwe macena nematema,
Ʋakatamba ʋakaimba ʋakanamata.

Zuʋa rakaŋge raʋa kupota,
Ʋanhu ʋese ʋakaŋge ʋaneta,
Mazwi akaŋge aʋa kuenda.
Mambo akaɓuɗa kubva mumba,
Cima icicema, ŋgoma icirira,
Iye aciɀituŋgamidza nemuɗonɀo.

All day long the drum continued to cry and the people danced a dance without joy. The King spent the day in his house, he did not come out even for a little while. But the Queen, the chief wife of the King, she it was who came forth and danced with might, a strange might since it came not from food. Curu the old spent the day seated in the court, beating the drum to summon all the people saying, "Gather together, all you Manyika, that day has come at last, the day of ending, for Nyatene must hear us today, if ever he will hear us in this distress."

Many of the men were wearing cloths and skins of black and white, they danced, they sang and they prayed.

Now the sun was setting and all the people were tired, their voices were going. The King came forth from his house while the mournful drum-beat cried and reechoed, and he supported himself on his staff.

—H. W. CHITEPO, *Soko Risina Musoro*

Shona is the principal language of the Republic of Rhodesia, in southern Africa. It is spoken by about 4 million people, or 70 percent of the native population. Shona is another of the Bantu languages.

Afrikaans

Vanaand het ek weer so verlang,
in grondelose vrees
van eie gryse eensaamheid,
dat jy by my moet wees,

dat ek die wye koeltes van
jou stem om my kan voel,
soos die rimp'ling van die somerreën
vervlugtig oor my spoel.

En toe ek deur die duister wind
wat oor my huisie waai,
die knip hoor lig, het heel my hart
in vreugde opgelaai . . .

Nou sit ons voor die vuur en speel
die vlamlig deur ons hare . . .
Laag waai die reënwind buite deur
die afgevalle blare.

This evening once again I longed
in vague, abysmal fear
of my own old, grey loneliness
that you were with me here,

that the cool reaches of your voice
about me I were feeling,
like the rippling of the summer rain
so softly o'er me stealing.

And when above the dark, cold wind
that round my cottage blew
I heard the latch, my heart leapt up
with joy to welcome you . . .

And now we sit before the fire,
its flame-glow in our hair . . .
Meanwhile the rain-wind murmurs through
the fallen leaves out there.

—W. E. G. LOUW, *Quiet Evening*

Afrikaans is one of the two official languages of the Republic of South Africa, the other being English. It is spoken by over 4 million people—the $2\frac{1}{4}$ million white Afrikaaners, plus about 2 million "coloreds," or persons of mixed descent. The former live mainly in the northeastern provinces of Transvaal and Orange Free State; the latter mainly in the western part of Cape Province in the west.

Afrikaans is a development of 17th-century Dutch brought to South Africa by the first settlers from Holland. The subsequent isolation of the people and their descendants caused increasing deviations from the original Dutch, so that Afrikaans may now be considered a separate language. Written Afrikaans can be most easily distinguished from Dutch by the indefinite article *'n*, which in Dutch is *een*.

Zulu

Ngimbeleni ngaphansi kotshani
Duze nezihlahla zomyezane
Lapho amagatsh' eyongembesa
Ngamaqaɓung' agcwel' uɓuhlaza.
Ngozwa nami ngilele ngaphansi
Utshani ngaphezulu ɓuhleɓa :
" Lala sithandwa, lal' uphumule."

Ngimbeleni endawen' enjena :
Laph' izinsungulo zezilimi
Zenkathazo zingenakuthola
Sango lokwahlukanis' umhlaɓa
Zingivus' eɓuthongwen' oɓuhle.
Uma wen' ofunda leminqana,
Ungifica, ungimbele lapho
Utshani ngaphezulu ɓuyothi :
" Lala sithandwa, lal' uphumule."

Bury me where the grasses grow
Below the weeping willow trees
To let their branches shed upon me
Leaves of varied greens.
Then, as I lie there, I shall hear
The grasses sigh a soft behest:
"Sleep, beloved one, sleep and rest."

Bury me in a place like this:
Where those who scheme and give their tongues
To plots and anger, never can
Displace the earth that covers me
Nor ever keep me from my sleep.
If you who read these lines should chance
To find me, O then bury me
Where grasses whisper this behest:
"Sleep, beloved one, sleep and rest."

—BENEDICT WALLET VILAKAZI, *If Death Should Steal Upon Me*

Zulu is one of the major Bantu languages of South Africa. The home of the Zulus, Zululand, is located in the province of Natal, in the easternmost part of the Republic of South Africa. The language is closely related to Xhosa and Swazi, the three belonging to the Nguni branch of the Bantu family. There are about 4 million speakers.

Xhosa

Nkosi, sikelel' i' Afrika
Malupakam' upondo Iwayo;
Yiva imitandazo yetu
Usisikelele

Yihla Moya, yihla Moya
Yihla Moya Oyingcwele

Sikelela iNkose zetu
Zimkumbule umDali wazo;
Zimoyike Zezimhlouele,
Azisikelele.

Lord, bless Africa
May her spirit rise high up;
Hear Thou our prayers
And bless us.

Descend, O Spirit
Descend, O Holy Spirit

Bless our chiefs;
May they remember their Creator,
Fear Him and revere Him,
That He may bless them.
—Xhosa National Anthem

Xhosa is spoken principally in the Transkei territory of South Africa, which borders Lesotho and faces the Indian Ocean. It is another of the Bantu languages with about 4 million speakers. The Xhosas have intermingled with the Hottentots and their language contains some of the Hottentot "click" sounds. The *Xh* at the beginning of their name represents one of these sounds.

Sotho

Le hoja 'muso ona o itlama ho sireletsa litokelo tsa botho tsa batsoali naheng ena, e leng tokelo ea ho nyalana le ho ba le bana, 'muso oa tlameha hape ho hopotsa baahi ba Lesotho ho hlokomela boikarabelo bo boholo ba sechaba ka kakaretso esitana le boiketlo ba sona ba nako e tlang. 'Muso ha o na ho kenakenana le taba ea hore na lelapa le be boholo bo bokae; 'muso ha o na ho seha moeli oa palo ea bana le hore na ba sieane ka lilemo tse kae, empa leha ho le joalo 'muso o kopa hore motho ka mong esitana le mekhatlo e ke e ele taba ena hloko le ho bona se tlisoang ke keketseho e potlakileng ena ea sechaba.

While this government does guarantee the protection of the human rights of every mother and father in the country, the right to marry and to procreate, it must remind the citizens of Lesotho to be aware of their great responsibility to the society as a whole, and to the future well-being of the entire nation. This government will not interfere with the size of anyone's family, it will not dictate any ideal number of children or the spacing of births, but it asks that private individuals and private organizations pay serious attention to all implications of the present rapid growth of our population.

Sotho, more correctly called Sesotho, is one of the major languages of southern Africa. Sotho proper refers to Southern Sotho, spoken by about one million people in Lesotho and another $1\frac{1}{2}$ million in the surrounding areas of South Africa. In its broader sense it includes Northern Sotho, or Pedi, spoken in northern Transvaal, South Africa, and Western Sotho, generally referred to as Tswana. Sotho is another of the Bantu languages.

Tswana

Mmina-Photi wa bo khama le Ngwato-a-Masilo
Ka kala fela jaaka lenong Marung
Motseng gaetsho ka go tlhoka ke go lebile
Ke kwaletse tsala yame kele kgakala
"A pelo tsa lona di se fuduege
Mme dumelang mo Modimong."
Nna ke leje je le tlhaotsweng go—Nna Motheo wa kago.

I, descendant of Khama, and Nwato of the line of Masilo, whose totem is the duiker,
Hovered like a vulture, high up in the clouds.
Even as I looked, my home eluded my eyes.
I wrote to my friend from far away,
"Let not your hearts be troubled,
But trust in the Lord . . ."
I am a rock chosen to be the cornerstone of a people.

Tswana, more correctly called Setswana, is another of the Bantu languages of southern Africa. Its speakers, the Tswana, number about $2\frac{1}{2}$ million—$1\frac{3}{4}$ million of whom live in South Africa, and 700,000 in the neighboring country of Botswana, which is named after them. Tswana is closely related to the Sotho language and, in fact, is often referred to as Western Sotho.

Swazi

Nkulunkulu, mnikati wetibusiso temaSwati,
Siyatibonga tonkhe tinhlanhla;
Sibonga iNggwenyama yetfhu,
Live, netintshaba, nemifula.
Busisa tiphatshimandla takaNggwane;
Nguwe wedvwa Somandla wetfhu.
Sinike kuhlakanipha lokungenabucili;
Simise, usicinise, Simakadze.

O God, bestower of the blessings of the Swazi,
We are thankful for all our good fortune;
We give praise and thanks for our King,
And for our country, its hills and rivers.
Bless those in authority in our land;
Thou only art our Almighty,
Give us wisdom without guile;
Establish and strengthen us, Thou Everlasting.
—Swazi National Anthem

Swazi, more correctly called Siswati, is the national language of the kingdom of Swaziland in southern Africa. It is spoken by virtually the entire native population of the country, or about 400,000 people, as well as an additional 500,000 in South Africa. Swazi is one of the Bantu languages, closely related to Zulu and Xhosa, and in fact can be readily understood by speakers of these languages.

Bushman

Kóroke̥n ‖χ̥au ǀki ‖kaúë, au ‖kaúëte̥n ǀkā wāï. Kóroke̥n ǀne ‖χéi‖χĕi, haṅ ǀne taṅ-ĩ ‖kaúë a͝u wāïta ă. ( ) Haṅ bó̱rŏ, haṅ taṅ-ĩ, a͝u haṅ tátti ē̱ kóro ǀkŭ ē̱. Hé̱ ti hiṅ ē̱, ha ǀkŭ bō̱rŏ, haṅ ‖kwaṅ táṅ-ĩ, haṅ tatti kóro ǀkú ē̱. Hē̱ ti hiṅ ē̱, ha ǀku bō̱rŏ a͝u ha táṅ-ĩ, haṅ ‖kwăṅ ká ‖kaúë ă ha ā̱, ha si hā̱, ha si ‖χ̇a̩m hā.

( ) Hē̱ ti hiṅ ē, ‖kaúëte̥n ǀne !koeiṅ í, ‖kaúëte̥n ǀne ǀkī ha, ‖kaúëte̥n ǀne ts'ī ǀkūke̥n ha, haṅ ǀne hō ha, haṅ ǀne ‖aṅ ǀkí lē ha au ǀkúbbi; ( ) hē ti hiṅ ē haṅ ǀne !naú tĩ hă.

The jackal watches the leopard when the leopard has killed a springbok. The jackal whines (with uplifted tongue), he begs the leopard for springbok flesh. He howls, he begs, for he is a jackal. Thus he howls, he indeed begs, because he is a jackal. Therefore he howls when he begs, he indeed wants the leopard to give him flesh, that he may eat, that he also may eat.

Then the leopard is angry, the leopard kills him, the leopard bites him dead, he lifts him up, he goes to put him into the bushes; thus he hides him.

Bushman is spoken principally in the Kalahari Desert of southern Africa. Its speakers, the Bushmen, number about 50,000—divided between three countries: Botswana (25,000), South West Africa (15,000), and South Africa (10,000). Like Hottentot, also spoken in South West Africa, Bushman is a member of the Khoisan family of languages.

The most notable feature of Bushman, and in fact of all the Khoisan languages, is the use of the so-called "click" consonants, produced by drawing air into the mouth and clicking the tongue. Since conventional spellings are obviously inadequate to represent these sounds, an assortment of lines, dots, and other marks are used.

Hottentot

≠Kam !ūi-aob gye //ĕib di gūna !homi !na gye !ũi hā i. /Gui tsĕb gye !gare-/uiï di !khareï ei heiï di somi !na gye ≠nõa i, tsĩb gye //om tsĩ sĩgurase gye !gan-tana, tanaba ra !hororose. Ob gye //ĕib /gūse gyere !ũ beiraba !ũi-aob ta !kamsa //goa bi, ti gye ≠ĕi. //Natib gye ≠nirase gye ≠homisęn, tsĩb gye //hei-≠nu ei bi nĩse !gũṅ, tsĩ /nĩ dā-!hararoti gose gye ≠gai-!oa-!oasęn, tsĩb gye !ũi-aob ei //hei-≠nũ tsĩ //khōse gye !khā bi.

Ob gye !ũi-aoba //khōse ≠kon ≠oms ăba χu ≠kei-≠keihe, tsĩ gye //gao tsĩb gye //eiχa hăse uri-khăi tsĩ beiraba gye !khō, tsĩ //nāba gye /gūse mā i tsouï !na gye /nami-//na bi. χawe //nāsan nĩ nou gūna mũ, tįmis /kan gye beiraba sau tsĩ tsoub !na gye uri-//gõa tsĩ /khom-/khomsase !garegu ei gye ≠ku. //Natib gye !ũi-aoba !gawua-!na hăse /ũn ăba ra tsuru-!ă gye ≠gei : „≠Kawa //eiba χu ≠gōsęn tama īs gye ≠khõas tsĩ /am-≠gōsęns tsĩna ra ū-hā."

One day a young shepherd was watching his sheep on a mountainside. While he was sitting on a rock in the shade of a tree, his head nodded forward and he fell asleep. A ram grazing nearby, seeing the shepherd lower his head, thought he was threatening to fight. So he got ready, and drawing himself back a few paces he launched himself at the shepherd and butted him severely.

The shepherd, thus rudely awakened from his sleep, arose angrily, caught the ram, and threw him into a well standing nearby. But the moment the other sheep saw their leader fall into the well, they followed him in and were dashed to pieces on the rocks. So the shepherd, tearing his hair, cried out: "What sorrow and trouble are brought about by useless anger!"

Hottentot is spoken in South West Africa. Its speakers are not numerous—about 50,000—and constitute about one-fifteenth of the country's population. Like Bushman, Hottentot belongs to the Khoisan family of languages.

Hottentot is another of the "click" languages, the sounds represented by such symbols as /, ≠, //, !, and #. When the earliest Dutch settlers in southern Africa first encountered this language, they described it as consisting of nothing more than the sounds *hot* and *tot*. Thus arose the term Hottentot. Today it has a somewhat derisive connotation and many people prefer the term Nama, the name of the largest Hottentot-speaking tribe.

Malagasy

Aza anontaniana izay anton'izao
Fanginako lalina ary feno tomany!
Aza anontaniana, satria fantatrao
Fa fahatsiarovana no anton'izany . . .

Tsaroako ny tsikin'ny androko omaly,
Izay manjary aloka foana, indrisy!
Tsaroako! . . . Antsoiko ta tsy mba mamaly,
Ary toa manadino, ary toa tsy mba nisy!

You shall not ask what the present tears
From the deep of my silence mean!
You shall not ask because you know
They are memories of long ago!

I recall the joys of days gone by,
They waned alas to flit away!
I claim and call them forth in vain
As though oblivious and never again!

—J. J. RABEARIVELO, *Love Song*

Malagasy, also known as Malgache, is spoken on the island of Madagascar which in 1960 became the Malagasy Republic. Its 7 million speakers include most of the population of the island.

It would be logical to assume that Malagasy belongs to one or another of the African language families but this is not the case. Investigation has established it as one of the Malayo-Polynesian languages, the rest of which are spoken thousands of miles to the east, in Southeast Asia and on islands in the Pacific. It is now believed that the inhabitants of Madagascar are descendants of settlers from present-day Indonesia (perhaps the island of Borneo), who arrived between 1,500 and 2,000 years ago.

Malagasy contains some words of Bantu, Arab, French, and English origin. It has a soft, musical quality somewhat reminiscent of Italian.

AN ARTIFICIAL LANGUAGE

Esperanto

Ne provizu al vi trezorojn sur la tero, kie tineo kaj rusto konsumas, kaj kie ŝtelistoj trafosas kaj ŝtelas; sed provizu al vi trezorojn en la ĉielo, kie nek tineo nek rusto konsumas, kaj kie ŝtelistoj nek trafosas nek ŝtelas; ĉar kie estas via trezoro, tie estos ankaŭ via koro. La lampo de la korpo estas la okulo; se do via okulo estas sendifekta, via tuta korpo estos luma. Sed se via okulo estas malbona, via tuta korpo estos malluma. Se do la lumo en vi estas mallumo, kiel densa estas la mallumo!

Lay not up for yourselves treasures upon earth, where moth and rust doth corrupt, and where thieves break through and steal; but lay up for yourselves treasures in heaven, where neither moth nor rust doth corrupt, and where thieves do not break through nor steal; for where your treasure is, there will your heart be also. The light of the body is the eye; if therefore thine eye be single, thy whole body shall be full of light. But if thine eye be evil, thy whole body shall be full of darkness. If therefore the light that is in thee be darkness, how great is the darkness!

—Portion of the Sermon on the
Mount, Matthew vi.19–23

Esperanto, the most important and influential of the so-called artificial languages, was devised in 1887 by Dr. Lazarus Ludwig Zamenhof of Warsaw, Poland. Based on the elements of the foremost Western languages, Esperanto is incomparably easier to master than any national tongue, for its grammar rules are completely consistent, and a relatively small number of basic roots can be expanded into an extensive vocabulary by means of numerous prefixes, suffixes, and infixes. The French Academy of Sciences has called Esperanto "a masterpiece of logic and simplicity."

The Esperanto alphabet consists of twenty-eight letters—twenty-two English letters plus ĉ, pronounced *ch* (*e.g.*, *ĉielo*—sky); ĝ, pronounced *j* (*aĝo*—age); ĥ, pronounced like the German *ch* but rarely used; ĵ, pronounced *zh* (*ĵurnalo*—newspaper); ŝ, pronounced *sh* (*fiŝo*—fish); and ŭ, used in forming diphthongs (*ankaŭ*—also). *C* is pronounced *ts* (*cento*—hundred), *j* is pronounced *y* (*jes*—yes), and *q*, *w*, *x*, and *y* are absent. Every word is pronounced exactly as it is spelled, with the stress always on the next to last syllable. There are no silent letters.

All nouns in Esperanto end in -o, adjectives in -a, adverbs in -e, and verb infinitives in -i. Notice the combination *varmo* (warmth), *varma* (warm), *varme* (warmly), and *varmi* (to warm). The suffix -j is added to nouns to form the plural and also to adjectives when the nouns they modify are plural. The present tense of a verb ends in -as, the past tense in -is, the future in -os, the conditional in -us, and the imperative in -u. No changes are made for person or for number. There is no indefinite article; the one definite article *la* stands for all numbers and genders.

A few examples of the Esperanto system of word formation will serve to illustrate the ease with which new words may be learned. The infix *-in-*, for example, indicates the feminine form (*frato*—brother, *fratino*—sister; *koko*—rooster, *kokino*—hen). The infix *-eg-* indicates intensity (*pluvo*—rain, *pluvego*—downpour); the infix *-ar-* indicates a collection of similar objects (*arbo*—tree, *arbaro*—forest); and the infix *-er-* indicates a unit of a whole (*ĉeno*—chain, *ĉenero*—link).

If the reader will examine the passage above, he will observe that all but a very few of the words have been adopted from one of the major Western European languages.

Part III

COUNTRY-BY-COUNTRY SURVEY

AFGHANISTAN (18 million). Persian, with 5 million speakers, and Pashto, with 10 million, are the two official languages, the former generally used in government circles. There are also about one million speakers of Uzbek and 400,000 speakers of Turkmen.

ALBANIA (2 million). Albanian is spoken by practically the entire population.

ALGERIA (15 million). Arabic is spoken by the vast majority of the population. About 2½ million people speak various Berber languages. Kabyle is spoken by over 2 million people in the mountains east of Algiers. Slightly to the south and east, in the region known as the Aurès, Shawia is spoken by about 150,000 people. Far to the south, in scattered parts of the Sahara Desert, about 10,000 Tuaregs speak Tamashek. French is spoken by the dwindling European community and by many educated Algerians.

ANDORRA (20,000). Catalan is spoken here.

ANGOLA (6 million). The official language is Portuguese, spoken by the country's 500,000 whites. The most important native language is Mbundu, a term that actually embraces two languages—Umbundu, with about 2 million speakers in central Angola, and Kimbundu, with about 1½ million speakers in the north. Kongo is spoken by about 500,000 people in the far north, Chokwe by a like number of people in the northeast. Lwena (Luvale) is spoken by about 250,000 people in the eastern panhandle. Lunda, closely related to Chokwe, is spoken by about 50,000 people in the northeast.

ARGENTINA (25 million). Spanish is the official language, spoken by the great majority of the population. Italian speakers number about one million, German 500,000, Yiddish 200,000. Indian languages are spoken in a few remote areas.

AUSTRALIA (13 million). English is spoken by everyone except for the 50,000 aborigines, who speak a great variety of languages. Aranda (Arunta), of the central regions, and Murngin, of Arnhem Land in the far north, are two of the more important.

AUSTRIA (7½ million). German is spoken by almost the entire population.

BAHAMAS (200,000). English is spoken here.

BAHRAIN (200,000). Arabic is spoken here.

BANGLADESH (75 million). Bengali is spoken by the vast majority of the population. A minority of about 500,000 people, referred to somewhat incorrectly as Biharis, speak Urdu.

BARBADOS (250,000). English is spoken here.

BELGIUM (10 million). Flemish, spoken in the north, and French, spoken in the south, are the two official languages. The dividing line extends east-west across the country just below Brussels, though Brussels itself is French-speaking. Flemish is native to about 5½ million people and French to about 4½ million, though about 2 million Belgians are bilingual. Near the German border about 150,000 people speak German.

BHUTAN (1 million). The national language is known as Jonkha. It is written in the Tibetan script. Nepali is spoken in the south.

BOLIVIA (5 million). This country has the highest percentage of Indians of any in the hemisphere. Spanish, the official language, is spoken by less than 40 percent of the population. The two major Indian languages are Quechua, with about 1½ million speakers, and Aymara, with about one million. Others include Chiquito, Guarani, and Tacana.

BOTSWANA (700,000). The official language is English but Tswana is spoken by almost the entire population. There are some 25,000 Bushman speakers in the west.

BRAZIL (100 million). Portuguese is spoken by the vast majority of the population. However, there are sizable colonies of speakers of German, Italian, Spanish, Polish, and Japanese. Indians number less than 200,000. Of their languages the most important are Tupi and Arawak, both spoken in the valley of the Amazon. Carib is spoken in the north, Ge in the east, Guarani in the south, and Panoan in the west.

BRITISH HONDURAS (125,000). English, the official language, is spoken by about three-fourths of the population. Spanish is the mother tongue of about 15 percent, many of whom speak English as well. Maya, or Yucatec, is widely spoken in the northern third of the country, while Kekchi, of the Mayan family, is spoken in a small area of the southwest. Carib is spoken along the southern coast.

BULGARIA (9 million). Bulgarian is spoken by about 90 percent of the population. The Turkish-speaking minority numbers some 750,000.

BURMA (30 million). Burmese is spoken by about three-fourths of the population. Two other important languages are Karen, with about 2½ million speakers in the south, and Shan, with about 1½ million speakers in the north. Chin (500,000) is spoken in the Chin Hills, bordering southern Assam, India, while Kachin, or Chingpaw (350,000) is spoken in the extreme north. Mon, once a major language of the region, now has about 350,000 speakers in the panhandle near the city of Moulmein. Other languages include Palaung (50,000), of the area to the north of Mandalay, and Wa, or Kawa (50,000), spoken along the Salween River as it enters Burma from China.

BURUNDI (4 million). Rundi is spoken by the entire population. It is co-official with French. Swahili serves as a commercial language.

CAMBODIA (7½ million). The national language is Khmer, spoken by about 85 percent of the population. It is co-official with French, which has perhaps 500,000 speakers. Chinese and Vietnamese are each spoken by about 400,000 people. Among tribal languages, Cham is the most important, with about 100,000 speakers.

CAMEROON (6 million). French and English are both official languages, though the latter has relatively few speakers. Native languages number well over 100. Bantu languages predominate in the south, the most important being the closely related Fang and Bulu languages, with a total of 1½ million speakers. Also in the Bantu family are Yaundé and Duala, each spoken in and around the city of the same name. A variety of Pidgin English is widely spoken along the coast. Mbum is spoken in the central regions, while Fulani is the principal language of the north.

CANADA (22 million). English and French are the two official languages. English is the mother tongue of approximately 13 million Canadians, French of approximately 6 million. Nearly 5 million of the 6 million French speakers live in the province of Quebec, where they outnumber speakers of English by two to one. Many Canadians are bilingual, speaking both English and French with equal, or nearly equal, facility.

Some 3 million Canadians claim another language as their mother tongue. According to the 1971 census, German is the mother tongue of 560,000 people, Italian of 540,000, Ukrainian of 310,000, Dutch of 145,000, and Polish of 135,000. Others include Chinese (95,000), Portuguese (85,000), Hungarian (85,000), Serbo-Croatian (75,000), and Yiddish (50,000).

Many Indian languages are also spoken in Canada. The two most important are Cree (30,000 speakers) and Ojibwa, or Chippewa (20,000), both spoken in Ontario, Manitoba, and Saskatchewan. Micmac is spoken by about 4,000 people, mainly in Nova Scotia, Naskapi by about the same number in northern Quebec. Mohawk has about 2,000 speakers in Ontario and Quebec. Chipewyan is spoken by about 3,000 people in northern Manitoba, Saskatchewan, and Alberta; Assiniboin by about 1,000 people in Saskatchewan and Alberta. In Alberta there is also Blackfoot, with about 2,500 speakers. British Columbia has a large number of Indian languages, most with fewer than 1,000 speakers. Okanagan is spoken along the river of the same name, Lillooet, Shuswap, Thompson, and Carrier along the Fraser River, Chilcotin along the Chilcotin River, and Tsimshian along the Skeena and Nass rivers. Nootka is spoken on Vancouver Island, Kwakiutl on northern Vancouver and the adjacent mainland facing Hecate Strait, and Haida on the Queen Charlotte Islands. In the far north there are about 15,000 speakers of Eskimo.

CENTRAL AFRICAN REPUBLIC ($1\frac{1}{2}$ million). The official language is French. Sango, originally the language of a single tribe living on the banks of the Ubangi River, has become the lingua franca of most of the country. Gbaya is an important language of the west, Banda of the central and eastern regions.

CEYLON. *See* Sri Lanka.

CHAD (4 million). The official language is French. The most widespread native language is Sara, with about 750,000 speakers in the southern half of the country. Arabic, in the north, ranks second, with about 500,000. Maba is spoken by about 200,000 people in the area of the east known as Wadai. Teda (Tibbu), of the north, and Mbum, of the south, each have about 100,000 speakers.

CHILE (10 million). Spanish is spoken by the great majority of the population. There is a sizable German minority in a few of the southern provinces. Among Indian languages the most important is Araucanian, with about 200,000 speakers in the area between Concepción and Valdivia.

CHINA (800 million). About 95 percent of the population of China speaks Chinese or one of its dialects. Here we shall treat the remaining 5 percent.

The largest ethnic minority in China is the Chuang, who number about 8 million. Their language, which belongs to the Tai family, is spoken primarily in the Kwangsi Chuang Autonomous Region, which borders Vietnam. Other major groups are the Uigurs (4 million), of the Sinkiang Uigur Autonomous Region, northwest China, who speak a Turkic language; the Yi, or Lolo (3 million), of Yunnan Province, southern China, whose language is of the Tibeto-Burman family; the Miao ($2\frac{1}{2}$ million), residing mainly in Kweichow Province, south-central China, whose language belongs to a separate branch of the Sino-Tibetan family; and the Puyi, or Chungchia ($1\frac{1}{4}$ million), also of Kweichow Province, whose language is also of the Tai family. Three other national languages are spoken by more than a million people in China: Tibetan ($2\frac{3}{4}$ million), Mongolian ($1\frac{1}{2}$ million), and Korean (one million).

Languages whose speakers in China number between 100,000 and one million are: (1) Tung (700,000), a Tai language spoken in Kweichow and Kwangsi; (2) Yao (650,000), related to the above-mentioned Miao, spoken in southeastern China; (3) Kazakh (500,000), a Turkic language spoken in northern Sinkiang; (4) Lisu (320,000), a Tibeto-Burman language spoken in Yunnan Province; (5) Wa, or Kawa (200,000), a Mon-Khmer language spoken in the Chinese-Burmese border area; (6) Nung (170,000), a Tai language spoken in southeastern Yunnan near the border with Vietnam; (7) three Tibeto-Burman languages spoken in Yunnan Province: Nakhi, or Moso (140,000), Lahu (140,000), and Kachin, or Chingpaw (100,000).

For languages with fewer than 100,000 speakers, information is scanty. A few that might be mentioned are (1) Salar (30,000), a

Turkic language of Tsinghai Province; (2) Sibo (20,000), a Tungusic language spoken near the Soviet border; (3) Nanai, or Gold (5,000), also a Tungusic language, which has an additional 7,000 speakers in the Soviet Union.

COLOMBIA (25 million). Spanish is spoken by the vast majority of the population. Indian languages include Arawak and Carib.

CONGO (Brazzaville) (1 million). The official language is French. The most important native languages are Lingala, of the north, and Kongo, of the south, each with about 300,000 speakers. In the south Kituba, a creole language based on Kongo, serves as the lingua franca.

CONGO (Kinshasa). *See* Zaïre.

COSTA RICA (2 million). Spanish is spoken by the vast majority of the population. Two Indian languages spoken are Bribri, with about 4,000 speakers, and Cabecar, with about 1,500.

CUBA (9 million). Spanish is spoken by almost everyone.

CYPRUS (650,000). Greek and Turkish are this island's two languages, the former with about 500,000 speakers, the latter with about 125,000.

CZECHOSLOVAKIA (15 million). Czech, with about 10 million speakers, is spoken in the western provinces of Bohemia and Moravia, while Slovak, with about $4\frac{1}{2}$ million, is spoken in Slovakia. The Hungarian-speaking community numbers about 400,000.

DAHOMEY (3 million). The official language is French. Fon is the most important native language, with about one million speakers in the southern half of the country. Bariba is spoken by about 200,000 people in the north, while Yoruba has a like number of speakers along the eastern border.

DENMARK (5 million). Danish is spoken by virtually everyone.

DOMINICAN REPUBLIC (5 million). Spanish is spoken by almost the entire population.

ECUADOR (7 million). The official language is Spanish. Quechua is the most important Indian language, with about 500,000 speakers. Of the lesser languages, Jivaro is the most important, with about 10,000 speakers.

EGYPT (35 million). Arabic is spoken by almost the entire population.

EL SALVADOR (4 million). Spanish is spoken by the vast majority of the population.

EQUATORIAL GUINEA (300,000). The official language is Spanish. In the mainland province of Río Muni (pop. 220,000) the principal language is Fang. On the island of Fernando Po (pop. 80,000) the natives, who number about 20,000, speak Bubi. Much of the rest of the population consists of workers and settlers from Nigeria and Cameroon.

ETHIOPIA (27 million). Amharic, the national language, is spoken by about a third of the population, or approximately 9 million people. Tigrinya ($2\frac{1}{2}$ million speakers) is spoken in the northern provinces of Tigre and Eritrea, while Tigre (500,000) is spoken in northernmost Eritrea. Gurage (350,000) is spoken southwest of Addis Ababa, and Harari (50,000) in the city of Harar. All of these languages are of the Semitic family and are descended from Geez, the classical literary language of Ethiopia.

The other major languages are of the Cushitic family. The most important is Galla (8 million speakers), spoken to the west, south, and east of Addis Ababa. Sidamo (4 million) is spoken in the southwest, and Somali ($1\frac{1}{2}$ million) in the southeast. Also in the Cushitic family are Beja, Afar, and Saho, with a few hundred thousand speakers each in Eritrea.

English is widely spoken in official circles in Ethiopia, while Arabic and Italian are understood in a number of places.

FIJI (500,000). The indigenous language, Fijian, is spoken by about 40 percent of the population. About half the population is of Indian descent, speaking mainly Hindi and Urdu, but also Tamil, Telugu, and other languages. Most of the population also speaks English, which is the official language.

FINLAND (5 million). Finnish is spoken by over 90 percent of the population. There are about 300,000 Swedish speakers on the southwestern and southern coasts. Of Finland's 2,500 Lapps, about 1,850 speak the Lappish language.

FRANCE (50 million). French is the national language. In southeastern France, the region known historically as Provence, several million people speak Provençal. Near the German border, in the region formerly known as Alsace-Lorraine, there are about $1\frac{1}{2}$ million speakers of German. In Britanny about one million people speak Breton. Along the border with Spain there are 250,000 speakers of Catalan in an area near the eastern end, and 100,000 speakers of Basque in an area near the western end. On Corsica a dialect of Italian is spoken.

FRENCH GUIANA (60,000). French is the official language, but the majority speak a French creole.

GABON (500,000). The official language is French. About forty Bantu languages are spoken, the most important being Fang, of the north, with about 175,000 speakers.

GAMBIA (400,000). The official language is English. Native languages include Malinke (150,000 speakers), and Wolof and Fulani, with about 50,000 each.

GERMANY (80 million). German is almost universal. The only minority language is Sorbian (Lusatian), a Slavic language spoken by about 50,000 people in the southeasternmost part of East Germany.

GHANA (10 million). The official language is English. The most important native languages are the closely related Twi and Fanti, spoken by about 4 million people in the forest area west of the Volta River. Ewe ranks next with about one million speakers in the Volta region. Ga and Adangme are each spoken by about 250,000 people in the Accra plains. The two main languages of the north are Gurma and Dagomba (Dagbane), each with about 250,000 speakers.

GIBRALTAR (30,000). The official language is English. The permanent residents speak mainly Spanish, but most of them know English as well.

GREAT BRITAIN. *See* United Kingdom.

GREECE (9 million). Greek is spoken by almost the entire population. Minority languages include Turkish (250,000 speakers), Macedonian (50,000), and Albanian (50,000).

GREENLAND (50,000). Eskimo is spoken by the great majority of the population. The 7,000 Danes in Greenland speak Danish, which is the official language.

GRENADA (100,000). English is the language here. French Creole, once widely spoken, is now on the verge of extinction.

GUATEMALA (6 million). The official language is Spanish. Indians, who constitute about half the population, speak more than a dozen different languages of the Mayan family. The big four are Quiché (750,000 speakers), Cakchiquel (400,000), Mam (350,000), and Kekchi (300,000).

GUINEA (4 million). The official language is French. The major African languages are Fulani ($1\frac{1}{4}$ million speakers), in central Guinea; Malinke (one million), in the north; and Susu (250,000), in the southwest. Kissi, Gola, and Loma are spoken near the border with Liberia and Sierra Leone.

GUINEA-BISSAU (500,000). The official language is Portuguese. Native languages include Balante (200,000 speakers), Fulani (125,000), and Malinke (80,000). A Portuguese creole serves as the lingua franca.

GUYANA (750,000). English is spoken by the vast majority of the population. It is rapidly replacing Hindi and Tamil, originally spoken by the large East Indian population. Among American Indian languages Arawak is spoken along the coast and Carib inland.

HAITI (5 million). The official language is French, but the majority of the population speaks a French creole, containing a number of Spanish, English, African, and American Indian words.

HONDURAS (3 million). Spanish is spoken by the vast majority of the population. Lenca, an Indian language, is spoken in the central and western parts of the country. Carib is spoken along a stretch of the northern coast. On the Bahía (Bay) Islands off the coast the predominant language is English.

HONG KONG (4 million). The official language is English but the vast majority of the population speaks Chinese.

HUNGARY (10 million). Hungarian is spoken by almost the entire population.

ICELAND (200,000). Icelandic is the official and universal language.

INDIA (600 million). India has the unenviable distinction of being the most linguistically diverse country in the world. More than 150 languages are spoken, including twelve major ones, and none by more than 30 percent of the population.

The most widely spoken language is Hindi, with about 180 million speakers in the north-central part of the country. To this may be added Urdu, which it closely resembles, with another 30 million. The two other most important languages of northern and central India are Bengali, spoken in West Bengal (45 million speakers), and Marathi, spoken in Maharashtra (42 million). After that come Bihari, spoken in Bihar (40 million), Gujarati, spoken in Gujarat (25 million), Oriya, in Orissa (20 million), Punjabi, in the Punjab (15 million), Rajasthani, a collection of dialects spoken in Rajasthan (15 million), Assamese, in Assam (9 million), Bhili, in west-central India (2 million), and Sindhi, in western India ($1\frac{1}{2}$ million). All the above languages are descended from Sanskrit and thus of the Indo-European family.

The southern third of India is the home of the Dravidian languages, totally unrelated to those of the north. The four major languages of this family are Telugu, spoken in Andhra Pradesh (45 million speakers), Tamil, in Tamil Nadu (38 million), Kanarese, or Kannada, in Karnataka (22 million), and Malayalam, in Kerala (22 million). Other Dravidian languages are Gondi ($1\frac{1}{2}$ million), Kurukh, or Oraon (one million), and Kui (500,000), all spoken in central India, and Tulu (one million), spoken around the city of Mangalore.

A third group of languages, called the Munda languages, is spoken in scattered areas of northern and central India. The most important of these is Santali, with about 3 million speakers. Others are Mundari (750,000), Ho (750,000), Savara, or Sora (250,000), and Korku (200,000). The Tibeto-Burman family is represented by a great number of languages in the state of Assam. Ranging from 250,000 to 500,000 speakers are Bodo, spoken north of the Brahmaputra River; Garo, spoken in the Garo Hills; Meithei, spoken in Manipur; and Lushei, spoken in the southernmost districts. Finally, there is one Mon-Khmer language in India—Khasi, with about 400,000 speakers in the Khasi Hills, west of the city of Shillong.

A major element in the Indian linguistic picture is a non-Indian language—English. Though understood by only a small percentage of the population, it is still the most likely means of communication between people from different parts of the country. Although the Indian constitution provided that Hindi would become the official language of India in 1965, it was decided in that year that English would continue for the time being as "associate official language."

INDONESIA (125 million). Indonesian is the national language. Though it is the native tongue of only 12 million people, it is spoken or understood by as much as three-fourths of the population. Other major languages are Javanese (45 million speakers), Sundanese, also spoken on Java (13 million), and Madurese, spoken on Java and also on the island of Madura (8 million). The principal languages spoken on Sumatra are Minangkabau (3 million), Achinese (2 million), and Batak ($1\frac{1}{2}$ million). On Borneo, Indonesian is spoken in the coastal areas, but inland the Dayak peoples, who number about one million, speak a variety of languages. On Celebes the major language is Buginese ($2\frac{1}{2}$ million), and on Bali, Balinese (2 million). In West Irian (formerly Netherlands New Guinea) some fifty languages of the Papuan family are spoken. Two of the better known are Marind and Nimboran.

IRAN (30 million). The national language is Persian, with more than 20 million speakers. In the province of Azerbaijan in the northwest there are about 4 million speakers of Azerbaijani. Kurdish-speaking Kurds number about $1\frac{1}{2}$ million. Baluchi is spoken by about 500,000 people in the extreme southeast, near the border with Pakistan. Armenian speakers number about 100,000, Assyrian speakers about 20,000.

IRAQ (10 million). The national language is Arabic. There is a sizable Kurdish-speaking minority in the north, numbering about $1\frac{1}{2}$ million. Armenian and Assyrian are also spoken.

IRELAND (3 million). English and Irish (Gaelic) are the two official languages. The latter, however, is spoken by less than 20 percent of the population, all of whom speak English as well.

ISRAEL (3 million). The great majority of the Jewish population speaks Hebrew, the younger generation as their mother tongue. The older generation for the most part still speaks a number of other languages—Yiddish, German, Russian, Polish, Rumanian, Arabic, Persian, Ladino, etc.—but most have mastered Hebrew since their arrival in Israel. Arabic, which is co-official with Hebrew, is spoken by the Arab minority of 350,000.

ITALY (55 million). Italian is the national language. In the region of Alto Adige, bordering Austria, German is spoken by about 200,000 people and is co-official with Italian. French is spoken by about 100,000 people in the region of Aosta in the northwest. Rhaeto-Romanic has about 500,000 speakers mainly in Friuli, near the border with Austria and Yugoslavia. In southern Italy there is an Albanian minority of about 75,000, as well as about 25,000 speakers of Greek. On Sardinia about one million people speak Sardinian.

IVORY COAST ($4\frac{1}{2}$ million). The official language is French. More than fifty tribal languages are spoken here, none by more than 15 percent of the population. Among the more important are Dyula and Senufo, spoken in the north; the closely related Agni (Anyi) and Baule languages, spoken in the southeast; and Malinke, spoken in the northwest.

JAMAICA (2 million). The official language is English. Much of the population, however, speaks a local patois, generally referred to as Jamaican English, which is often unintelligible to the outsider. It contains a number of archaic English words as well as some from Africa.

JAPAN (100 million). Japanese is the national language. There are about 500,000 speakers of Korean. Ainu, apparently unrelated to any other language in the world, is now spoken by only a handful of people on Hokkaido and appears on the verge of extinction.

JORDAN ($2\frac{1}{2}$ million). Arabic is spoken by virtually the entire population.

KASHMIR (5 million). The major language is Kashmiri, spoken by about 3 million people. A number of minor languages are spoken in the northwest, including Burushaski, which appears unrelated to any other in the world.

KENYA (12 million). The official language, Swahili, is spoken over much of the country, though usually as a second language. English is also widely used, especially for commercial purposes. Two other major Bantu languages are Kikuyu, with about 2 million speakers just to the north of Nairobi, and Kamba, with about one million speakers in the southeastern part of the country. Luo, a Nilotic language, is spoken by about one million people in the area adjacent to Lake Victoria. In the Nilo-Hamitic family are Masai, with about 150,000 speakers along the border with Tanzania, and Turkana, with a like number of speakers in the northwestern corner of the country. In another branch of the Nilotic family are Nandi, with about 150,000 speakers in west-central Kenya, and Suk (Pokot), with 75,000 speakers to the north, along the border with Uganda. Two Cushitic languages are spoken in the east and northeast—Somali, with about 300,000 speakers, and Galla, with 100,000.

KOREA (50 million). Korean is the official and universal language.

KUWAIT (1 million). Arabic is spoken here.

LAOS (3 million). Lao is spoken by about 80 percent of the population. Tribal languages include Miao, or Meo, with about 100,000 speakers, and Yao, with about 50,000. There are also some speakers of Vietnamese and Chinese. French is widely spoken in official circles.

LEBANON (3 million). Arabic is the official and dominant language, though French is also widely spoken. Armenian speakers number about 150,000. There are also about 15,000 speakers of Assyrian.

LESOTHO (1 million). English is the official language, Sotho the most important native language.

LIBERIA ($1\frac{1}{2}$ million). The official language is English. Of the native languages the most important is Kpelle, with about 500,000 speakers. Vai, with a script of its own dating back to the early 19th century, is spoken along the coast at the western end of the country. Also on the coast are Bassa, in central Liberia; Kru, farther south; and Grebo, in the southeastern corner. Kissi, Gola, and Loma are spoken in the north, near the border with Guinea and Sierra Leone.

LIBYA (2 million). Arabic is spoken by the great majority of the population. There are some Tuareg (Tamashek) speakers in the west.

LIECHTENSTEIN (20,000). German is spoken here.

LUXEMBOURG (350,000). French is official but German is also much used as a written language. Among themselves the people speak Luxembourgian.

MALAGASY REPUBLIC ($7\frac{1}{2}$ million). Malagasy is spoken by almost the entire native population. It is co-official with French.

MALAWI (5 million). Nyanja, known as Chewa in Malawi, is the major language, with over $2\frac{1}{2}$ million speakers. It is co-official with English. Other languages include Yao, with about 500,000 speakers along the southern shore of Lake Nyasa, and Tumbuka, with about 200,000 speakers in the north.

MALAYSIA (12 million). The official language is Malay, spoken by about 6 million people. Chinese ranks second, with about 4 million; Tamil third, with about one million. Malay and Chinese are also spoken in Sarawak and Sabah, but there are many tribal languages as well.

MALDIVES (125,000). The language spoken here is Maldivian, an offshoot of Sinhalese.

MALI (5 million). The official language is French. Bambara is the most important native language, with about $1\frac{1}{2}$ million speakers in the eastern part of the southern portion of the country. Fulani (750,000), Soninke (500,000), and Malinke (250,000) are spoken in the west, Songhai (250,000) near the town of Timbuktu, and Tuareg, or Tamashek (200,000), in the eastern regions. Dyula and Senufo are spoken in the south, near the border with Ivory Coast.

MALTA (300,000). The native language is Maltese, though most people speak English as well.

MAURITANIA (1,250,000). The official language is French, but Arabic is spoken by about 80 percent of the population. There is a large Fulani-speaking minority in the south, numbering about 150,000 people. About 50,000 people speak Soninke.

MAURITIUS (1 million). This racially diverse island presents a wide variety of languages. A French creole is the mother tongue of about 300,000 people; it is also the principal spoken language of 200,000 more and serves as the lingua franca for much of the country. Of the 600,000 people of Indian origin, about half speak Hindi, 10 percent Urdu, 5 percent Tamil, the rest mainly French Creole. French speakers number about 50,000, Chinese about 15,000. The official language is English but it is spoken very little.

MEXICO (55 million). Spanish, the official language, is spoken by the vast majority of the population. Speakers of Indian languages number about 3 million (three-fourths of whom also speak Spanish), most of them in the southern part of the country. The most important Indian language is Nahuatl, with about 800,000 speakers in the area north, east, and south of Mexico City. Second place goes to Maya, or Yucatec, with about 450,000 speakers on the Yucatán Peninsula. In the state of Chiapas there are Tzotzil (100,000 speakers), Tzeltal (100,000), Chol (50,000), and Zoque (25,000), while in Tabasco there is Chontal (20,000). In Oaxaca there are Zapotec (300,000), Mixtec (225,000), Mazatec (100,000), Mixe (50,000), and Chinantec (50,000). Other languages include Otomi, spoken chiefly in México and Hidalgo (225,000); Totonac, of Veracruz and Puebla (125,000); Mazahua, of México (100,000); Huastec, of Veracruz and San Luis Potosí (65,000); and Tarasco, of Michoacán (60,000). In northern Mexico the most important Indian languages are Tarahumara, of Chihuahua, and Mayo, of Sonora and Sinaloa, each with about 25,000 speakers.

MONACO (25,000). French is the major language, though there is also an Italian-speaking minority.

MONGOLIA (1,300,000). Mongolian is spoken by the vast majority of the population. There are about 50,000 speakers of Kazakh in the west.

MOROCCO (17 million). Arabic is spoken by the majority of the population. The 5 million Berbers speak a number of different languages. Shluh, of the south, and Tamazight, of the central regions, each has over 2 million speakers. Riffian is spoken by about 500,000 people in the north. French and Spanish are widely spoken, the latter principally in the former Spanish zone.

MOZAMBIQUE (8 million). The official language is Portuguese, spoken by the country's 200,000 whites. The two most important native languages are Makua, of the north (2½ million speakers), and Thonga (Tsonga), of the south (1½ million). Yao and Makonde are spoken in the extreme north, near the border with Tanzania. Zulu is spoken in the extreme south, near the border with Swaziland.

NEPAL (12 million). The national language is Nepali, the mother tongue of about 6 million people in Nepal, with an additional 2 million speaking it as a second language. Bihari is spoken by about one million people in the south. In the Katmandu Valley there are some 500,000 speakers of Newari, while just to the north Murmi is spoken by about 500,000 people. Over one million Nepalese speak Tibetan as a second language.

NETHERLANDS (13 million). Dutch is spoken by almost the entire population. In the northern province of Friesland about 300,000 people speak Frisian in addition to Dutch.

NETHERLANDS ANTILLES (200,000). The official language is Dutch, but on the southern islands Papiamento is widely spoken.

NEW ZEALAND (3 million). English is spoken by the vast majority of the population. The Maori, the native inhabitants of New Zealand, number about 200,000, about half of whom speak the Maori language.

NICARAGUA (2 million). Spanish is spoken by the vast majority of the population. Miskito, or Mosquito, an Indian language, is spoken by about 25,000 people along the eastern coast.

NIGER (4 million). The official language is French. The most important native language is Hausa, with about 2 million speakers in the central and southeastern parts of the country. Djerma (750,000 speakers) is spoken in the southwest, in the area that includes

Niamey, the capital. Fulani (500,000) and Tuareg, or Tamashek (300,000), are spoken in the north and central regions, while Teda, or Tibbu (50,000), is spoken in the northeast.

NIGERIA (70 million). This, the most populous nation in Africa, also has the greatest number of languages—about 250. The official language is English. The most important native language is Hausa, of the north, the mother tongue of about 15 million people, but spoken by close to 20 million in all. Ranking next are Yoruba (12 million), spoken in the southwest; Ibo (8 million), spoken in the southeast; and Fulani (6 million), also spoken in the north. Other important languages are Kanuri (2 million), of the Bornu region in the northeast; the closely related Efik and Ibibio languages ($1\frac{1}{2}$ million), the former spoken in and around the town of Calabar in the southeast, the latter adjacent to it on the west; and Tiv (one million), of Benue-Plateau state, central Nigeria. Ijo, or Ijaw (500,000), is spoken in the Niger River delta; Edo (500,000) in Mid-Western state near Benin City; Urhobo (500,000) in Mid-Western state south of Benin City; Nupe (500,000) near the junction of the Niger and Kaduna rivers; and Idoma (250,000) in Benue-Plateau state.

NORWAY (4 million). Norwegian is spoken by almost the entire population. Most of the country's 20,000 Lapps speak Lappish.

OMAN (750,000). Arabic is spoken here.

PAKISTAN (65 million). The official language is Urdu. It is the mother tongue of only 5 million people but is spoken fluently as a second language by as much as two-thirds of the population. The other major language is Punjabi, with about 45 million speakers. Sindhi is spoken by about 7 million people in the province of Sind, while Pashto is spoken by about 6 million in the North-West Frontier Province. In the province of Baluchistan in the southwest there are about one million speakers of Baluchi, an Iranian language, and 500,000 speakers of Brahui, a Dravidian language.

PANAMA ($1\frac{1}{2}$ million). Spanish is the national language, though a number of minor Indian languages are also spoken. The two most important are Guaymi, with about 25,000 speakers in the northwest, and Cuna, with about 20,000 speakers on the islands of the San Blas Archipelago.

PAPUA NEW GUINEA (2½ million). Many hundreds of languages are spoken here. The majority are of the Papuan family, though a number of Melanesian languages are spoken in the coastal areas. In Papua, the southern half of the country, a few of the better known languages are Motu, Kiwai, and Orokolo. In New Guinea, the northern half, there are Enga, Kâte, and Yabim. But the two major lingua francas of Papua New Guinea are Pidgin English, spoken mainly in the north but also in and around Port Moresby on the southern coast, and Police Motu, a simplified form of Motu spoken throughout much of Papua. Both these languages have official status in the country.

PARAGUAY (2½ million). More than half the population of Paraguay is bilingual. Spanish is the official language, spoken by about 75 percent of the population. Guarani, an Indian language, has almost as many speakers, though it is more common in the rural areas.

PERU (15 million). The official language is Spanish, but Indian languages are widely spoken in the highlands. Quechua speakers number about 5 million, Aymara about 500,000. Others include Panoan and Jivaro.

PHILIPPINES (40 million). Tagalog, the language of southern Luzon, has been declared the national language and given the new official name of Pilipino. It is the mother tongue of about 10 million people, but is now spoken by about half the population. The three Visayan languages, Cebuano (8 million speakers), Hiligaynon (3 million), and Samaran (1½ million), are spoken in the middle islands and on northern Mindanao. Ilocano (3 million) is spoken in northern Luzon, while Bikol (2 million) is spoken on the Bikol peninsula in the southeast. On Luzon northwest of Manila are Pampangan (650,000), spoken in Pampanga province, and Pangasinan (500,000), spoken in the province of the same name. In Mountain province, in the north-central part of the island, there is Igorot, with about 250,000 speakers. Among the Moro peoples of Mindanao the most important language is Maranao, with some 400,000 speakers. At least 10 million Filipinos speak English fluently as a second language.

POLAND (33 million). Polish is practically universal. Kashubian, considered by some a separate language, by others a dialect of

Polish, is spoken by about 100,000 people in the province of Gdańsk.

PORTUGAL (10 million). Portuguese is spoken almost universally.

PORTUGUESE GUINEA. *See* Guinea-Bissau.

PUERTO RICO (3 million). Spanish is spoken everywhere, but English is taught as a second language and is commonly heard in the cities.

QATAR (170,000). Arabic is spoken here.

RHODESIA (6 million). The official language is English, spoken by the country's 250,000 whites. Among the natives, Shona is the most important language, with about 4 million speakers. Matabele (Ndebele), a dialect of Zulu, is spoken by about one million people in the southwest.

RUMANIA (20 million). Rumanian is spoken by about 90 percent of the population. There is a sizable Hungarian minority of about $1\frac{1}{2}$ million people living in Transylvania. The German-speaking community numbers about 400,000.

RUSSIA. *See* Union of Soviet Socialist Republics.

RWANDA (4 million). Ruanda is spoken by virtually the entire population. It is co-official with French. Swahili serves as a commercial language.

SAN MARINO (20,000). Italian is spoken here.

SAUDI ARABIA (8 million). Arabic is spoken everywhere.

SENEGAL (4 million). The official language is French. Wolof is the most important African language, with about $1\frac{1}{2}$ million speakers mainly in the western part of the country. Other languages include Fulani (750,000 speakers), Serer (650,000), Dyola (350,000), and Malinke (250,000).

SIERRA LEONE (3 million). The official language is English. Among the native languages Mende is the most important, with more than one million speakers in the southern half of the country. Temne is spoken by about 750,000 people in the central and northwestern districts. Vai is spoken along the coast near the border with Liberia, while Kissi and Gola are spoken in the interior near the border with Liberia and Guinea. A variety of Pidgin English known as Krio is also widely spoken.

SIKKIM (200,000). Nepali speakers constitute about 75 percent of Sikkim's population. Another group speaks a dialect related to Jonkha of Bhutan. The aboriginal Lepchas have their own language.

SINGAPORE (2 million). Chinese is spoken by about 75 percent of the population, or $1\frac{1}{2}$ million people. Malay speakers number about 250,000, Tamil about 200,000. Malay has been designated the "national language," while English, Chinese, Tamil, and also Malay are known as "official languages."

SOMALIA (3 million). Somali is spoken by the vast majority of the population. Arabic is widely understood as are, to a lesser degree, Italian and English.

SOUTH AFRICA (23 million). The official languages are Afrikaans and English, the former spoken by over 4 million people, the latter by about $1\frac{1}{2}$ million. Of the African languages the most important are Zulu, spoken principally in Natal (4 million speakers); Xhosa, spoken in Transkei (4 million); Tswana, spoken near the border with Botswana ($1\frac{3}{4}$ million); Sotho, spoken near the border with Lesotho ($1\frac{1}{2}$ million); and Pedi, spoken in Transvaal ($1\frac{1}{2}$ million). Swazi (500,000) is spoken in the area adjoining Swaziland, while Venda (350,000) is spoken in northern Transvaal. Fanakalo, a jargon based on Zulu with numerous English and some Afrikaans words added, is spoken among workers in the mines. There are also some 10,000 speakers of Bushman.

SOUTHERN YEMEN ($1\frac{1}{2}$ million). South Arabic, a collective term for a number of dialects that are quite different from Arabic, is generally spoken here. Standard Arabic, however, is the official language.

SOUTH WEST AFRICA (750,000). The most widespread language here is Ambo, spoken by the 350,000 Ovambos of the northern part of the country. Herero is spoken by about 50,000 people in the east and central regions. Speakers of Hottentot number about 50,000, of Bushman about 15,000. Among the whites about 50,000 speak English, 30,000 speak German, and 10,000 speak Afrikaans.

SOVIET UNION. *See* Union of Soviet Socialist Republics.

SPAIN (35 million). Spanish is the national language. However, in northeastern Spain there are about 5 million speakers of Catalan, while in northwestern Spain about 3 million people speak Galician, a dialect of Portuguese. Near the French border, in the provinces facing the Bay of Biscay, there are about 600,000 speakers of Basque.

SRI LANKA (formerly CEYLON; 13 million). Sinhalese is the official language, spoken by about 9 million people, or 70 percent of the population. The remainder are Tamil speakers, living mainly in the north and on the east coast of the island.

SUDAN (17 million). Arabic, the official language, is spoken by about half the population, mainly in the northern two-thirds of the country. Also in the north is Nubian, one dialect of which is spoken by about 500,000 people in the central province of Kordofan, another by about 175,000 people in Northern Province. Beja is spoken by about 500,000 people in the province of Kassala facing the Red Sea; Fur by about 175,000 in the western province of Darfur. Of the dozens of languages of the south the two most important are Dinka ($1\frac{1}{2}$ million speakers) and Nuer (750,000). Shilluk (100,000) is spoken in Upper Nile Province; Zande (250,000) near the border with Zaïre; and Bari (250,000) and Lotuko (100,000) near the border with Uganda.

SURINAM (400,000). The official language is Dutch, but Taki-Taki, a variety of Pidgin English, serves as the lingua franca. Other languages include Hindi (100,000 speakers), Javanese (50,000), Saramacca, the creole language of the 30,000 Bush Negroes of the interior, and Carib, spoken by a few thousand Indians.

SWAZILAND (400,000). Swazi is spoken by almost the entire African population. The official language is English.

SWEDEN (8 million). Swedish is practically universal, except for 30,000 speakers of Finnish and 10,000 speakers of Lappish, both in the far north.

SWITZERLAND (6½ million). Switzerland has four official languages. German ranks first with about 4 million speakers. Standard German is the written language and is used in the parliament, universities, courts, and churches, but Swiss German, a distinctly different local dialect, is used in everyday speech. French is spoken by about 1¼ million people in the west, in an area that includes Geneva. Italian is spoken by about 750,000 people living mainly in the south. Romansch, a Rhaeto-Romanic dialect, is spoken by about 50,000 people in the canton of Graubünden.

SYRIA (7 million). Arabic is spoken by the vast majority of the population. French is spoken by many people as a second language. Other languages include Kurdish (250,000 speakers), Armenian (150,000), Circassian (50,000), Turkmen (50,000), Assyrian (15,000), and Aramaic (2,000).

TAIWAN (15 million). Chinese is the national language, the Mandarin dialect being official, but the 13 million native Taiwanese speak the southern Fukienese, or Amoy, dialect. There are about 200,000 aborigines who speak a group of languages belonging to the Malayo-Polynesian family.

TANZANIA (14 million). About 120 languages are spoken here. Swahili is the language of administration and is spoken by much of the population, usually as a second language. English is also widely used, especially for commercial purposes. Most of the tribal languages are of the Bantu family and include Sukuma, spoken in the north (one million speakers); closely related Nyamwezi, spoken in the western region (350,000); Chagga, spoken on the slopes of Mt. Kilimanjaro (250,000); Hehe, of Iringa district, south-central Tanzania (200,000); and Makonde (200,000) and Yao (100,000), spoken near the border with Mozambique. Masai, a Nilo-Hamitic language, is spoken by about 75,000 people near the border with Kenya. In the Khoisan family are Sandawe (25,000), spoken near the town of Kondoa, and Hatsa, or Hadzapi, with fewer than 1,000 speakers around the perimeter of Lake Eyasi. On Zanzibar Swahili is the dominant language, though Arabic and a number of Indian languages are also spoken.

THAILAND (40 million). Thai is spoken by about 85 percent of the population. Chinese speakers form the largest minority, numbering about 4 million. Other languages include Malay, with about one million speakers in the extreme south, and Khmer, with about 350,000 speakers in the southeast. Among tribal languages the most important are Mon (75,000), spoken near the western border, and Karen (75,000) and Miao, or Meo (50,000), spoken in the north.

TOGO (2 million). The official language is French. Ewe is the most important native language, with about 750,000 speakers, mostly in the south. In the north the major languages are Kabre and Gurma.

TRINIDAD AND TOBAGO (1 million). The official and dominant language is English. A French creole, once widely spoken, is still heard in scattered areas. The large East Indian population speaks Hindi, Tamil, and a number of other languages in addition to English.

TUNISIA (5½ million). Arabic is spoken by the vast majority of the population. French is widely used in official circles.

TURKEY (40 million). Turkish is spoken by over 95 percent of the population. Kurdish-speaking Kurds of southeastern Turkey form the largest minority, numbering about 1½ million. Other languages include Arabic (300,000 speakers), Circassian (75,000), Armenian (50,000), Greek (50,000), Georgian (50,000), Ladino (20,000), and Aramaic (1,000).

UGANDA (10 million). The official language is English. Among the African languages the most important is Ganda, or Luganda, a Bantu language with about 2 million speakers in an area that includes Kampala, the capital. Other Bantu languages include Nkole, or Nyankole (750,000 speakers), of the southwest near Tanzania; Chiga, or Kiga (350,000), of the extreme southwest; Gisu (350,000), of the southeast; Toro (250,000), of the southwest; and Nyoro (250,000), spoken east of Lake Albert. In the Nilotic family are Lango (500,000) and Acholi (350,000), of north-central Uganda, and Alur (150,000), of the northwest. In the Nilo-Hamitic family are Teso (750,000) and Karamojong (250,000), both spoken in the northeast. In the Central Sudanic family are Lugbara (300,000) and Madi (100,000), both spoken in the northwest. Swahili is not widely used in Uganda but sometimes serves as a lingua franca between speakers of different languages.

UNION OF SOVIET SOCIALIST REPUBLICS (250 million). With its tremendous expanse of territory, the Soviet Union embraces a great number of diverse peoples and languages. The figure usually given is 130, about half of which have been reduced to writing. In the 1970 census 142 million people listed Russian as their mother tongue, with another 42 million speaking it fluently as a second language. Some sixty other languages are listed below. The majority are spoken by a people of the same name who inhabit a republic or other administrative division of the same name (*e.g.*, Georgian S.S.R., Bashkir A.S.S.R., Khakass Autonomous Region, Chukchi National District).

Besides Russian, the two other Slavic languages of the Soviet Union are Ukrainian (35 million speakers) and Belorussian (7 million). Also in the Indo-European family are the two Baltic languages, Lithuanian (2½ million), and Latvian (1½ million); one Romance language, Moldavian (2½ million); and three Iranian languages, Tadzhik (2 million), Ossetian (400,000), and Kurdish (80,000). Finally there are Armenian, with 3¼ million speakers, and Yiddish, spoken by about one-fourth of Russia's 2 million Jews.

In the Finno-Ugric family there is Estonian, with one million speakers, plus four languages in European Russia: Mordvin (one million speakers); Udmurt, or Votyak (600,000); Mari, or Cheremis (500,000); and Komi (400,000). Two Ugric languages, of the subgroup that includes Hungarian, are Ostyak, or Khanty (15,000), and Vogul, or Mansi (4,000), both spoken in the Ob River basin of western Siberia. Combining with the Finno-Ugric languages to form the Uralic family are the four Samoyed languages of northernmost Russia: Nenets, or Yurak (25,000), Selkup, or Ostyak-Samoyed (2,000), plus Nganasan, or Tavgi, and Enets, or Yenisei-Samoyed, each with fewer than 1,000 speakers.

About twenty-five languages of the Soviet Union are of the Altaic family. The largest subgroup is the Turkic which includes: Uzbek (9 million speakers), Tatar (5 million), Kazakh (5 million), Azerbaijani (4 million), Chuvash, Turkmen, and Kirgiz (1½ million each), Bashkir (one million), Yakut (300,000), Kara-Kalpak (225,000), Kumyk (200,000), Uigur (150,000), Tuvinian (135,000), Karachai (100,000), Khakass (60,000), Balkar (60,000), Altai (50,000), and Nogai (50,000). Two Mongolian languages are Buryat (300,000) and

Kalmyk (125,000). The Tungusic subgroup of the Soviet Far East includes Evenki, or Tungus (15,000), Even, or Lamut (7,000), and Nanai, or Gold (7,000).

Still another language family of the Soviet Union is the Caucasian, located in the Caucasus, between the Black and the Caspian seas. These languages number about forty in all, thirty of them spoken in a single republic, the Dagestan A.S.S.R. The most important Caucasian language by far is Georgian, with over 3 million speakers. The others that have been reduced to writing are Chechen (600,000), Avar (400,000), Kabardian (320,000), Lezgin (300,000), Dargin (225,000), Ingush (150,000), Adygei (100,000), Abkhazian (80,000), Lak (80,000), Tabasaran (50,000), and Abazinian (25,000).

One Semitic language is spoken in the Soviet Union—Assyrian, with about 15,000 speakers. In the Paleo-Asiatic family are Chukchi (12,000), Koryak (6,000), Nivkh, or Gilyak (2,000), Ket, or Yenisei-Ostyak (1,000), and Itelmen, or Kamchadal, and Yukagir, or Odul, each spoken by only a few hundred people. Lastly there are 1,000 speakers of Lappish, 1,000 speakers of Eskimo, and a hundred speakers of Aleut.

UNITED KINGDOM (55 million). English is spoken universally. About 600,000 people in Wales speak Welsh and about 75,000 in Scotland speak Scottish Gaelic, but all these people speak English as well.

UNITED STATES OF AMERICA (210 million). English is the national language, spoken by the vast majority of the population. However, the continuous arrival of immigrants in America, representing virtually every country in the world, has resulted in dozens of other languages being spoken. According to the 1970 census, Spanish is the mother tongue of about 8 million people in the United States, German of 6 million, Italian of 4 million, French of 2½ million, Polish of 2½ million, and Yiddish of 1½ million. Others include Swedish and Norwegian (600,000 each), Slovak (500,000), Greek, Czech, and Hungarian (450,000), Japanese (400,000), Portuguese, Dutch, Russian, and Chinese (350,000), Lithuanian (300,000), and Ukrainian and Serbo-Croatian (250,000).

The census also reports that of America's 792,000 Indians, 268,000, or about one-third, speak an Indian language as their mother tongue. The most important by far is Navajo, with about 100,000 speakers in Arizona, New Mexico, and Utah. Next in line come Ojibwa, or Chippewa (30,000), and Sioux, or Dakota (20,000), both spoken in the northern Midwest; Cherokee, with about 10,000 speakers in Oklahoma and 1,000 in North Carolina; Apache (10,000) and Papago (8,000), of Arizona; Creek (7,500), of Oklahoma; Choctaw (7,000), of Oklahoma and Mississippi; Keresan (7,000), of New Mexico; Blackfoot (6,000), of Montana; Pima (5,000), of Arizona; and Shoshone (5,000), spoken in a number of western states. Also in Oklahoma are Chickasaw (2,500), Kiowa (2,000), Comanche (1,500), and Caddo, Pawnee, Osage, and Delaware, each with only a few hundred speakers. Cheyenne (3,500) is divided between Oklahoma and Montana, Arapaho (2,500) between Oklahoma and Wyoming, and Fox (1,500) between Oklahoma and Iowa.

In the Midwest there are also Omaha, with about 2,000 speakers in Nebraska, and Winnebago, with about 1,500 in Wisconsin and Nebraska. In Montana there are also Crow (3,500), Assiniboin (1,000), and Flathead (1,000). In New Mexico there are also Zuñi (3,500); Tiwa, spoken by the Taos and Isleta Indians (2,500); Tewa (2,000); and Towa, spoken by the Jemez Indians (1,000). In Arizona there are also Hopi (4,000), Yuma (1,000), and Mohave (1,000). Ute is spoken by about 3,000 people in Utah and Colorado, Yakima by about 1,000 in Washington, Nez Perce by about 1,000 in Idaho, and Klamath by a few hundred people in Oregon. Paiute (2,000) is spoken in a number of western states. In New York there are Seneca (4,000), Mohawk (2,000), and Oneida (1,500 including some in Wisconsin). Passamaquoddy, of Maine, and Seminole, of Florida, are each spoken by a few hundred people.

In Alaska there are about 25,000 speakers of Eskimo, as well as about 1,000 speakers each of Aleut, spoken in the Aleutian Islands, and Tlingit and Haida, spoken in the Alaskan panhandle. In Hawaii about 7,500 people speak Hawaiian.

UPPER VOLTA (6 million). The official language is French. The most important native language is Mossi (Moré), with about 3 million speakers. Gurma is spoken in the east, Fulani and Tuareg (Tamashek) in the north, and Dyula in the west.

URUGUAY (3 million). Spanish is spoken by almost the entire population.

VENEZUELA (12 million). Spanish is spoken by the vast majority of the population. Indian languages include Arawak and Carib.

VIETNAM (40 million). Vietnamese is spoken by the great majority of the population. Chinese speakers form the largest minority, numbering about one million. Thai is spoken by about 800,000 people in the north, Khmer by about 400,000 near the Cambodian border. Dozens of tribal languages are also spoken. In North Vietnam there are Muong, the only language actually related to Vietnamese (400,000 speakers), as well as Nung (300,000), Miao, or Meo (200,000), and Yao (175,000). In South Vietnam the various Montagnard peoples speak Jarai (150,000), Rhade (125,000), Bahnar (100,000), Sedang (80,000), and many other languages. In the lowlands there is Cham, with about 50,000 speakers. French is widely spoken in official circles.

YEMEN (6 million). Arabic is spoken by the entire population.

YUGOSLAVIA (20 million). Serbo-Croatian is spoken by about three-fourths of the population. The two other official languages are Slovenian, spoken in Slovenia ($1\frac{1}{2}$ million speakers), and Macedonian, spoken in Macedonia (one million). There are also about one million speakers of Albanian and 500,000 of Hungarian.

ZAÏRE (25 million). The official language is French. The four major African languages are Kingwana, a dialect of Swahili, with about 3 million speakers in the northeast, east, and south; Luba (3 million speakers), of the southeast; Kongo (2 million), of the west; Lingala $1\frac{1}{2}$ million), of the north and northwest. Each of these serves as the language of trade in its respective region and is thus spoken as a second language by many inhabitants. Among the many other languages are Mongo (2 million speakers), of the central regions; Ruanda (one million), of the east; Mangbetu (500,000), of the north; Zande (500,000), near the border with the Sudan; and Lunda (200,000), of the south.

ZAMBIA (5 million). The official language is English. Bemba is the most important native language, with about $1\frac{1}{2}$ million speakers in the northeastern part of the country. Tonga, of the south, and Nyanja, of the east and central regions, are each spoken by about 750,000 people. Lozi, of the southwest, and Lwena (Luvale) and Lunda, of the northwest, each have about 100,000 speakers.

SOURCES OF INDIVIDUAL PASSAGES

Afrikaans	Translation by C. J. D. Harvey, in *Afrikaans Poems with English Translations*, ed. by A. P. Grové and C. J. D. Harvey, Oxford University Press, Cape Town and New York, 1962.
Albanian	Stuart Edward Mann, *Albanian Literature*, B. Quaritch, London, 1955.
Aleut	Richard Henry Geoghegan, *The Aleut Language*, U.S. Department of the Interior, 1944.
Amharic	Martino Mario Moreno, *Cent Fables Amhariques*, Imprimerie Nationale, Paris, 1947.
Avar	A. Akhlakov, *Heroic-Historic Songs of the Avars*, Makhachkala, U.S.S.R., 1968.
Basque	Resurrección María de Azkue, *Euskaleŕiaren Yakintza*, Espasa-Calpe, S.A., Madrid, 1942.
Batak	H. N. van der Tuuk, *Bataksch Leesboek*, Frederik Muller, Amsterdam, 1860.
Belorussian	Serialized in the magazine *Polymya*. This extract appeared in the issue of November 1968.
Bengali	*Collected Poems and Plays of Rabindranath Tagore*, Macmillan Company, London, 1936.
Bihari	*The Songs of Vidyapati*, ed. by Subhadra Jha, Motilal Banarasidass, Banaras, India.
Breton	François Marie Luzel, *Contes bretons*, Quimperlé. T. Clairet, 1870.
Bulgarian	Translation by Marguerite Alexieva and Theodora Atanassova, Narodna Kultura, Sofia, 1955.
Burushaski	D. L. R. Lorimer, *The Burushaski Language*, H. Aschehoug & Co., Oslo, 1935.
Buryat	T. A. Bertagaev and Ts. B. Tsydendambaev, *Grammatika Buryatskogo Yazyka* ("Buryat Grammar"), Oriental Literature Publishing House, Moscow, 1962.

Bushman	W. H. I. Bleek and L. C. Lloyd, *Specimens of Bushmen Folklore*, C. Struik (Pty.) Ltd., Cape Town, 1968.
Chamorro	Donald M. Topping, *Spoken Chamorro*, University of Hawaii Press, Honolulu, 1969.
Chechen	N. F. Yakovlev, *Sintaksis Chechenskogo Yazyka* ("Chechen Syntax"), Academy of Sciences of the U.S.S.R., 1940.
Chinese	*Selected Readings from the Works of Mao Tse-tung*, Foreign Languages Press, Peking, 1967.
Chuang	A. A. Moskalev, *Grammatika Yazyka Chzhuan* ("Chuang Grammar"), Nauka, Moscow, 1971.
Coptic	*Coptic Texts*, ed. by William H. Worrell, University of Michigan Press, Ann Arbor, 1942.
Creek	*Tchikilli's Kasi'hta Legend*, with a commentary by Albert S. Gratschet, Academy of Science of St. Louis, 1888.
Croatian	Translation by Zora G. Depolo, Lincoln-Prager Publishers Ltd., London, 1959.
Czech	Translation by M. and R. Weatherall, George Allen & Unwin Ltd., London, 1948.
Danish	*Andersen's Fairy Tales*, Macmillan Company, New York, 1966.
Delaware	Frank G. Speck, *A Study of the Delaware Indian Big House Ceremony*, Pennsylvania Historical Commission, Harrisburg, 1931.
Dutch	Translation by B. M. Mooyaart-Doubleday, Doubleday & Company, Garden City, N.Y., 1952.
English (Old)	Translation by E. Talbot Donaldson, W. W. Norton & Company, New York, 1966.
English (Middle)	Vincent F. Hopper, *Chaucer's Canterbury Tales, An Interlinear Translation*, Barron's Educational Series Inc., Woodbury, N.Y., 1948.
Estonian	William K. Matthews, *Child of Man*, Boreas Publishing Company, London, 1955.
Evenki	V. D. Kolesnikova, *Sintaksis Evenkiiskogo Yazyka* ("Evenki Syntax"), Nauka, Moscow, 1966.
Ewe	Diedrich Westermann, *A Study of the Ewe Language*, Oxford University Press, London, 1930.
Faroese	William B. Lockwood, *An Introduction to Modern Faroese*, E. Munksgaard, Copenhagen, 1955.

Fijian	G. B. Milner, *Fijian Grammar*, Government Press, Suva.
Finnish	Translation by Naomi Walford, G. P. Putnam's Sons, New York, 1949.
Flemish	Translation by C. B. Bodde, Harper & Bros., New York, 1924.
Fox	Truman Michelson, *Fox Miscellany*, Smithsonian Institution, Bureau of American Ethnology, Bulletin 114, Washington, 1937.
French	Translation by Eleanor Marx Aveling, Dodd, Mead & Company, New York.
Frisian	"The Literature of Frisian Immigrants in America," *De Tsjerne*, Volume V, 1950.
Fulani	Frank William Taylor, *A First Grammar of the Adamawa Dialect of the Fulani Language*, Clarendon Press, Oxford, 1921.
Gaelic	*Short Stories of Padraic Pearse*, selected and adapted by Desmond Maguire, The Mercier Press, Cork, 1968.
Georgian	Translation by Marjory Scott Wardrop, Co-operative Publishing Society of Foreign Workers in the U.S.S.R., Moscow, 1938.
German	Translation by H. T. Lowe-Porter, Alfred A. Knopf, New York, 1958.
Greek (Classical)	Translation by Seth G. Benardete, in *The Complete Greek Tragedies*, ed. by David Grene and Richmond Lattimore, Modern Library, New York, 1956.
Greek (Modern)	Translation by Jonathan Griffin, Simon and Schuster, New York, 1966.
Hausa	R. C. Abraham, *Hausa Literature and the Hausa Sound System*, University of London Press Ltd., London, 1959.
Hawaiian	Jane Comstock Clarke, *Where the Red Lehua Grows*, Honolulu Star-Bulletin, Ltd., Honolulu, 1943.
Hottentot	D. M. Beach, *The Phonetics of the Hottentot Language*, Cambridge University Press, Cambridge, 1938.
Hungarian	Translation by Frances A. Gerard, Harper & Bros., New York, 1896.
Icelandic	Hallberg Hallmundsson, *An Anthology of Scandinavian Literature*, Macmillan Company, New York, 1965.

Indonesian	A. Teeuw, *Modern Indonesian Literature*, Martinus Nijhoff, The Hague, 1967.
Italian	Translation by Eric Mosbacher, Grove Press, New York, 1953.
Japanese	Translation by Edward G. Seidensticker, Alfred A. Knopf, New York, 1969.
Kalmyk	*Yazyki Narodov SSSR* ("The Languages of the Peoples of the U.S.S.R."), Nauka, Leningrad, 1968.
Kashmiri	*Paramananda-Sukti-Sara*, edited and translated by Zinda Kaul, Durga Press, Srinagar, 1941.
Kazakh	Translation by Lev Navrozov, Foreign Languages Publishing House, Moscow.
Korean	*A Pageant of Korean Poetry*, selected and translated by In-Sŏb-Zŏng, Eomun-Gag, Seoul, 1963.
Lao	*Chansons Lao*, Ministère des Beaux Arts, Kingdom of Laos.
Lappish	Björn Collinder, *The Lapps*, Princeton University Press, Princeton, 1949.
Latin	Norbert Guterman, *A Book of Latin Quotations*, Anchor Books, Garden City, N.Y., 1966.
Latvian	Juris Silenieks, in *Quinto Lingo*, February, 1969.
Lingala	L. B. de Boeck, *Manuel de Lingála*, Éditions de Scheut, Brussels, 1952.
Luba	H. W. Beckett, *Hand Book of Kiluba*, produced under the supervision and direction of Chevalier John Alexander Clarke, Garenganze Evangelical Mission, Mulongo, D.P. Lubumbashi, Zaïre, 1951.
Malay	M. B. Lewis, *Teach Yourself Malay*, The English Universities Press Ltd., London, 1947.
Maori	Bruce Biggs, *Let's Learn Maori*, A. H. & A. W. Reed, Wellington, 1969.
Marathi	T. E. Katenina, *Yazyk Maratkhi* ("The Marathi Language"), Nauka, Moscow, 1967.
Marshallese	Byron W. Bender, *Spoken Marshallese: An intensive language course with grammatical notes and glossary*, University of Hawaii Press, Honolulu, 1969.
Maya	Text by R. P. F. Ximenez with Spanish translation by Dora M. de Burgess and Patricio Xec, Quezaltenango, Guatemala City, 1955.

Mende	Gordon Innes, *A Practical Introduction to Mende*, School of Oriental and African Studies, University of London, London, 1967.
Mohawk	*The Iroquois Book of Rites*, edited by Horatio Hale, reprinted by the University of Toronto Press, Toronto, 1963.
Mossi	F. Froger, *Manuel Pratique de Langue Môré*, L. Fournier, Paris, 1923.
Nahuatl	Translation by Thelma D. Sullivan, in *Estudios de Cultura Náhuatl*, Volume V, 1965.
Nakhi	Joseph F. Rock, *The Zhi ma Funeral Ceremony of the Na-Khi of Southwest China*, St. Gabriel's Mission Press, Vienna, 1955.
Nenets	Z. N. Kupriyanova, L. V. Khomich, A. M. Shcherbakova, *Nenetsky Yazyk* ("The Nenets Language"), State Educational-Pedagogical Publishers, Leningrad, 1957.
Nepali	Nikolai I. Koroliov, *Yazyk Nepali* ("The Nepali Language"), Nauka, Moscow, 1965.
Norwegian	*Aku Aku*, Rand McNally & Company, Chicago, 1958.
Ojibwa	Leonard Bloomfield, *Eastern Ojibwa*, University of Michigan Press, Ann Arbor, 1957.
Oriya	Boris M. Karpushkin, *Yazyk Oriya* ("The Oriya Language"), Nauka, Moscow, 1964.
Osage	Francis La Flesche, *War Ceremony and Peace Ceremony of the Osage Indians*, Smithsonian Institution, Bureau of American Ethnology, Bulletin 101, 1939.
Ostyak	János Gulya, *Eastern Ostyak Chrestomathy*, Indiana University, Bloomington, 1966.
Papiamento	W. M. Hoyer, *A Brief Historical Description of the Island of Aruba*, Boekhandel Bethencourt, Curaçao, 1945.
Pashto	Translation by Olaf Caroe, in *The Poems of Khushhal Khan Khatak* by Evelyn Howell and Olaf Caroe. Distributed by the Oxford University Press for the Pashto Academy, University of Peshawar, Peshawar, 1963.
Persian	Translation by J. Payne, in *Fifty Poems of Hafiz*, collected and made, introduced and annotated by Arthur J. Arberry, Cambridge University Press, Cambridge, 1953.
Portuguese	Translation by Roy Campbell, The Noonday Press, New York, 1953.

Provençal	Translation by Maro Beath Jones, Saunders Studio Press, Claremont, California, 1937.
Quechua	Translation by Clements R. Markham, Trübner & Company, London, 1871.
Romany	Jan Kochanowski, *Gypsy Studies*, International Academy of Indian Culture, New Delhi, 1963.
Rumanian	*Introduction to Rumanian Literature*, ed. by Jacob Steinberg, Twayne Publishers, New York, 1966.
Russian	Translation by Constance Garnett, The Modern Library, New York.
Samoan	C. C. Marsack, *Teach Yourself Samoan*, The English Universities Press Ltd., London, 1962.
Sanskrit	Charles Rockwell Lanman, *Sanskrit Reader*, Ginn and Company, Boston, 1888.
Seneca	Nils M. Holmer, *The Seneca Language*, Upsala Canadian Studies, Lund, 1954.
Serbian	Translation by Drenka Willen, Harcourt, Brace & World, New York, 1962.
Shona	Translated and edited with notes by Hazel Carter, Oxford University Press, London and Cape Town, 1958.
Sinhalese	Translation by S. Radhakrishnan, Oxford University Press, London, 1950.
Slovak	Translation by Jean Rosemary Edwards, Artia Prague, Prague, 1961.
Slovenian	Translation by Sidonie Yeras and H. C. Sewell Grant, The Pushkin Press, London, 1930.
Somali	B. W. Andrzejewski and I. M. Lewis, *Somali Poetry*, Clarendon Press, Oxford, 1964.
Spanish	Translation by John Ormsby, The Heritage Press, New York.
Swedish	Translation by Leif Sjöberg and W. H. Auden, Alfred A. Knopf, New York, 1964.
Syriac	*The New Testament and Psalms in Syriac*, The British and Foreign Bible Society, London, 1919.
Tagalog	E. San Juan Jr., *Rice Grains*, International Publishers, New York, 1966.

Tahitian	R. D. Lovy and L. J. Bouge, *Grammaire de la langue tahitienne*, Publications de la Société des Océanistes, Musée de l'Homme, Paris, 1953.
Tamil	J. M. Somasundaram Pillai, *Two Thousand Years of Tamil Literature*, Madras, 1959.
Telugu	Translation by Charles Philip Brown, College Press, Madras, 1829.
Tibetan	George N. Roerich, *Selected Works*, Nauka, Moscow, 1967.
Tongan	E. E. V. Collocott, *Tales and Poems of Tonga*, The Museum, Honolulu, 1928.
Turkish	*Fazıl Hüsnü Dağlarca, Selected Poems*, translated by Talât Sait Halman, University of Pittsburgh Press, Pittsburgh, 1969.
Twi	E. L. Rapp, *An Introduction to Twi*, Basel, 1936.
Uigur	E. N. Nadzhip, *Sovremenny Uigurski Yazyk* ("Modern Uigur"), Oriental Literature Publishing House, Moscow, 1960.
Ukrainian	*The Poetical Works of Taras Shevchenko*, translated by C. H. Andrusyshen and Watson Kirkconnell, University of Toronto Press, Toronto, 1964.
Urdu	Muhammad Sadiq, *A History of Urdu Literature*, Oxford University Press, London, 1964.
Vietnamese	Translation by Nguyen Van Vinh, Vinhbao (Saigon) and Hoanhson (Hanoi), 1952.
Visayan	John U. Wolff, *Beginning Cebuano*, Yale University Press, New Haven, 1966.
Welsh	J. Gwilym Jones, *William Williams Pantycelyn*, University of Wales Press, Cardiff, 1969.
Yiddish	Translation by Sol Liptsin, in *Yiddish Stories for Young People*, ed. by Itche Goldberg, Kinderbuch Publishers, New York, 1966.
Yoruba	J. A. de Gaye and W. S. Beecroft, *Yoruba Composition*, Routledge & Kegan Paul Ltd., London, 1951.
Zulu	*Zulu Horizons*, The Vilakazi Poems rendered into English by D. McK. Malcolm and Florence Louie Friedman, Howard Timmins, Cape Town, 1962.

ACKNOWLEDGMENTS

The author is greatly indebted to the following people who have furnished passages and translations in the language indicated, and also provided valuable assistance and information.

V. I. ABAEV, Institute of Linguistics, Moscow. (Ossetian)

P. N. K. BAMZAI, New Delhi, author, *A History of Kashmir.* (Kashmiri)

JOHN F. BRYDE, University of South Dakota, Vermillion, South Dakota, U.S.A. (Sioux)

RAJNIKANT C. DESAI, formerly Deputy Director, Office for Science and Technology, Division of Economic and Social Affairs, United Nations. (Gujarati)

G. I. ERMUSHKIN, Institute of Linguistics, Moscow. (Mordvin)

G. C. GOSWAMI, Gauhati University, Gauhati, Assam, India. (Assamese)

ERIK HOLTVED, Professor Emeritus, University of Copenhagen. (Eskimo)

PYOTR I. INENLIKEI, Institute of Linguistics, Leningrad. (Chukchi)

NIKOLAI I. IVANOV, Chuvash State University, Cheboksary, U.S.S.R. (Chuvash)

AKHMED JAFARZADE, Kazimagomed, Azerbaidzhan S.S.R., U.S.S.R. (Azerbaijani)

RICHARD A. JARAMILLO, Reservation Programs Officer, Crow Indian Agency, Montana, U.S.A. (Crow)

ANDREW JOHNSON, Sheldon Jackson College, Sitka, Alaska, U.S.A. (Tlingit)

MAINA KAGOMBE, Editor-in-Chief, *Pan African Journal*, New York, U.S.A. (Kikuyu)

BÉLA KÁLMÁN, Lajos Kossuth University, Debrecen, Hungary. (Ostyak)

ASAN K. KARYBAEV, Kirgiz State University, Frunze, U.S.S.R. (Kirgiz)

NIKOLAI I. KAZAKOV, Ioshkar-Ola, U.S.S.R. (Mari)

LELAND D. KEEL, Deputy Director, Chickasaw Housing Authority, Ada, Oklahoma, U.S.A. (Chickasaw)

TEMBOT KERASHEV, Maikop, U.S.S.R. (Kabardian)

IVANKA KOVILOSKA-POPOSKA, University of Skopje, Skopje, Yugoslavia. (Macedonian)

ROBERT A. LOGAN, Duluth, Minnesota, U.S.A., author *The Books of Kapuwamit*. (Cree)

VASILI I. LYTKIN, Institute of Linguistics, Moscow. (Komi)

ATHMANI MAGOMA, Information Officer, United Nations Radio. (Swahili)

MA-THAN-E-FEN, United Nations Information Centres Service. (Burmese)

CELINE MATHEW, University of Kerala, Trivandrum, India. (Malayalam)

MATTULADA, University of Hasanuddin, Macassar, Celebes, Indonesia. (Buginese)

REV. FRANCIS MIHALIC, Wantok Publications Inc., Wewak, Papua New Guinea. (Pidgin English)

MYKOLAS MIKALAJUNAS, Vilnius, Lithuania, U.S.S.R. (Lithuanian)

CONSTANCE NASH, Sheldon Jackson College, Sitka, Alaska. (Tlingit)

N. B. G. QAZI, University of Sind, Hyderabad, Pakistan. (Sindhi)

SHAFIQ QAZZAZ, Silver Spring, Maryland, U.S.A. (Kurdish)

JOHN W. RAEDE, Westmont College, Santa Barbara, California, U.S.A. (Sorbian)

A. K. RAMANUJAN, The University of Chicago, Chicago, Illinois, U.S.A. (Kanarese)

PETER REDHORN, Browning, Montana, U.S.A. (Blackfoot)

DEAN SAXTON, Sells, Arizona, U.S.A., author, *Papago & Pima—English Dictionary*. (Papago)

GEORGES H. SCHMIDT, Chief, Terminology Section, United Nations. (General Linguistics)

SHIH-FENG YANG, Academia Sinica, Taipei, Taiwan. (Miao, Sibo, Yi)

LEONID SHOIKHET, Samarkand, U.S.S.R. (Uzbek)

TEONGGOEL P. SIAGIAN, University of Wisconsin, Madison, Wisconsin, U.S.A. (Batak)

CHOON SILASUVAN, translator and announcer, Asian Languages Service, United Nations Radio. (Thai)

JASVINDER SINGH, Flushing, New York, U.S.A. (Punjabi)

ELIZABETH SMITH, Muskogee, Oklahoma, U.S.A. (Cherokee)

JESSIE STILL, Muskogee, Oklahoma, U.S.A. (Cherokee)

ROBERT W. YOUNG, Area Tribal Operations Officer, Bureau of Indian Affairs, Albuquerque, New Mexico, U.S.A. (Navajo)

Index of Languages and Language Families